In the Scent of Horses, Hay, and Old Barns

In the Scent of Horses, Hay, and Old Barns

The Story of Eleanor Prince
Intrepid American Horsemanship Educator

PAMELA GALBREATH

FOUR
IN HAND
PRESS

First published in 2025 by
Four-in-Hand Press
an imprint of Trafalgar Square Books
The Stable Book Group
32 Court Street, Suite 2109
Brooklyn, NY, 11201

Library of Congress Control Number: 2025946051
ISBN: 978-1-64601-301-2
eISBN: 978-1-64601-302-9

Photos: Unless otherwise noted, photographs are courtesy of Carl Prince.
Interior design: Abbey Gregory
Cover design: RM Didier

Printed in
10 9 8 7 6 5 4 3 2 1

This is a work of nonfiction. The events and experiences detailed herein are all true and have been faithfully rendered as the author has remembered them, to the best of her ability. However, some names, identities, and circumstances have been changed in order to protect the privacy and/or anonymity of particular individuals involved.

Author's Note: Misremembering is a part of the recounting of our lives. Ellie Prince, all those interviewed, and I did our best, they to accurately recall, I to accurately weave the narrative.

A version of Michelle's story from chapter 22, "Travels and Horse Treats," was originally published as "Time for Wyoming Horses" in the February 2024 issue (Vol. 70, No. 1, Linden Press Inc., Fort Collins, CO) of *WREN Magazine*.

For

Carl and Lynn

In Memory of

Bill Prince
August 21, 1925 – April 21, 2012

George Prince
April 9, 1958 – February 3, 2012

Eleanor Fracker Prince
November 17, 1926 – March 19, 2024

"You're like me, Henry," [Jake] continued,
"as long as there's a breath left in your body,
you'll want to be around horses
and nothing in this world will keep you from 'em."

~ *The Black Stallion,* by Walter Farley

"One night I went down to the barn around 10:30 to join Ellie, and we sat talking, waiting, chilly, but wrapped in the scent of horse and hay and old wood. In the quiet night hours with the mare, my Peggy, and Ellie's Minx and Scamper, we girls talked intimately of our dreams, hopes, and disappointments."

~ *Just Beyond Harmony*, by Gaydell Collier

Contents

I Want a Horse

Chapter 1

ASK THOSE WHO HAVE GIVEN THEIR LIVES TO THE LOVE OF HORSES TO RECALL when it all started. They will perhaps say that it was in those first moments in the saddle or bareback, when with a simple command or the tug of a lead rope, the magnificent animal began to move forward. His strong muscles rippled, his ears twitched forward and back, and the movement of his head and neck gently invited the new rider to give and take the reins, and to be one as horse and rider.

That wasn't the case for a four-year-old girl named Eleanor Harmon Fracker, who wore on a particular day a special dress of tatting and frills for the purpose of visiting, with her parents and sister, close friends who were to be addressed by the children as Aunt Emma and Uncle George. The Frackers had traveled twenty miles from their home in Melrose, Massachusetts to Cape Cod for the special visit. On that summer day in 1931, early model cars and horse-drawn buggies were equally represented on the streets, and Aunt Emma and Uncle George's lane was certainly no exception. Outside their home, someone had parked a buggy. The horse in harness, securely tied to a post, had a reputation, according to his owners, for being at minimum cantankerous and unpredictable—with a predisposition to kick whenever he felt the urge to do so.

It might be accurate to say that at some point, with the adult conversation a dull droning in her ears, little Eleanor, named after Eleanor Roosevelt, took a walk toward her destiny. More likely, boredom sparked curiosity, and she wandered until she spied that most magnificent animal. To the buggy she fearlessly marched. When her parents found her, Eleanor was sitting calmly on the ground between and just behind the two front legs of the horse. The animal was calm as well. An observer might suggest that the two seemed to trust one another. Unbeknownst to the little girl, her passion and life's work had begun, and she would never be deterred.

Trust and determination, Eleanor would discover ninety years later in her family genealogy, were significant qualities in her New World ancestry. The ancestral story began in 1630, according to Colonial-era records of Essex County in Massachusetts. Eleanor's father, William Fracker Jr., was a direct descendant of Thomas Newhall Sr. and his wife Mary Woodland Newhall, participants in the Great Puritan Migration. In 1630, with fifty other male settlers, the Newhalls established the settlement of Lynn, located roughly twelve miles up the coast from central Boston. Thomas Newhall Sr. received thirty acres, which was a small plot of land but nevertheless a plot of land where he determined to build his family's dream.[1]

Almost three hundred years later, Eleanor's father would be an influential player in his older daughter's determination to own and work with horses. In 1920, twenty-year-old Walter Fracker Jr. set off, with his father and his best friend Jack, on a road trip out west that took them from some unrecorded town in Colorado to Seattle, Washington. This trip to the great American West revealed, in his penciled journal, a young Walter who was intrepid, inventive, adventurous, and resolute, in spite of a journey of "flat tires all the way." He could as well have been writing of the eventual westward journey, many years hence—the flat tires metaphorical—of his daughter Eleanor.

Quite a few of the Fracker party's automobile parts were lost along the gravel and dirt roads, requiring too-frequent delays and repairs. Harrowing moments involved arguments with other travelers as to who had the right-of-way on the edge of a precipice and the nearly impossible navigation of deeply rutted roads on the west side of the Continental Divide. However, Walter Fracker's account indicated that he laughed at the hardships, set his eyes on the destination of the day, and was thankful for and content with every mile covered: "The country was beautiful … it made me want to jump off [the vehicle] and stay." Luckily, the party of three was in no hurry and could be generous with their time and skills in repairs. Walter wrote, "We met [a driver] and cleaned his spark plugs and pushed him up and over a hill. He in return gave us a Bible. God knows we need it." He also recorded that near Eureka, Washington, he found a job which involved "taking care of nine head of horses." Acquiring the journal years later, Eleanor discovered in her father's notes that he justified to the family that for the job, it had been of the utmost importance that he purchase a horse and a saddle, the saddle costing much more than the horse. Savoring both the hardships and joys her father detailed in the journal, Eleanor was sure that "from my dad I got my desire to go west, regardless of hardship, and own horses."

The pleasure of the adventurous and fearless Mr. Fracker's participation in his older daughter's life began on November 17, 1926, when Eleanor was born in Lawrence Memorial Hospital in Medford, Massachusetts, a suburb of Boston. Her parents brought her home to 11 Kenmore Road, in Malden, and soon after moved to Melrose. The family expanded to include Eleanor's younger sister Carolyn, and they lived in Melrose until 1952, when Walter then inherited his father's property in Freedom, New Hampshire.

Settled in 1682 and incorporated in 1850, the town of Melrose in the 1920s appeared unaffected by the rush of industry into the Boston area, a mere seven miles south. As if the early settlers had drawn up a decree, the city center remained compact, and the surrounding countryside gave way to well-kept farmland, vast hills, forests, and fells. Numerous healthy ponds included Ell and Spot and the large Crystal Lake. Forests were thick and vast. Main Street and Upham Street were the city's only main thoroughfares—wide and graveled, displaying in their time trolley, wagon, and Ford tracks. Two- and three-story brick shops, with common walls throughout a block, indicated that store owners and their families lived just above their businesses. Elm trees grew curbside, vying for space with sparsely wired telephone poles before Dutch Elm disease killed the elms.[2]

In the 1920s, Melrose, of Middlesex County, boasted an elementary school, just across Upham Street from Norman Road, and a large public library. Edwin Carl Kemp described the town as a quiet community with no major businesses, clean and well-kept. Its population was 20,865, and its dwellings, both modest and mansion-sized, registered 4,449. The train station, built in 1900 by Boston and Maine Railroad, served the town. It was called "Wyoming Station."[3]

Walter Fracker Jr. worked in Melrose for a company that repaired and painted car bodies. Eleanor insisted that "if a car was bashed in, Dad could fix it, and no one would ever know it had been damaged." He traveled all over the United States to network and demonstrate for the company, Automotive Finishers of Detroit, which eventually was affiliated with Burgess Forbes, a paint manufacturer in Maine. For a time, he even hosted what would now be considered a do-it-yourself radio show. When Eleanor, whose nickname "El" was sticking, announced to her dad that her sixth-grade class was studying Sir Galahad and Lancelot and she therefore needed a shield, he exuberantly led her through the process of making a shield that would be a replica of those of old.

As El watched, her father cut plywood to scale. The two of them drew the lines for the design. Then, carefully explaining the use and contrast of colors and mixes and types of paint, El's father suggested that the background of the shield be red. He guided his daughter in using gold leaf to adorn the shield's edges and its requisite lion. El then patiently applied thirty layers of varnish, lightly sanding each of the dried thirty layers to effect a sheen. The shield looked like glass. Marveling at the finished project and what she had learned, El soon became intrigued with art. She also intuited from her father's instruction a lesson that she would carry throughout her life: "that I could do just about anything I wanted or needed to do, and the only way to do it was the right way."

El's tutelage under her father extended, with less precision and skill, to sports. At some point in El's early school days, roller skating became the rage. Mr. Fracker stepped forward to tutor El and Carolyn. He chose for the lesson a downhill sidewalk. "It was an easy slope," El explained, "down by Mrs. Fuller's place." Starting out, Mr. Fracker gained the traction that he wanted, but he soon lost control, careened down the hill, and fell into a hedge, badly scraping and cutting his knees. In reminiscent admiration, El said, "And that's how my father taught me to roller skate." His fearless escapades soon earned him, among his friends, the nickname "Andy Gump," after a popular cartoon character whose inventions and escapades often indicated a lack of planning and forethought.

The days of roller skating may have been short-lived, but Eleanor's talent for drawing and painting was not. She soon started sketching horses, paying exact attention to the composition of their heads and musculature. All other interests were suddenly adapted to horses, as if her existing world were a funnel to a new world featuring these alluring animals. In fifth grade, yearning for a horse, she read nearly every book in the school library that pertained in some way to horses. *My Friend Flicka*, *Black Beauty*, and *The Black Stallion* were remembered favorites. "Even though school wasn't my thing," El said, "I eventually read so many of the library's horse books that the teacher refused to let me read any more books on that topic." Her parents stepped in and started buying her the horse books she wanted. However, El's mother was growing somewhat concerned about her daughter's development as a young lady. For a subsequent birthday, she bought El books on topics such as, El remembered, "how to conduct oneself." Oh, how El cried! She hated those books! Her dad whisked her away to the Woolworth's Five & Ten store to buy whatever Westerns and horse books the store sold.

"All I wanted at this point," El said, "was to go west. There were more horses out west than back east. Only rich people had horses in the east. We weren't poor, but we weren't rich either. Besides, where we lived, my parents reasoned that there was just not enough space to keep a horse, and it was too expensive. Maybe the Depression figured into my parents' stance. I don't remember. I just know that I was nutty about horses and couldn't see life any other way."

There was certainly no space at 76 Norman Road for a horse, and Melrose's physical layout was not one that could easily accommodate horses. Close to Boston, the town was bordered by an immaculate golf course, which provided a significant level of quiet. It was not a rich area, but El described it as pleasant and nice. "Even though we didn't have a lot of money, it didn't stop us from doing things. It was also a friendly and trusting place. Once, when my parents went to Mexico, Mrs. Fuller, who lived on the corner, invited me to stay at her house. She didn't need to since I was grown by then. But she did. I think she knew I was feeling a bit lonely for my family. My loneliness was her only concern."

El remembered that "we had a big back yard, close to the corner of a larger road, and the house was on a hill, with the city down below. My favorite memory of the city was the Five & Ten. It had a soda fountain, but more importantly, it sold books. All I remember is the book section, especially the Westerns, and of course the books Mom bought me about courtesy and all that stuff."

Eleanor could walk or ride her bike the half-mile or more to Winthrop School, grades four through eight, and then later to high school. "One day, on my way home from Winthrop, not thinking of what was around me, probably thinking about horses, my head down, pumping with resolve up the big hill, I rammed into a parked car. It didn't hurt me, just my ego."

El wondered if she might have inherited her dad's tendency toward accidents. The house in Melrose had brick front steps with no sides. Once, El took a plunge off those steps and landed hard. Her parents thought she had broken her back. The injury was serious enough that El would spend the rest of her life doing exercises to avoid back pain.

"Another time," El recalled, "I was coming up the steep basement steps with my bike and wasn't paying attention as I passed under a part of the stairwell wall that jutted out considerably. I raised my head up so quickly that when my head hit the underside of the wall, it slammed my mouth shut and broke a front tooth. What a mess that was. The dentist had to put black stuff on it until the nerve retreated. That was terrible. I still have a cap on that tooth.

"I still have the bike, too. It's interesting what you keep and what gets lost. Some things stay and some things disappear. I don't know how that works, but I still have the teddy bear that I loved as a child. Thankfully, I grew out of my clumsiness.

"I remember so much of our house in Melrose," El said. "Our house was the second house on the corner, and our neighborhood had sidewalks. We often played kickball in the front yard with friends, after supper. There wasn't much room between the houses and garages. A stand of oak trees was in the back, and we had elm trees until they all died. The life of most of the house was in our big kitchen—ironing, meals, everything. Eventually my mother, clearly out of love, yielded the always-sparkling-clean floor to me. It was where I made belts from leather hides to raise money for my first horse."

Mrs. Fracker was an impeccable housekeeper, always making sure that clothing, rooms, and rugs were neat, clean, and organized. She insisted on no shoes in the house. She probably would be mortified to know that El carried all her life this favorite memory: "It was summer, and Mom had left a container of marshmallow fluff on top of the fridge in the back hall when we went to Freedom, New Hampshire, to see our grandparents. It grew too warm in the back hall, causing the top of the container to blow off. There were sticky fluff stalactites and stalagmites in the back hall, all over the shelves, in the pantry, and on the fridge. Fluff was all over the ceiling." El was fascinated by "the artistry of the small explosion."

In raising her adolescent daughter, Mrs. Fracker had more than marshmallow fluff to contend with. They loved each other dearly, but El and her mother had very little in common. Quite attentive to her looks and figure, Mrs. Fracker loved the social life that she had inherited when she, Miss Maxine F. Griffith, married Mr. Walter S. Fracker Jr. Her intent was to gently and lovingly mold her two daughters into socialites as well. As a member of the prestigious Melrose Women's Club, Mrs. Fracker seized every opportunity to teach her girls how to be proper ladies. El was not pleased. "There was a proper way to conduct yourself at a tea—pinkie finger up!—and she insisted on teaching me how to use a finger bowl. There was a proper way to sit—ankles crossed!—and there was a proper way to speak and to dress. Too often, I was forced to trot around behind her when she went into Boston to clothes-shop."

All this was not, however, to dismiss the value of education, opinions, and certain skills. "To the contrary. My mother worked in a bank. She taught me a great deal about safely managing money and keeping a checking and savings book. A lot of that is not taught now, and that puts young people at a disadvantage." Her mother was also shrewd and sought to impart her knowledge of the ways of humankind to El. "Mother taught me that if you don't want something known, don't tell anybody." Her mother also weathered the storms in the family's life by "being a shadowy person regarding making up her own mind. If Daddy announced that something was going to happen, if he announced that we were going to get a dog, she at first argued against it, but if the dog showed up, and it often did, she would decide it was okay and actually showed support. She graciously accepted inevitable outcomes rather than getting upset."

Even as she appreciated her mother's tutelage in all things financial, understanding that such knowledge would secure her independence in the future, El could not squeeze herself into the lifestyle and future her mother saw for her. It didn't help that Carolyn was not only compliant but also eager to emulate her mother. "I loved Carolyn, but we really had nothing in common. She loved dolls and babies, and I loved teddy bears and animals." Carolyn delighted in all that the shops displayed, while El's take on the sometimes day-long shopping trip was that she was "dragged under duress" to try on dresses. "Silk stockings, garter belts! I hated all that! When WWII came, so many of those things were no longer available, but we girls still were not supposed to wear sensible pants. So, in the 6th grade, rebelling against the dress code, I was sent home for wearing shorts." El's style, even as a young girl, was leisure wear or britches or, eventually, riding clothes. Calling herself "no dainty miss," she constantly wore out her shoes and pants.

"I did, for a short time, show an interest in cooking, even though Mother feared my making a mess in the kitchen. One day, when my parents were gone, I got out the cookbook and decided to make fudge. All went well until I spilled the wash water into the batter. The fudge came out beautifully, though, and I never told anyone about the added ingredient."

El knew she was blessed to live in Melrose, but no interests could compare to her absorbing, relentless passion for horses. Since sitting under the cantankerous horse, she could think of little else. Horses permeated every part of her being.

Lucky to have her own room in Melrose, she found it hard, years later, to recall any of the typical artifacts of a young teenage girl. What she did remember was the streetlight out front, which shone through her bedroom window facing Norman Road. After her parents wished her goodnight and told her to turn out the lights, she could still read her horse books by that streetlight. The greater advantage, though, was that her window gave her access to a precious daily event. A horse-drawn wagon wheeled by at dawn, laden with glass bottles of fresh milk. As the delivery man quietly stole from house to house, placing the chilled bottles on the porches, El's gaze was riveted on the horse. This daily event was more exciting to El than the earthquake that woke her one early morning. She knew immediately what it was and was grateful that there was no damage. She was equally grateful that the horse would deliver milk the coming day.

During the family summers in Freedom, New Hampshire, where her father's parents owned a summer home, El fed her growing passion with "borrowed horses." Early pictures show her sitting on a paint horse, surely a loaner from generous folks. Her parents soon paid for her to take riding lessons. The lessons may have been only trail riding, with no instruction in a ring, but El found it exciting that the woman had El ride with an English saddle. Once, while cantering, which El admitted she should not have been doing, she fell from the saddle. Luckily, she was not dragged, but the horse's right foreleg struck her stomach, knocking the wind out of her. The instructor got her right back on the horse. "From then on," El said, "I was riding. I loved the lessons and was rather pleased that I was the only student. I kept wondering, though, why no one else was interested in lessons." That her instructor loved and felt an intense responsibility for her horses' well-being was not lost on the young El. When her instructor grew old, rather than have her horses go to possibly unreliable owners, she had them all put down. At first, El thought that was awful. "But years later, I would understand."

During haying season, El rode a horse belonging to Mr. Peabody, whose house and barn were in the village. He owned chickens, a cow, and a draft horse. Sensitive to El's need to gratify her love of horses, and with his hay meadow not far from his home, he invited El to go along with him to gather his hay. When the hay rack, a rickety but reliable wagon, was full, Mr. Peabody positioned himself to walk beside his faithful old horse. He explained to El that if someone was riding a horse, they used "reins." He, however, in walking his horse, was using "lines" to "drive" the animal. El pocketed in her heart this one of many lessons she would receive and cherish over the years from people who truly knew horses. Mr. Peabody turned the horse toward home, and for many a summer, atop that massive but gentle animal rode the young and blissful Eleanor.

As Eleanor watched Mr. Peabody work, her heart was happy. Here was a kind man gathering food for his and possibly others' horses. He was, she recalled, "a typical farmer married to a typical farm wife, both hard-working, down-to-earth stewards of the land, and fit. And Mrs. Peabody was a wonderful cook."

Most of Mr. Peabody's work with hay was done by hand: cutting, drying, gathering into swaths, loading into the wagon. There was mention of a horse-drawn mowing machine, but El never saw it. She was there "only when it was time to get in the hay with its heavy scent," and get it in she did, working alongside the gentle farmer.

Borrowed horses came as well from an unlikely source: the radio. El's younger sister Carolyn vividly remembered the days when she and El leaned into the radio to listen to the adventures of *The Lone Ranger*. Carolyn recalled that "we'd shout 'Hi ho, Silver!' right along with our hero in the black mask as his beautiful white horse reared and pawed the sky! My hero, of course, was the handsome ranger, but Eleanor's was always the horse."

Soon, borrowed horses, milk wagon horses of the early dawn, and afternoon radio shows were not enough. El needed her own horse. The moment this idea took root in her, she would not be deterred. The year of the issuance of her edict may have been as early as 1936, when she was 10. In a most deliberate, confident, and nearly defiant manner, El announced to her parents, "I want my own horse." It was not so much a request as a declaration of how she intended to spend the rest of her life.

According to Lori Gray, in her June 8, 1980 article "True Grit,"[4] El's parents countered with these conditions: El had to buy the horse with her own earned money, and she had to find a place for it and be able to pay the boarding fee. This might have been a great deal to ask of a teen, but Mr. and Mrs. Fracker were not oblivious to their daughter's long-held desire. They knew she was clever and resourceful. They knew she was determined and, as her Winthrop School grades indicated, she was responsible, excusing that she received only an "average" for obedience and self-control.

El banked on the fact that, if the request was logically stated, "my parents always let me fly." Mrs. Fracker did express initial reluctance, but El said her father "grinned with delight and got right in step."

El's dad helped her set up her big money-making project. Mr. Fracker's brother, Seymour, was married to the paymaster in a shoe factory. She agreed to take orders for belts, cut from whole cowhides that El's dad, and probably his brother, purchased. The hides were delivered to the floor of Mrs. Fracker's spotless kitchen, where El cut them to various belt sizes, depending on the orders. Using her artistic ability and a leather burning tool set, El drew and burned into the belts all manner of lovely scenes. Her aunt then delivered to and received payments from El's customers. El reminisced that "the whole kitchen smelled like a Wyoming branding. I was already into the Western way of life long before I went west."

As El's belt sales proved lucrative, bringing her closer to her dream of owning her own horse, her dad started taking her to horse sales in New Hampshire and Maine. One such excursion took them to a railroad yard in Maine, where trains were bringing in sale horses from the West. Dealers met the trains and haggled with potential customers. In the midst of the chaos of the buying and selling, El learned a lesson. If a horse became ill or injured and went down in the cattle car, he had to suffer all the way to Maine. These horses may have been potential military mounts or may have been destined for camps for kids, but the bottom line was that they were being sold for profit, with little thought of care from the dealers. The horses packed onto the trains were probably from ranches far away, where they had once known freedom. But here they were now, stuffed in cattle cars on cattle trains. Seeing that setting, at that early age, El vowed that she would never tolerate inhumanity to living beings. She vowed that her horses "would never be treated in any way but with loving kindness, excellent care, and unwavering respect."

Several years after El's announcement that she would have her own horse, a stable was found and a horse was finally purchased, a big, powerful dapple-gray gelding that was a "ride and drive" horse. El's parents reasoned that with the effects of the war, a horse-drawn buggy would be a gas-saver for family trips to the grocery store. However, the dapple-gray would not prove himself as a driving horse.

On one trial trip, El's father, intent on giving El a lesson, drove the horse, hitched to a buggy, through the village square toward a steep hill. His intent was to drive the horse up the hill on one of the roads leading out of the square, presumably to tire and settle the horse. However, a group of four ladies was walking down the hill on their way to church. Mr. Fracker had to choose a lower, flat road and urged the horse to go straight. The horse spooked for no apparent reason and took off. Gaining control of the horse, Mr. Fracker descended from the buggy and started to lead the nervous animal. The horse took off. Mr. Fracker tried to halt him by hanging on and was dragged miserably on his knees.

Leaving Mr. Fracker behind, the horse headed toward a house owned by a couple who had not long ago lamented that they might sell their house "because nothing ever happens here." The horse galloped into a narrow pathway between their house and its garage. The buggy stuck; the horse somersaulted, broke free of the buggy harness, and eventually stopped with not one scratch on him. Mr. Fracker was not as fortunate. His knees were in bad shape. In Freedom's newspaper the next day, he was described as someone looking like he had "just survived a war battle." It was not lost on El that when her father tried to teach her something, "it was always very hard on his knees." The dapple-gray was returned to its previous owner.

Not long after the village square incident, during a summer in New Hampshire, Eleanor Harmon Fracker found her horse. Purchased trustingly from the same Maine dealer who had taken back the dapple-gray, the horse's name was Sammy. Sammy corroborated, many years later, the hand-written note on a draft of Eleanor's nearly completed professional resumé: "Owned horses all my life."

Sammy

★

Chapter 2

It didn't take long for the teenaged Eleanor, in 1940, to become inseparable from Sammy. "I got a good education at Melrose High School, even though school just wasn't my thing. Sammy was." The stable for Sammy was near Franklin Park, which featured trails and ponds. Whether walking or riding her bike, the young El was intent on getting to the stable to practice the grooming and riding she had learned from her years of reading horse books. She wanted no interruptions lest her efforts be imperfect.

Every day, as soon as school let out, El hurried to the stable and readied Sammy for a ride on the trails of the Middlesex Fells. She liked taking the trail that went behind the high school so that she could wave hello to the teachers smiling out their windows at the young rider. She also admitted that she enjoyed the attention paid her by the students as she trotted by. In spite of her focus on horses, El had a circle of friends who loved to play kick ball on her family's wide lawn. She did have one close friend, Beverly, "until we just casually drifted away." For the most part, though, she described herself as a loner throughout high school. "It was okay. I had my horse. I was out riding, or I was doing what I needed to do to keep and care for that horse.

"Somehow," El said, "I got my homework done because I did graduate. I liked my Latin teacher, not just because she taught the roots of the language but because she had traveled, and I wanted to travel. I loved to hear her stories of far away and wide-open places." Even at an early age, El was learning that connections, relationships, and friendships could afford her knowledge, wisdom, and experiences. Astride her own horse now, the young El daydreamed of her desired faraway and wide-open place, the American West.

El had ridden most of her borrowed horses bareback, and she did the same with Sammy until she could afford a saddle. She paid fifty dollars for a U.S. cavalry saddle, called a McClellan saddle, "which was the type of saddle I wanted. They're somewhat uncomfortable for the rider but very comfortable for the horse." El's philosophy of horsemanship was budding early: "Nothing is good for the rider unless it is good for the horse." What was good for El and Sammy meant never being apart. It was therefore decided that Sammy would make the journey with the family, every summer and spring break, to Freedom, New Hampshire. The family would be the guests of Mr. Walter Fracker Sr. and his wife, Angie Harmon Fracker, at the summer home to which Walter and Angie would retire in 1945. The dirt road into the resort town, not ideal for a vehicle towing a small horse trailer, was in such bad condition that "Mud Time" was how the family referred to their stays in Freedom. Any other negative feature ended there, however. To all the Frackers, the large white house on Maple Avenue, with huge windows and black shutters, was truly freedom. El called her childhood in Freedom "ideal." The entire family concurred. In fact, Mr. Walter Fracker Sr. willed the house—named Acorn after its noticeable acorn-shaped cupola—to El's father, and El's sister Carolyn would ultimately fill the home with her own family.

El's grandmother, Angie Harmon Fracker, mentioned often and referred to in the Society sections of the Freedom newspaper as Mrs. Walter S. Fracker, had been quite the social figure in Chelsea, Massachusetts, where she and Mr. Walter Fracker Sr. lived when they weren't in Freedom. Of critical note was Mrs. Fracker's long-standing involvement in the Chelsea Women's Club, which was affiliated with the General Federation of Women's Clubs. In 1912, Angie Fracker became President of the Chelsea Women's Club, which performed "work of vast import for the uplifting and betterment of the women in America. This organization, which reaches into the homes of the people of nearly every town and city in the United States, has perhaps a greater grasp of the real needs and aspirations of the masses of citizenship than do the political parties which are dominated by men."[5] Millions of middle-class women joined what became known as "women's clubs" in the 1880s and 1890s. Turn-of-the-century feminist novelist Charlotte Perkins Gilman called women's clubs "one of the most important sociological phenomena of the century."[6]

Despite appearing "frivolous" to more radical feminists in the suffragist, socialist, and anarchist movements, the clubs provided many women an independent platform outside the home. Their work often resulted in immediate, if more modest, changes, from purifying a city's drinking water to assisting orphanages, establishing parent-teacher conferences to boost public schools, or funding scholarships for girls and women. At the state and local level, these clubs focused on community service and social progress rather than culture, creating a "sense of unity … among women." Credibility was further attained with the creation of women's clubs at the national level, notably the General Federation of Women's Clubs, which emerged in 1910 as the largest organization, with branches in every state, eventually boasting one million members.[7]

It can be argued that Mrs. Walter S. Fracker Sr.'s leadership in the Chelsea Women's Club had an effect, albeit indirectly, on her granddaughter Eleanor.

While perhaps not one to join a women's club, El was already clearly indicating that nothing could stand in the way of her plans to own, care for, and learn all that she could from Sammy in order to eventually realize her goal. El was becoming a determined, independent young woman with an unfettered vision. Surely, Angie Fracker was delighted.

Despite her social resumé, which suggested a lady of poise and polish, Angie Fracker loved the unfettered phenomenon of speed—not unlike another of El's ancestors, great-grandmother Frances Fracker, who, against the norm, owned her own car and delighted in motoring. Sammy, to Angie's delight, was a willing horse. It was a glorious day when Gammy, as El referred to her grandmother, no longer had to endure a slow buggy ride to the grocery store, seven miles south in the town of Effingham. Sammy could walk out, and Sammy could proudly trot, and Gammy was nothing less than thrilled with her granddaughter, who was driving the buggy she had bought for $50. Surely the socialite Mrs. Walter S. Fracker Sr. was impressed that the buggy had originally been owned by Frank Swett Black, a Freedom retiree, the 32nd governor of New York from 1897 to 1898, and a member of the United States House of Representatives from 1895 to 1897.[8] With unleashed pleasure herself, El remembered the buggy as all black, with lanterns, a plush seat (probably stuffed with horsehair), gold stripes on the spokes and along the edging, and pin stripes all around. Sammy himself was a small sorrel horse with white markings and a star on his forehead. He resembled a Morgan horse, which suited Eleanor, who listed *Justin Morgan Had a Horse* as a favorite childhood book.

Sammy, despite his fame as a horse in harness, was not without his early flaws. He had a tendency, the young El learned, to step whenever and wherever he chose. According to El's sister Carolyn, "He was always backing up, often onto people's lawns." Once, he backed up until he broke through an eight-foot-high storefront glass window. El's dad was called upon to repair the damage. "Perhaps maintenance and repair," El said, "was one of the ways that my parents showed support for my love of horses."

Young Eleanor herself was not without mischievous moments. As she described it, "The through route around Freedom, New Hampshire, had just been newly resurfaced, and I was out riding Sammy near it. I wanted to try out the surface. I didn't know the repercussions. Eventually someone came to our house and told my parents that I had messed up the pavement with hoofprints. I guess I was not the best kid in the world. That was quite a naughty thing to do."

Happiest when she was active, El devised the game of "Indians" for herself and Sammy, with safety definitely not an issue. Space for the game *was* an issue, so Freedom provided an ideal setting. El set up hay bales, and, mounted on Sammy, shot them with arrows, first at a standstill, then a walk, then a trot, and then a canter. "Sammy was great for stuff like that. He didn't seem to care what we did together, as long as we were together." Clearly, the belief that communication between horse and rider was critical was forming in the young rider.

El's paternal grandfather was pleased with El's purchase of a horse and arranged, that first summer, for Sammy to be boarded at a stable near Freedom's town square. It was close enough to Acorn for El to ride her bike to the stable every morning. Filled with determination, she was set on a single objective: to groom and ride her horse. There was one rather touchy obstacle, though. A friend of the family, whom El and her sister were to always greet as "Aunt Ellis," lived over a store in the town square. She was a bit eccentric in that she always hung her used tea bags on a line to dry for reuse. She loved to talk, and she would invite just about any familiar face for a visit. El did not want to be snared, did not want to be robbed of time with Sammy, but she did not want to be impolite to this nice lady. "So I bolted as fast as I could on my bike, and shot past her house before she could see me."

The next summer, new boarding was arranged for Sammy. He would stable in the barn-shed—more a shed than a barn—attached to Acorn. El was pleased with the accommodations since her grandfather explained that horses, who like to go in and out when they choose, prefer sheds to barns. Her grandfather would provide Sammy's boarding but, he explained to El, she would be responsible for everything else. He wanted her to understand what it meant to own an animal that was fully dependent on her, from food to fun. He explained that Sammy's comforts would always come before hers, with no exception. Ever. Grandfather Fracker displayed his belief in El, and her confidence in her own ability to care for Sammy grew. "That may be why I never rode Sammy in the evenings. I think I was concerned about dangers and about taking care of him. He deserved his evenings off. He had rights and needs just as I did."

Her grandfather did not have to coax El to meet her end of the bargain: that she not only care for but also feed Sammy every day, since he had no pasture in which to graze. This condition included El learning to cut and gather hay from her grandfather's two-acre field behind the house. He taught her to use his large scythe, a tool which El would eventually carry with her to Wyoming. El made sure to take care of all of Sammy's needs. It wasn't hard. She loved her horse, and she adored her grandfather, who was knowledgeable about horse care and, to El's fascination, was also a wood carver. El especially loved the beautiful sideboard he had built. "It was heavy and couldn't be on the second floor. It took up a good part of a wall, with spiral columns at either end of the front. Oak leaves and acorns were carved into the yellowish wood. It took him years to make, and it was absolutely wonderful. My grandmother stored her good glasses and plates in the sideboard. If there was one thing I could have had, it would have been his tools. They were a part of him."

A bit of spoiling was also a part of Grandfather Fracker. He doted on Eleanor, and when, as a small girl, she asked him if she could have a kitty, he agreed and took her to get a kitten that she could keep for the two weeks that her family would be in Freedom. Grandfather Fracker drove her to get the temporary pet in his Oldsmobile, one of the first automatic transmission cars. When the time came to return the kitten, El's grandfather again drove. As they got in the car to return home, Grandfather Fracker asked El—always up for a challenge, especially one that involved an exciting bit of learning—if she would like to drive the car home. With no fear or hesitation, El said yes, and, in just a slow mile or so, bumped into a tree. Grandfather Fracker took it in stride. Mistakes made in the face of learning were all right for grandfather and granddaughter.

Love, independence, patience, and room to grow and discover were all intertwined in the cherished moments between El and her grandfather. El held influence over her grandfather, sometimes getting the two of them into trouble. "He was affable and laid back, and I could lead him into anything. He tried to do just about anything I asked of him." In his canoe, they often embarked on fishing trips where El, a bit impishly, would distract her grandfather into more time for learning the skills of catching a fish or for showing her the natural world that surrounded them. They soon forgot the time and returned home to a late meal and an irate Gammy.

El's memories of her grandfather included "fishing at a little pond on the other side of the road from a swimming hole. Since Gammy would not clean fish, my grandfather and I would clean what we caught and then cook and eat them. Gammy's rule, which she said was centuries old, was that if you caught it, you cleaned it."

On one fishing excursion, El hooked a good-sized snapping turtle. They dragged it to land, and her granddad killed it. El wanted the shell, so her grandfather helped her clean it as best they could. He then explained that they would put it on an ant hill, so that the ants could finish the job of cleaning. Sadly, some animal came along later and destroyed it. "It was sad," El said. "It was a pretty shell. But my grandfather taught me something so interesting about the ants, so the disappointment was worth it."

He might have instilled in El too much exuberance about the natural world. Needing to be closer to living things, El started catching them. "I'd put my catches in one of those tall, tubular Quaker Oats containers, and keep the animal for a little while. I loved to draw them, study them. Once I caught some garter snakes and wanted my grandmother to see them. I came from the barn and into the kitchen about the same time that the bottom fell out of the container. I remember that was another time Gammy was irate."

Perhaps Mr. Walter S. Fracker Sr. took cherished time to instill in his granddaughter a sense of business and a sense of philanthropy, for Mr. Fracker was experienced in both. With only one year of college, Walter S. Fracker Sr. began his business life as a bookkeeper at the Winnisimmet National Bank in Chelsea. He soon transferred to the city's County Savings Bank and was promptly promoted to treasurer. In 1921, the boy who was once a messenger and a clerk was named vice president of County Savings Bank of Chelsea. In this position, he served his community well. Most remarkable, the County Savings Bank, managing to survive the 1929 crash that led to the Depression, cooperated with four other banks in 1932 to loan the city of Chelsea $300,000 to pay municipal and school employees, including teachers.[9]

On December 7, 1941, when Pearl Harbor was bombed, El was a sophomore in high school. Her parents tried to shield Eleanor and Carolyn from much of the war news, but El soon took a part-time job after school with a company outside of Melrose that made coats for the Navy men fighting the war. She called what she did "piece work," the intricacy of which suited her. "The faster you worked, the more money you made. It was right up my alley." And it was a way for her to support the war effort and make money for Sammy's feed and boarding costs. El was one of many workers who stuffed the coats with "kapok," a fiber that comes from the seed pods of tropical kapok trees. El learned that kapok did not compress, was buoyant and lightweight, and was an excellent insulation. The coats, which sported zippers, pockets, and canvas covers, were close-fitting as well as strong, sturdy, warm, and utilitarian. They were a means to survival. El purchased one of the coats and found it to be great for riding. She would wear the coat for nearly her entire life.

During the war, no car route had yet been built around the town of Freedom. Troops therefore came through the village, right through the town square, where assembled crowds cheered and waved their American flags with patriotic zeal. El's grandmother was appalled that her granddaughter was wearing shorts when the troops came through, but El didn't care. She didn't want to miss showing the troops her support. "Otherwise, I wasn't really in touch with the war. There was the gas situation, and not much on the store shelves. That was really all I saw. Being there for the troops then, shorts or not, was important to me."

With the United States drawn into the war, all the land around the Fells Reservoir, including the trails El loved to take Sammy on, were closed to the public. The reservoir, about a mile from the city of Melrose, was an emergency water source and thus considered a prime place for sabotage. El's primary place to exercise Sammy was thus cut off. She soon learned, however, that the Massachusetts Mounted Patrol, as part of the city's Defense Program, had been called up to maintain vigil over the land surrounding the reservoir. Without a thought as to age or qualifications, El decided that the Horse Patrol was her means to show her patriotism and to continue riding in Melrose. She volunteered and was accepted. She felt important writing the official reports of human activity near the reservoir and eagerly attended the Sunday meetings, when the patrol practiced formation, or cavalry, riding. The patrol was comprised of retired adults, but El, the only teenager, fit right in. "They must have liked me because they let me stay on the patrol. The only problem was that the horse you rode had to be one that was nice to other horses. You had to tie a red bow on your horse's tail if it was a kicker. Sammy was a kicker, so he had to wear a red bow on his tail."

El was not the only family volunteer. She was so proud of her beloved dad when he became a volunteer police officer for the Melrose Police Department, replacing one of the many policemen who had gone to war. "My dad could do anything, and he also took his civic responsibilities seriously." It meant a great deal to El that both of her parents "were attuned to being helpful whenever it was necessary. Donating their time and helping others was just as important to them as donating money. They were good community members, just like my grandparents in Freedom."

Despite—or because of—the effects of the Depression and the war, young El knew that she lived a good life. She did not take for granted that she was surrounded by an extended family that loved her and believed in her and encouraged her in her dreams. She knew she was a lucky girl to own her own horse. Throughout her high school years, El and Sammy were inseparable.

Recalling the thrill of her early days with her new horse, El described her mood as exuberant. "I finally had my very own horse. I rode him the first day I got him. My time in the country, on the trails, on my horse was bliss. Every time I rode, I was on vacation. Sammy gave me a sense of freedom. I was in a beautiful place. Being out in nature, on my horse, was like a religious experience. I felt close to God in the beautiful areas, closer than in a church. Alone on my horse, I was able to see so much more wildlife, and the wildlife wasn't afraid of me. Because of all that, I felt that much more appreciation and love for Sammy. I poured all my love into that horse."

El had paid very little for Sammy, soon learning that his stubbornness had driven down the price. "I finally got him to go, and soon I could go everywhere with him. No one rode Sammy but me because he wouldn't go forward with them. My mom never rode him, but she liked him. Every afternoon, after she had worked in Gammy's Chelsea tearoom, she had an ice cream cone ready for Sammy."

During the Freedom summers, Sammy was icing on El's cake. Acorn was the candles. El loved the house's massive Victorian furniture and that it went on forever, all the rooms attached in a line: living room, dining room, woodshed, and eventually the barn. The house was well kept, but, unlike at home in Melrose, El was allowed to wear her shoes inside. The property abounded with oaks and four huge elm trees. The lawn, which her bedroom looked out on, was flawless. Sloping south to the town proper, it was impeccably maintained for many years with a hand mower.

El remembered a metal roof on the house's widow's walk, on which no one was allowed. "I could hear the rain on the metal. I loved that sound." Downstairs, a window opened out onto the veranda, where a porch swing had been hung.

The veranda was screened in, "and we could watch the thunderstorms coming over Green Mountain, which I climbed several times. It was just one of the things you did."

The elder Frackers kept their cars in the barn, away from Sammy. El was fascinated to learn from her grandfather that the acid in horse urine can take the paint right off a car. Her loving grandparents didn't seem to mind the necessity for constant surveillance of the barn, to prevent any potential damage by the horse their granddaughter adored.

El appreciated that Freedom was a small and friendly town. Her sister remembered it as a town of generous and kind people and wonderful neighbors. "There was one small post office," Carolyn said, "and one little store in the square in the center of town. Right in the middle of the square was a huge urn with greens and flowers. The store sold bread, milk, and a few other staples. If you wanted more, you had to go out of town, but who wanted to go out of Freedom?"

Photographs and drawn images of Freedom in the early to mid-1900s depicted a town nestled in Carroll County where, indeed, anyone would want to settle. The houses, barns, and shops were quaint, with a harmony of design that emitted peacefulness. The houses were not unlike those of other colonial towns—two- or three-story white boxes with pitched roofs, elongated windows, black shutters, and small dormer windows suggesting attics for members of the large families. The exacting craftsmanship of the nearby barns indicated agricultural pride. The town gave evidence of small trades: blacksmiths; bedstead builders; door, sash and blind woodworkers; and shoe repairmen. Most houses had porches that ran the length of the fronts of the houses, their decks painted gray, the roof overhangs stabilized by ornately carved, white porch posts. With a population of less than 1,000, the traffic of Fords, buggies, and wagons saw no congestion as they wended their way along the wide, curving, dirt roads. Sweeping lawns nestled on hilly contours, and huge, thick-trunked deciduous trees, exploding with striking foliage every autumn, grew on both sides of the town square's few sidewalks, which were lined with locally owned shops that might in later decades be called boutiques. A worn and weathered sign welcomed travelers "to Freedom." A substantial, babbling creek ran through the town, and the rare single-lane bridges consisted of planks, with narrow logs set as structures upon rock foundations. Farmlands outside of the town proper were ribboned by stout and sturdy New England stone fences. At least two churches served the population, the only difference in structure from the houses being the tall spires atop the steeples. Beyond the town were hills, thick forests, and large ponds, including the huge Loon Lake to the south and the wide and vast Ossipee Pond forty-eight miles west of town. The forest-covered White Mountains, probably named for the oft-present snow dotting the centuries-smoothed peaks, loomed to the northwest beyond the lakes. Snug against Maine's western border, Freedom was only 48 miles inland from the Atlantic coast.[10]

The earliest long-term residents of nearby Effingham, where Angie Fracker preferred to do her grocery shopping, were primarily colonials who had settled in the area before 1788, when New Hampshire was granted statehood. At some point in the early 1800s, Effingham experienced an influx of colonists from Maine. These emigrants settled in the north section of Effingham, and for some unrecorded reason, they soon grew dissatisfied with being under the jurisdiction of Effingham. They filed, spoke for their claim, and when they gained their freedom and incorporated in 1831, they named their new town just that: Freedom. One of the men who engaged in Freedom's peaceful secession from Effingham carried the last name of Harmon. It probably was Phineas Harmon, born in 1788 and great-grandfather to Angie Harmon Fracker, Eleanor Harmon Fracker's grandmother.[11]

El recalled that it was a practice in both Melrose and Freedom for the younger children to visit their elderly family members and other older folks. Politeness, courtesy, respect, and the art of conversation were learned during visits to "these nice old people," a skill that El would master and carry throughout her life, as well as the memory of the kindness, attention, and love bestowed by the elderly.

El remembered that her family was "always all together, and it was a loving atmosphere. The adults were good about letting the kids loose to roam and explore and have adventures. We lived with each other's idiosyncrasies. My grandmother always ran to get her jewelry and held it throughout a thunderstorm. When the storm passed, she returned it. We never criticized or made judgments of idiosyncrasies. Respect was everything."

El and her sister had little in common, but there was never animosity. "We weren't close. Carolyn had her dolls and indoor things and tennis. She liked cats, and I would grow to love big dogs. Carolyn was always neat and down-to-earth. I was the black sheep. Someone was always reminding me to pick up after myself. I had more important things to do. Carolyn wasn't a nutjob like I was, not in any way. I was always a nutjob for horses."

In Freedom, though, the two sisters had moments of togetherness. Carolyn recalled that "even though we weren't all that close, I always enjoyed being her younger sister. She was a great gal, always coming up with games." They gathered acorns to make animals and people, using match sticks for legs. They also played a game using one finger and the thumb to throw jackknives at targets. "That was fun, and," remembering her older sister's practicality, Carolyn added, "it helped El eventually learn to handle a knife for wood carving."

According to El, "Carolyn always thought it a bit unfair that I got a horse. She did have little Inky, but Inky was more or less the family dog. Also, even though I hated my middle name, Harmon, and was always complaining about it, I did have a middle name. For some reason, Carolyn wasn't given one. But,"

El emphasized, "she got to be famous at the 1939 New York World's Fair, and I didn't. And I guess that was really nice." El was fourteen, and television had just been invented. At the Fair, El remembered that there was, at one exhibit, a huge revolving stage. As it went around, a group of people appeared on the stage, the group growing larger with each revolution. Somehow Carolyn, only nine years old, had managed to get on the stage and was being interviewed on a large television screen, one of the first. El was delighted that she suddenly had a famous sister. That might have been as good as having a horse, she figured.

Both sisters remembered with fondness that their grandfather maintained a garden in Freedom. There was always something new to plant, and always something for him and El to compete over. One summer he tried broccoli, which grew into a huge bush which El could nearly sit under. Her grandmother, piqued with curiosity, as tended to be the norm in the Fracker households, cooked the leaves, which were later determined to be poisonous, in a large pot. The pot turned black, and the family unanimously decided that no harvested broccoli would be eaten. "But what an adventure that was," said El, and her grandfather agreed. He redeemed his loss with his apple cider. It was made from his own cider mill late in the summer, from the fruit of the many apple trees on his property, and, El contended, "It was so good! And it was good that he made gallons."

Carolyn remembered waking up in the summer mornings to the sound of her grandfather hoeing. "I could hear the click of the hoe on the rocks. That way, we always knew where he was, and we always wanted to know where he was, we loved him that much." Freedom spelled freedom, but it was also the place where stability, trust, and the love of family, nature, and discovery were a way of life.

Freedom was a resort area, attracting people from all the neighboring states, including New York. El remembered that "there was a thing between the summer people and the regulars. Nothing mean, of course, but the regulars were grateful when all the summer people left." The Fracker Jr. family saw themselves as both regulars and summer people. Surely a horse lent permanency to the situation. Every time the family drove into Freedom for summer or spring break, Sammy traveled behind in his trailer on the bumpy and muddy road, the pretty town square and the well-kept houses coming into view. Every time the family left to return to Melrose, the young El watched the retreating town view, somewhat blocked by Sammy's trailer, and wondered if the small resort town might someday be a forever home, for her and a horse.

Assuring More Than One Horse

Chapter 3

THE YEAR WAS 1944, AND ELEANOR WOULD SOON GRADUATE WITH HER class at Melrose High School. Any thoughts of summer fun were obscured by the difficult decision she had to make. Accepted at Boston University, she knew she needed a bachelor's degree if she wanted to eventually hold her own in the world of business. She was set on working with horses; her life would be horses. Beyond that, she wasn't yet sure, but she was determined to grab every affordable opportunity to make herself credible and her dream real. In the mid-1940s, a young woman with a college degree was saleable and respected. At least that was the belief of the citizens of Boston, the seed of academia since colonial times and the hub of universities, including Harvard, the Massachusetts Institute of Technology, and Boston University. Wellesley, founded in 1870, was internationally recognized as the first all-female college in the state. Smith College in Northampton, Radcliffe in Cambridge, and Simmons College in Boston would follow the trend established by Wellesley.

The sad truth was that El knew that she could not attend Boston University fulltime, make and save money, and devote time and attention to the care of her horse. As hard as it was, she sold Sammy and made the decision to attend BU and work part-time. "My reason for going to college was this: If I went to college, I could eventually have more than one horse. If I didn't go to college, I wouldn't make enough money to have even one horse." She added, "That was probably not the best way to think of higher education, but it was my way."

El could not have parted with Sammy had her father not been part of the sale process. He arranged for all the interviews, ensuring that with each contact, he and El could weed out those who were not deserving of her loyal equine friend. Eventually, a little girl as crazy about horses as El was came forward. El was able to meet the girl and her family and was pleased. There were no 4-H programs at that time, but the girl shared El's attitude that "having a horse, even with no riding programs available, was everything." El was relieved that "this sweet little girl was going to work with Sammy and would appreciate all the tricks I had taught him, such as shaking hands." When she learned that the family lived on a farm, El was reassured that Sammy would receive excellent care. "That little girl and I were both happy."

Eleanor's grandmother was one of El's first employers. Mrs. Walter S. Fracker Sr., genteel and society minded, owned a tearoom in Freedom. Not in a million years would the girl who got muddy riding horses have chosen this type of employment had it not been for her love and respect for Gammy. Gammy, part Scottish and bestowed with the honor of Daughter of the American Revolution through every fight from King Phillips' War to the Civil War, had flair, which attracted the young El. "Gammy owned a Ford car with a back that sloped. She loved that car because of its get-up-and-go. She loved that thing, one minute stationary and the next, boom, and away it went."

Gammy's flair extended into her philanthropic work, both before and during her marriage. A member of the choir of the People's Church in Boston, she also mounted theatrical productions and musical events for community building, fundraising, and awareness of partisan issues. Even at women's club meetings, orchestral and chorale music was on the agenda. Pops concerts were used to raise money for tuberculosis research, children's homes, and veterans' needs. In nearly every production, Angie Harmon Fracker showed her talents as singer, pianist, and organist, and, for a short stint, director and playwright.[12] "When Gammy's voice began to fail," El said, "she was very frustrated. People loved to hear her sing, and she loved to sing. She had been in the public eye quite a bit, and she was a hard act to follow."

El inherited Gammy's talents in the fine arts. She could sing and play the piano, but she much preferred developing and utilizing her abilities in drawing and painting. The tearoom provided no obvious artistic outlet for the young El. Nevertheless, El worked diligently at her grandmother's business, waiting and bussing tables "and everything else, including sweeping floors." She worked in the afternoons, her mornings set aside for riding Sammy during their final days together. She had little time for her friends, who were always going out to Loon Lake for fun. "Sometimes I felt stuck, but I held to my dream of lots of horses."

Soon, an idea insinuated itself, one that would draw on the entrepreneurial instincts El had unwittingly inherited from her grandmother and her finance-savvy mother. It would draw as well on El's artistic skills and her love of horses. She started to design notecards, the covers of which included her paintings of, not surprisingly, horses. Her grandmother's customers bought them up. El received 50 cents for every card she sold.

El enjoyed the customers as much as she enjoyed her work at the tearoom. One woman in particular piqued El's growing interest in business. The woman, a frequent customer, never gave tips until one day, when she told El to go into her barn and take out anything that El would like. That would be her tip. Why, thought El, impressed with the woman's innovative business acumen, would anyone not want to work for such a motivating tip? The question, and the business model it represented, would remain with El throughout her professional life. As if prescient regarding the long and fierce Wyoming winters that would someday be a part of her story, El chose a pair of snowshoes hanging on pegs in the old barn.

The tearoom was a family affair. El remembered that her father made a wonderful Welsh Rarebit, and her mother's specialties were cakes and pies. These foods were featured weekend staples for the loyal customers. El described her grandmother "as a wonderful cook, but she made a terrible mess in the kitchen, which my mother usually had to clean up and wasn't too happy about." Fond of *The Fanny Farmer Cookbook*, Angie Fracker could boast of such specialties as muffins and spice cakes on Saturday mornings, but her signature recipe was chocolate cake with mocha icing. According to El, "That cake was totally delicious."

However, it was the mocha icing alone that would eventually claim fame, as revealed in a yellowed newspaper clipping. *The Paducah Sun* newspaper, of Paducah, Kentucky, ran an article on March 18, 1981, that told of the 1976 bicentennial horseback ride across the United States by Colonel James D. Langstaff. Colonel Langstaff decided that rather than keep a journal, he would record favorite recipes of the households of hospitable folks who had befriended him and bid him stay with them during his journey. One recipe that made its way into his recipe collection, supposedly published in 1981 and titled *Host to Host Coast to Coast*, was supplied by Eleanor Fracker Prince, of Sodergreen Ranch, Laramie County, Wyoming. The recipe for mocha icing, over 100 years old, was indeed El's grandmother's.[13] As a grown woman, Eleanor shared the cake and icing recipe with her many friends, "but," she said, "everyone had to make adjustments to the cake ingredients because we all lived at high altitude."

Sadly, the recipe for the chocolate cake itself was lost. Eleanor explained that "it was on a piece of paper that I stuck in my *Fanny Farmer* book, along with other recipes I sometimes cut out if they sounded good, even though I didn't have time to cook. I may have loaned that cookbook to a friend, but if I clean out the kitchen sink cupboard and find it, I'll let everyone know."

Enrolled at Boston University, El found a job working in sales at a nearby store that sold high-end dresses and other women's apparel. El worked part time, late afternoons, for three to five hours. Jobs were hard to come by for young people enrolled in school, and the jobs didn't pay much. El appreciated what she could get. Her customers "did no browsing. They were waited on, sitting comfortably as the salesperson brought out clothes based on the customer's voiced needs and desires. The volumes of trips we had to make were of no concern; the customer's satisfaction was everything." The job reminded El of the many times her mother urged her and her sister into dress shops, so that El might eventually dress, fix her hair, and wear makeup in the styles appreciated by her mother. "I dearly loved my mother, but I wasn't having any of it," El said, but she held to the job, for money meant education and savings, and education and savings meant horses. Despite their differences, Maxine Fracker enthusiastically supported her oldest daughter as a college student. From her salary came money for El's tuition and books, and both parents welcomed El to live at home all four years, rent-free.

When the fussiness of tearooms and dress shops got to El, she happily retreated to her grandfather's world. He was pivotal in her life. When El owned Sammy and even after he was sold, she saw her early mornings as a cherished time to be with her grandfather. They had breakfast together. No one else was up; he was all El's. She recalled that they each had a window to sit by while eating and that he had "his own wonderful rocking chair," which she later wished she had been able to take west with her. "I loved this time because I loved my grandfather. I loved having him all to myself. He had a whimsical side. Our breakfasts were always apple pie and ice cream. He sang the menu with his wonderful voice." The banker with the wonderful voice had once been the manager of the Chelsea Academy of Music and was known to have appeared in his wife's theatrical productions as a frequent soloist.

It was probably this frequent soloist who offered El a more immediate path to lots of horses. About five years before Eleanor made the decision to attend Boston University, her doting grandfather encouraged his son and daughter-in-law to send El off to summer camp, as was the vogue in the '30s and '40s. In 1939, 1940, and 1941, Eleanor left the care of Sammy to her grandfather and father and spent eight weeks of each summer at Camp Winnemont, described in a camp brochure simply titled *Winnemont 1940* as "A Summer Camp for Girls on Lake Ossipee." The opening sentences of the brochure revealed that "the genuinely happy spirit of Winnemont girls is the first thing to impress most visitors. It is the very essence of the camp." El, the young camper, was indeed happy.

Close to Mt. Whittier, in New Hampshire, the camp, with rustic wood-framed and tent-topped cabins, was surrounded by vast lawns, huge trees, and a wide lake. El wasn't too keen on the dancing lessons, but she reveled in time set aside for reading and for crafts that included carving and wood working, crafts which had been her grandfather's hobbies. What made her heart soar was revealed in several sentences under "Equipment": "Adjoining the athletic field is the riding ring, and back along the main road is the large stable accommodating fourteen horses. Riding is so popular with girls these days that Winnemont makes provision that all campers shall have riding without extra charge." The camp in fact housed 25 horses. El quickly convinced the staff that she was an experienced rider and spent much of her time chaperoning riders on afternoon trail rides and on supper and overnight trips. She also helped riders prepare for the August horse show. "I was so happy," she said, "around all those horses."

It should be noted that El took away two consequential aspects of the Winnemont riding program, long before she developed the notion of becoming a riding instructor. First, even though trail riding was a feature of the program, all instruction appropriately took place in a riding ring. Second, one of the instructors was Lieutenant Stanley W. Dziuban, from the Schofield Barracks of the United States Military Academy, who most assuredly instilled in young El the importance of cavalry—dressage—training for both horse and rider.

In the summers of 1944 to 1947, El again attended camp, but these summer sessions found her at Merrymeeting Camp for Girls, established in 1916 in Bath, Maine. Instead of being a camper, she was hired as a camp counselor. Her job was to tutor the young girls in English and Latin. "I didn't teach poetry or contribute to the Merrymeeting journal, which was mostly poetry. I've never bought a book of poetry." Poetry wasn't practical, and to El, the value of anything was in its practicality. As far as she was concerned, the most practical and therefore the most valuable of skills was learning how to ride a horse.

El was ecstatic when she was chosen to be a riding instructor at Merrymeeting. The camp covered fifty acres. Surrounded on three sides by the Kennebec River and Merrymeeting Bay, the camp boasted virgin forests and the White Mountains. According to El, the junior and senior girls' cabins were equipped with electrical lighting and were fully screened and solidly constructed. Each counselor and her ten assigned girls lived in their own cabin.

According to its 1947 brochure, *Merrymeeting: A Camp for Girls*, the camp, "through its counselor staff, wish[es] to help girls … learn to meet the problem of leisure time in a cultural way, develop and maintain physical health, nourish social adjustment through true friendship, [and] attain high ideals and balanced perspectives of life." At the camp, El displayed and continued to develop what she had learned from her family: a vigorous respect for culture, nature, health, friendship, high ideals, and varied perspectives. As the camp did not stress competitiveness in activities, El began to nurture a firm belief in cooperation over competition.

For El, Merrymeeting's jewel in the crown was the camp's robust horsemanship program. Pictures of young campers exhibiting relaxed, correct posture in the saddle and low hands on the reins were featured in the brochure in an enticing section titled "Horseback Riding." "Our camp," it reads, "is particularly well adapted for this ever-popular sport, with innumerable trails through the pine forests and deserted country roads. … In the course of a season our girls develop into excellent riders." The section explained that the girls, divided into groups according to age and experience, were "always accompanied by an experienced riding master."

On a separate page of the same brochure, titled "Counselors and Representatives," Miss Eleanor Fracker's high school picture is displayed. She wears a white blouse and a touch of color on her lips. Her face, as would be the case for the entirety of her life, is just seconds away from a wide and genuine smile. Her long, wavy hair is pulled back with what would become, for as long as she taught horsemanship, her signature barrettes. She is listed as a student at Boston University, living at 76 Norman Road, Melrose, Massachusetts. She had become an "experienced riding master," and was thus given leeway by the staff. "They left me alone to teach whatever, and as a result, they taught me how to teach."

As she would do many years later, El delighted in mixing riding instruction with other joys, including the world of nature. She took the students through blueberry and raspberry fields, a familiar feature of Maine flora. She had her students, to their delight, "dismount, eat, and mount." That, she said, "was a great way of teaching by reward."

As an instructor, Eleanor was an avid and constant learner, taking in every bit of knowledge she could about horsemanship. She was assisted in the riding program by "a wonderful old horseman," whose name, sadly, she could not recall. A pleasant man, he was then in his 70s, always neatly dressed in his work clothes. He fed the horses well and kept them in good condition. As he bridled and saddled the students' horses, he taught El much about groundwork, gentleness, grooming, and the quirks and personalities of horses, beyond their being just horses. "He was generous with his knowledge," El observed, but was otherwise a quiet man. He understood and respected the animals and worked to ensure the safety of both horse and rider. "He clearly loved the horses," El said, "and was a horse whisperer long before the horse whisperers of today."

Until Merrymeeting, El had received only minimal riding instruction, in spite of her nearly constant contact with horses. There were no schools that taught a rider how to teach other riders. At Merrymeeting, El's philosophy as an instructor began to take shape. The wonderful old horseman readied the horses, but El soon decided that if she were ever able to teach, she would have the students catch, lead, and groom their horses, including checking their feet for injury or damaging objects, such as stones. They would saddle and bridle them as well. "That way," she reasoned, "they'd feel the horses more. If you just get on and ride for an hour, you don't learn about the horse or become sensitive to him. The longer you are doing things with your horse, the more you enjoy the horse. Even smelling is important, for you and the horse!" El grew adamant in her insistence that she would teach in a ring, whether it was outside or in an indoor arena. She would not use trail rides as main venues for instruction, "where you're riding ahead of everybody and can't look at the riders, can't see all the things they're doing, how they sit, how they hold their hands. You can check, but you can't teach. It's just not efficient."

Instruction, El decided, would also extend beyond formal ring work. At the camp, the girls paid for an extra "breakfast ride." The girls were required to do their own cooking on the trail, after tying their horses to tree limbs. El noted that "breakfast was awful-looking stuff, gray eggs and half-done bacon," but she described the overall event as "delightful and instructional." The girls shared with El that "everything was the most wonderful in the world. They really loved that breakfast ride." However, it was a great deal of work, and El believed that the breakfast ride showed value in teaching the girls "about trying out and experimenting, about figuring out how to do things and what worked." They also learned how to live with their horses, attending first to the animals' needs ahead of their own. In addition, they learned how to live with and help each other, without any competition. Trail rides definitely had their benefits.

The young counselors were treated and trusted like reliable adults. El had her Sundays off, as did a number of the other counselors. The counselors were loaned cars by the camp directors, with the stipulation that the girls would travel no farther than 50 miles. On frequent Sundays, El drove to a designated place to meet her parents, who then took her to Freedom for the day. That evening they returned her to the camp's car. In the later summers, a gentleman named Robert Kingston Smith met Eleanor on those Sundays.

When Eleanor Harmon Fracker entered Boston University, in the fall of 1944, she was, thanks to the love and trust of her parents and grandparents, entering as an independent, confident, intelligent, and creative young woman, with a dream that would not be assuaged. She was indeed entering into a world that, since the Great Puritan Migration, was dominated by the influence of her direct ancestors: scholars, enterprising merchants, craftpersons, courageous soldiers, and even those who loved horses.

It was in the 1600s that ships brought El's ancestors, who were Congregationalists, from Southampton, England, to what is now Massachusetts. Learned and adventurous, the families came from far England and Scotland. Thomas Newhall Sr., ancestor—many generations removed—of Walter S. Fracker Jr., helped to establish one of the first permanent settlements in the town of Lynn, in the area that would become Massachusetts.[14] Eleanor's father could also trace roots in the Fracker family back to Thomas Kendall, church deacon in the mid-1600s;[15] Thomas Bancroft,[16] who helped to establish the first Congregational meeting house; and John Bancroft Jr., born in 1682, who, as a deacon at the church in Lynnfield, donated the "oldest book" to the church in Lynn.[17]

John Harmon, ancestor to El's paternal grandmother, Angie Harmon, arrived in the New World in 1660 as an indentured servant and soon became a freeman and a citizen, swearing, in 1677, an oath of allegiance to the Massachusetts Bay Colony.[18] John W. Fracker, Eleanor's great grandfather, was active in the governance of the Universalist Church.[19]

The shots fired at Lexington and Concord and subsequent wars drew Eleanor's ancestors into military service. Moses Harmon, also an ancestor to Angie Harmon, enlisted in the 15th Massachusetts Regiment of the Continental Army at age 18, in the winter of 1777. He is also listed in the 11th Massachusetts Regiment. He eventually settled and was buried in what would become Freedom, New Hampshire, listing as part of his 1820 property inventory "one old horse."[20] Jonathan Thompson, ancestor to El's father, enlisted in 1775 in the Seventh Continental Infantry, and Ezra Newhall, a possible descendant of Thomas Newhall Sr., enlisted in a Massachusetts Regiment.[21] Benjamin Wilson Jr., descendent from the Bancroft line, served in the War of 1812.[22]

The 1800s teemed with the likes of labor union organizers, transcendentalists, and crusaders for human rights causes. Abolitionists formed their networks and platforms. Committed and enterprising citizens, including those from whom Eleanor descended, created the businesses that would form the backbone of the economic development of Boston. Thomas Fracker Sr., great-grandfather to Walter S. Fracker Sr., came to Boston from England in the mid-1700s as a shipwright.[23]Thomas Fracker Jr. developed his father's business and established a shipyard in Boston, in 1783. At his death in 1780, his assets totaled $23,596.48.[24] Robert Potter, descendent of the Bancroft line, established one of the first tanneries near Boston.[25] In the 1800s, William McIntosh's son, ancestor to Angie Harmon, worked as a cabinet maker.[26] John McWhirk, Angie Harmon's maternal great grandfather, was a successful farmer and owner of much farming machinery.[27] Elias Harmon, paternal great grandfather to Angie Harmon, owned a farm in Freedom that was valued at $800, and in 1874, his "Boot and Shoemaker" business on Main Street, Boston, thrived.[28] Shipbuilders; cordwainers; woodworkers; and industrial, seaport, and municipal workers—well educated in their arts, skills, and theology—filled Eleanor Harmon Fracker's family tree.

The ancestors fought as well for the Union when the fledgling country was torn asunder. George McIntosh served in Company E of the 7th Massachusetts Volunteer Infantry, which soon became a part of the Army of the Potomac. He survived the war, worked in Boston as a carpenter, and became Eleanor's great-great grandfather on the Harmon side.[29]

John W. Fracker, Eleanor's great grandfather, enlisted in 1862 in Company H, 43rd Regiment, Massachusetts Volunteer Militia, commanded by a series of famous generals: McClellan, Burnside, and Hooker.[30] Many who formed this militia hailed from Chelsea, the eventual birthplace of El's grandfather and father, and were some of the first to be shipped to battle via the ironclad *Merrimac*.[31] At Camp Rogers, during Christmas of 1862, these same "educated soldiers" from Chelsea, according to the journal of Edward Rogers, Company H, set up Bible and literary societies and "volunteered to educate the African-American refugees in nearby camps."[32] Edward Rogers indicated that these

Chelsea men also respected and loved their horses. Amid accounts of the raggedness of the troops and the carnage and fear to which they had been exposed, he wrote that to spare the horses during one horrific battle, the field officers dismounted and sent their horses to grooms waiting in the rear. "The horses were excessively frightened at the artillery discharges. I could see a nervous palpitation or vibration pervading their whole system at every explosion. The exquisite sensibility of the noble animals would manifest itself first at the nostrils and pass by a perceptible wave or shock along the whole body. It seemed as though they wanted to say, or to have someone say it for them, 'What cruel wretches you are to drag us into your bloody quarrels.'"[33]

John W. Fracker returned to Chelsea after the war and worked as an upholsterer. Active in the Unitarian Church and for the causes of war veterans, he also was "superintendent of street lamps." More precisely, according to his *Boston Globe* obituary, in 1914, "In early days, when the street lamps were lighted by hand, he was one of the lamplighters."[34]

Equally interesting was the tale of Frank Harmon, the father of Eleanor's grandmother, Gammy Fracker. Frank left his rural homestead in Freedom, worked for some time as a locomotive fireman, and then left the job to become a successful sausage maker. As Eleanor learned in her work with horses, "a person can be highly successful in any lifetime career, as long as they are dedicated, and have in their blood Boston ingenuity."

The women must be mentioned here. Decades-removed records usually listed the women as working at home or without any occupation. A name, sometimes partial or incorrect, was included, as was, for those more prominent or recent, the birth and death dates. The early history of the founding and maintenance of this country by El's ancestors indicates, if only vaguely, that its women were dedicated, intelligent, determined, and ingenious. Interestingly, a significant number of them could claim longevity as well. Many lived into their 90s.

A Freedom Feeling

Chapter 4

Eleanor Harmon Fracker entered Boston University as an undergraduate in the fall of 1944 with the same singleness of purpose that had governed her life to this point: to continue to learn everything that she could about horses and horsemanship. The College of Liberal Arts, where El enrolled as a candidate for an AB degree in Fine Arts, sat conveniently behind the Boston Public Library, where she read every book on horses that she could find, including the few she could find on training. She took thorough notes, finding it frustrating that most of the information was on "almost finished" horses and not on what she thought of as real training: from the ground up. She also frequented the nearby bookstores on Huntington Avenue. She loved those old stores and took advantage of every one of them, scouring the shelves for fiction and nonfiction alike—anything that related, she said, "to four hooves, a mane, and a tail."

As if the library stacks and bookstore shelves weren't enough, El discovered that conveniently nearby was the massive brick building that housed Boston Police Department's Station 16. Adjacent to the building were the brick stables that housed the horses of Station 16's mounted unit. The stables abutted the backs of tall brick city dwellings and businesses, all embellished with the scaffolding of iron fire escapes. Established in 1873, the mounted police unit, the oldest in U.S. history, boasted an equine staff of about 100 horses and remained in existence until it fell victim to budget cuts in 2009. Station 16 served as a training facility for the large and muscled horses, similar to Morgans, that were sold or donated to the patrol. On duty, the horses and their riders exhibited with precision their training in cavalry maneuvers. The horses proudly wore thick blue blankets decorated with the city crest and the words "Boston Police, Mounted Patrol, Nation's First."[35] Impeccably groomed and attentive, they were magnificent yet friendly ambassadors to the citizens of Boston.

The mounted unit was nothing less than a treasure for El, who made it a point to detour toward Station 16 as often as she could. She was impressed by the obvious care and training given to the horses, and particularly remembered that when it was time to ready the horses, the animals were groomed and brought into their stalls, and the large saddles, on pulley systems above each stall, were lowered onto their backs. With every visit, El assiduously observed how the police officers conveyed respect, concern, calm, and love toward their tall, strong, proud, and trustworthy mounts. She was drawn to Station 16 almost daily, sometimes linking her equine-related detour to a shard of a memory of a relative whose livelihood was dependent on the reliability of horses. In the spring of her 97th year, El would learn that her great-grandfather on her mother's side, George Griffith (1832–1873), had been a "teamster,"[36] hauling critical goods via a wagon with a team of well-cared-for and trustworthy horses.

El soon realized that reading and observing weren't enough to satisfy her craving for equine education. She sought and found a riding facility in Conway, New Hampshire, where she could work intermittently, during and between semesters, as a counselor, specifically in riding education. "At Bald Hill Lodge, we weren't counselors like those at a camp. People who used the lodge's stable were not allowed to ride out alone, so we gave instruction in the morning and then took them out on trail rides in the afternoon."

El's experiences at Bald Hill Lodge were new and valuable. Throughout El's earlier camp experiences, she had never met a problem student. At the lodge, she met "the guy who made it clear that he knew everything about riding horses." She put up with "this miserable person's bragging and condescension" for only so long and then matched him up with a horse that would buck if the rider did anything wrong. The inevitable happened, and El, noting the rider's crestfallen demeanor and silent obedience, was satisfied that "the guy was humbled, and only his ego certainly bruised."

It was also at the lodge that El had one of her first intimate experiences with horses. An old gentleman horse trader received a contract to supply horses to the lodge. The only way to move the horses from the supplier to Bald Hill Lodge was to ride them. El volunteered for the seven-hour journey. Her assigned mount was a little mare. In just a short time, El grew concerned about the mare's obvious discomfort. Clearly, she was having abdominal pains. Fearing the girth was too tight, El dismounted, loosened it, and then led the mare rather than ride her. "I was so worried about her. I didn't want her to be sick. She was such a sweet little thing." A grateful El and a tired mare took it slowly, and El discovered that walking, all the while murmuring encouragement, is sometimes the best remedy for equine indigestion. The little mare recuperated, and, urged on by mutual trust, they finished the journey.

At the lodge, El's room with a bunk was separated from the barn where the horses were stabled by only a thin partition. She didn't recollect having any trouble falling asleep despite the slow and cadenced clicking of the horses' hooves and their soft, muffled nickering. "It was a normal, natural thing, those horses moving around, those horses I loved. After a while, I got used to their peaceful noises, and they lulled me to sleep."

El appreciated the knowledge she gained from the Boston Public Library, Station 16, Bald Hill Lodge, and her camp counseling experiences. She wisely committed to successfully completing her degree program at BU, driven by her constant hunger for new knowledge to study all that was available. Each semester, she took full loads. She completed two years of Spanish and an early semester class of Advanced French, where she mastered reading the language. She fulfilled her academic requirements in the sciences, English comp, history, education, and physical education. Her inner artist must have been frustrated, however, for although she completed four semesters in art history, she could only sign up for two semesters of Theory, Practical Drawing, and Painting. Perhaps the only discipline she avoided was mathematics. "I hated it unless it was the sensible, practical type of math, like banking. It was my mom who taught me practical math, and I knew how to be wary and careful with finances. I felt she had taught me all I needed to know to get started in the practical world."

El believed she succeeded in her college classes because of the high quality of education she had received in both elementary and high school. In those earlier years, most of her grades were A's and B's, and she didn't recall having any trouble as a student. Her parents and grandparents had instilled in her the respect for and love of learning that would make her a good scholar, always attentive and eager to discover new worlds and concepts. There was one lapse, however, and luckily it occurred early enough in El's life to make an impression but not to embed any negative attitudes about education.

From 1932 to 1933, El, just a wee tot, was enrolled in Miss Lowdon's Private School in Melrose. Her final report card indicated that she scored high grades in Reading, Spelling, Arithmetic, Attendance, Punctuality, Conduct, Politeness, and Order. However, El remembered in vivid detail Miss Lowdon's policy for naughty children. "You were sent to the attic. It was hot and dark, and you had to sit on a board on the floor, with the door closed shut. You had to wait until a teacher came for you. You were allowed out only when it was decided you were ready." Only those who had been to the attic knew the attic, and El knew the awful attic.

The little spark of misbehavior—what might also be construed as curiosity and an impatience and exuberance for adventure—might again have surfaced in Winthrop Elementary School, when, in both Miss Nickerson's fourth grade class and Mrs. Linekin's sixth grade class, El earned only an "average" in "Self Control" amongst all her A's and B's.

That same impatience and exuberance caused El, as a college student in her final semester, to rue that she hadn't had the foresight to enroll in college courses that would better prepare her to work with horses. "Why I took the classes I did, I have no idea. So many of them were of no value to me. I did well in my sophomore geography class, but I spent most of the class time filling a whole notebook with little drawings of horses. I didn't want to hear about the places in lecture. I wanted to go to those places. Why did I take Old English and philosophy? Why didn't I take more zoology?"

This is not to say that El had a narrow-minded view of scholarship. To the contrary, she loved to read, loved history, and loved to learn about other places and cultures. She admitted that she respected science and math. She had already learned that an instructor must make a subject interesting and animated if it was going to pique a student's interest. Ingrained in El was that the instructor must be lively and totally immersed in her subject. Immersion was no problem: El was clearly immersed in horses and horsemanship.

If what she called her extracurricular activities fostered her love for horses, the College of Liberal Arts Physical Education Department steered El, who entered Boston University with a tuition scholarship in basketball, volleyball, and archery, toward a definite path and passion for teaching. "I loved physical education more than any of my other courses. Especially the gymnastics equipment, which included climbing ropes. And of course the stationary horse, with its springboard that propelled you onto the apparatus, where you could hold the handles, turn around or do other maneuvers, and then leap off. I enjoyed that." She was also quite exuberant, perhaps a bit too much, about her modern dance class. One day, enveloped in the music and under the spell of her enthusiastic teacher, she almost put a girl's eye out leaping and flying through the air. She felt bad about the accident, explaining that "I was putting my all into my leaps." The explanation could have metaphorically described her way of living from then on.

El's abilities in her physical education classes did not go unnoticed. She was soon offered the opportunity to teach archery to small groups and riding lessons at a riding academy near campus. She mused, "Why didn't I go the physical education route? I will never understand why." She knew, though, the value of a liberal arts degree.

"In the 1940s," Eleanor explained, "college was the thing to do, even for women. It was a big deal. I lived in a place where they pushed women to succeed. I never thought myself a second-class citizen. I was never treated that way in my family and community. We learned that we could do what men do. My parents and grandparents pushed me to go to college." El knew she would be the first in her family to graduate from college, and she knew the experience would enrich her life. She was eager to learn about different places and meet different people. BU, she knew, provided that opportunity. "Because of being exposed to so much, I didn't have biases. I just didn't think that way. I met people at BU on their own merits."

So that El could save money, she and her parents decided that she would live at home and commute every day to the university campus, navigating the train route that ran from Melrose to Boston, and the pedestrian route that took her through Scollay Square. "I did a lot of walking. I wore out my penny loafers and my Saddle Oxfords, which I loved, and had to buy new ones. I honestly believe that my foot is wider now because of all that walking."

She described her route as a mile and a half from her house in Melrose to the train station. The train took her into the north Boston area. Her walk to her classes took her by Faneuil Hall and through Boston Gardens. "It was beautiful, with swan boats and public activities. Today it's not considered a safe walk, but back then I walked at night because of my work after classes in the upscale dress shop. There weren't any lights. I had to go home in the dark a lot of times, through the Gardens and back to the train station. My father might have picked me up at the train station, or I might have walked home. I was never afraid. Safety wasn't an issue."

Her independent-minded mother had trained her well for this experience of her life, nurturing El's confidence, independence, level-headedness, and delight in new experiences. When El was just starting high school, her parents recognized her artistic skill and recommended that she enroll in Saturday classes offered by the Boston Museum of Fine Arts. The commute would not be an easy one for a young girl whose life had not yet involved city streets. Her mother accompanied her only a few times, showing the way from Melrose to Boston, and then, as a pedestrian, through the town itself. After just a few trial runs, and not to anyone's surprise, El gained confidence, and for the next two years, arrived on time and immersed herself in her classes, all of which took place in the dead of winter. She absorbed every technique, skill, and recommendation offered by her instructors. Interestingly, she became fascinated with drawing nudes. "This was a wakeup call. I realized, even at my young age, that you have to know the skeleton to draw the form correctly." It didn't take long for El to apply what she was learning about human skeletons to horse skeletons. The intricate commute was worth it.

In later years, as a commuter student at Boston University, the gregarious El discovered one drawback to commuting: She had no connection with the dormitories and thus didn't make any close friends. "I was friendly with many, but I don't remember a single name. During my off times, I was running around by myself, usually in the library reading about horses or at Station 16, watching the horses. I remember one single date during college, and it was very uninteresting. All the good guys were gone, fighting in WWII. There were only a few men in the classes, conscientious objectors and those too young or who didn't qualify for service. College had a different atmosphere during the war."

There was eventually one strong acquaintance. On September 16, 1948, the *Melrose Leader*, of Melrose, Massachusetts, published that Eleanor Harmon Fracker, a Spring 1948 graduate of Boston University, had become engaged to Robert Kingston Smith, son of Mr. and Mrs. Frederic H. Smith, 135 Mt. Vernon

Avenue, in Melrose. This was the same gentleman who, before El's senior year in college, had met her on her few Sundays off from Merrymeeting. They spent their short days together hiking and biking. Eleanor recalled that "we didn't do anything together with horses. Eventually, he got more interested in them. It was a case of his needing to like them because I liked them. We actually got together over a white shirt. I wanted one, and he had one. Over he came to our house on his bike, with a white shirt on a hanger. That's really how we got to know each other, nothing really romantic, but it was practical."

The *Melrose Leader* shared that Rob was "attending the University of Massachusetts where he is studying chemical engineering. During the war he served three and one-half years with the Army in the Pacific Theatre." The announcement closed with the news that "a spring wedding is planned." The yellowed clipping had been securely preserved in the 4" x 6" leather-bound address notebook in which El's father had recorded his July 1920 trip from Colorado to Washington state.

Also in the spring of 1948, May 6 to be exact, El received a letter from the BU Graduate School, Office of the Dean, Chester M. Alter, Dean, which stated that the Department of Fine Arts "voted to admit you as a regular student and a candidate for the degree of Master of Arts on the basis of the usual requirements as listed in our bulletin, subject to your receiving the A.B. degree."

Although El knew that a master's degree would serve her well—perhaps allowing her to buy even more horses than she had originally imagined—she did not enter the Master of Arts program in the Boston University Graduate School that year. The pull to go west was too great, and her father was again heading in that direction, this time not on his own but with an invitation to his family. El would not be left behind. "Oh, Lordie," she remembered, "I wanted to go west so badly."

This would not be the first time the family had traveled westward. Because much of his professional work with Automotive Finishers of Detroit required trips to satellite offices, including Kansas City, Missouri, Mr. Fracker had rented a house in that city so that his eager family could join him when he traveled. His plan was to spend time in Kansas City and then head out west, to Denver, and then north through eastern Wyoming, a state with lots of horses.

With good-byes to El's fiancé Rob, and with the family's Cocker Spaniel, Inky, tucked into younger sister Carolyn's lap, the family set off in their station wagon in late 1948 for what proved to be a uniquely adventurous journey. Many years later, El wondered if her father and mother had helped her in making one of the biggest decisions of her life. Because of the family trip, a wiser El knew she could make a choice for her future based on what she had seen, rather than through sketches and snippets and journal entries of what others believed the Wild West looked like. She saw herself as having the ability to be prepared in planning her own journey west. She saw herself as quite practical and able in how she would deal with the uniqueness, vastness, and, especially, the wildness of the West.

It was late in December when the family headed north from Denver on the route that, ten years later, would be known as Interstate 25. According to El, "We made it to Cheyenne, and when we turned onto Route 30 eastward toward Nebraska, I looked up at the sky and knew I would never forget it. It was ominous, with dark and orange colors, maybe caused by a drop in pressure. By evening, the snow started to fall, and by night, it was horizontal, which I'd never seen before. I remember thinking that it was all just wildness. Looking back, we knew this as the winter of a series of harsh blizzards. I should have been frightened, but I wasn't. I was safe with my parents, my sister, and Inky, who Carolyn insisted was hers even though I knew he was Daddy's. Even as the storm raged, I wasn't nervous. I was thinking about how Carolyn was probably just jealous about Inky, since years earlier, I got a horse.

"All along Route 30," El recalled, "the snow drifts were humongous. We finally were stopped by snow drifts that were six feet or maybe higher. The only movement was troop trucks that were lumbering through in both directions. We had to pull over and spent the night in the station wagon. My parents became very serious, and I could tell they were worried. But early in the morning, my dad got out and spent a long time studying the railroad tracks that ran parallel to Route 30. Then, he navigated the station wagon onto the railroad tracks, which, because they were higher ground, had blown free of snow. He let some air out of the tires and drove the tracks, miraculously free of trains, all the way to a town somewhere near Omaha. We had to stop again, the drifts were so high, but my dad got us to a place where the townspeople were taking in folks. The owners of a Woolworth's Five & Ten store took us in."

The next day, plows came through, and the Frackers resumed their journey east and out of the edge of what would be remembered as the Blizzard of '49. El could not get over her father's ingenuity. "You couldn't stop my dad, not in just about any situation. He could fix or solve anything. He was just that determined and wise."

The family drove on to Freedom, New Hampshire. They were exhausted from the long trip, but El remembered that her sister insisted upon cleaning and tidying up her room and even making her bed before getting into it. "We were so different," El recalled. "I just rolled up in a blanket and went to sleep." Her sister was glad to be safely home, but El could not let go of the adventure that had made her dad a hero in her eyes. He was a bit of a chip off the old block. In 1891, his father, Walter Fracker Sr., lived with his mother and father at No. 15 Fourth Street in Chelsea. A burglar broke into the house on the night of Feb. 9, of the same year, according to the *Boston Globe* newspaper. Young Walter, age 27, caught the thief hiding in the closet and "ordered the intruder to leave the

Mr. and Mrs. Walter Fracker Sr. in Freedom.

El's father, Walter S. Fracker Jr.

El's mother, Maxine Griffith Fracker.

El and Carolyn, ready for camp.

Acorn, Freedom, NH.

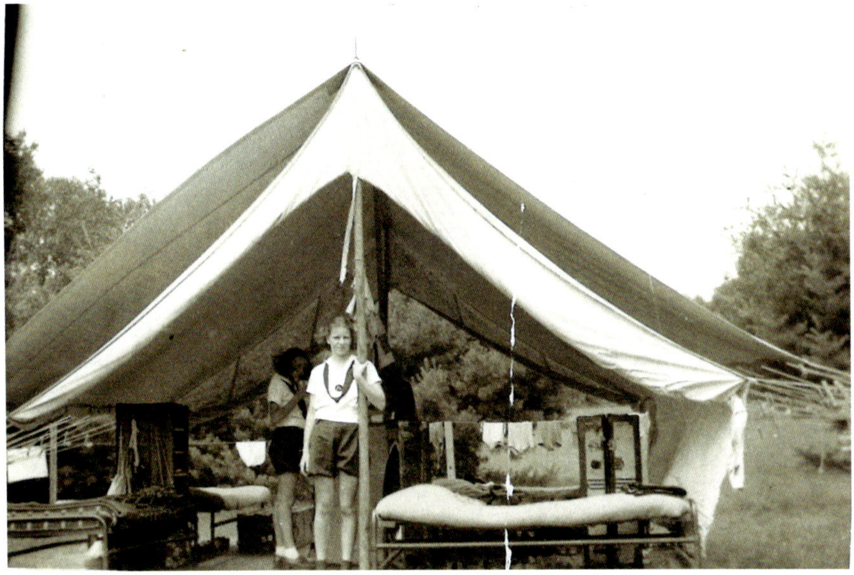

Camp Counselor El.

El and Sammy.

El and Inky.

El and her mother in the New England snow.

El's parents, 1930s.
The location is unknown.

El and Rob Smith in Austria.

El and Rob returning
from Germany, 1953.

El's first Wyoming home.

Photo taken by and courtesy of Rosemary McIntosh.

Margaret Johnson, mentor and friend to El in Wyoming.

Photo courtesy of Joyce Tyrell.

El with her signature smile.

The big house at old Sodergreen Ranch, summer 1966.

Barry.

house." The shaken would-be criminal fled, with Walter in hot pursuit, until police apprehended the man.[37]

As frightening as it was, the Blizzard of '49 did not in any way diminish Eleanor Fracker's desire to someday make the West her home. Echoing her admiration for her father, she stated, "You couldn't stop me." Not only did the West offer her a place to have many horses, she saw it as also offering "wide open spaces and beautiful sunsets and sunrises. Back east, everything was closed in by trees. You could get claustrophobic. In the West, you could see for miles. You could see the whole sky. You were lucky if you saw a tree. It was truly God's country. All that beauty was God's. In the West, everything was a little wilder. I realized I could do anything out there. There was more space to be alive. There was a sense of freedom. I loved New Hampshire, I loved Freedom, but in the West, there was a real freedom feeling."

West Via East

★

Chapter 5

THE WINTER OF '49 EVENTUALLY YIELDED TO SPRING, AND ELEANOR HARMON Fracker and Lieutenant Robert Kingston Smith were married in a simple ceremony, with no guests attending. El completed a four-month employment as the Art Director for the 1949 Boston Red Cross campaign, for which she created brochures and artwork for posters and which coincided with the celebration of Red Cross Month that March. When it was time for Rob to return to the University of Massachusetts to complete his undergraduate studies, the couple moved in with Rob's parents, who were newly settled in Springfield, Massachusetts. When they eventually found their own apartment, El remembered that "it had nothing in it, only a stove, a refrigerator, and pillows to sit on. The pillows were nice."

On May 13, 1949, Mrs. Eleanor Smith of 106 Marsden Street, Springfield, Massachusetts, received a letter confirming her job "as assistant in the Public Relations Department" for the non-profit Springfield Community Chest, starting May 23rd, annual salary $2,100, time off for lunch, and two weeks' vacation after one year. This was El's first salaried and benefitted job. With her mother's financial savvy, her father's self-confidence and love of adventure, and both paternal grandparents' ambitions, El had already determined she would not be a stay-at-home officer's wife.

In 1950, the independent El took on yet another job, as secretary to the Dean of Women at the University of Massachusetts in Amherst. "The Dean should have been in the Army," El said. "She'd have been just right. Everything was done her certain way, down to the tiny detail. The windows had to be open three inches, no more, no less. Everything had to be perfect. Even the plants had to be watered a certain way. We got along, though. I did whatever she wanted me to do the way she wanted me to do it. I didn't have any secretarial skills, but I wanted the job, so I set about to learn in what I called my own weekend class. I figured out every aspect of the job, and I did all right." El's major assignment, though, was nothing insignificant. She was responsible for putting out the weekly newsletter for the entire university.

Rob completed his degree in 1950 and returned to active duty in the Army as a commissioned officer. He soon received orders to Fort Lee, which, post-WWII, became the headquarters for the U.S. Army Quartermaster School. Lieutenant Smith was transferred to Ft. Lee, in Virginia, to receive training as a Quartermaster in the U.S. Army. His wife did not "follow" her husband. She "joined" him.

For some bureaucratic reason, the young couple didn't receive Rob's first monthly paycheck. They rented the small downstairs of a house because it was all they could afford, and El even went to the Red Cross to ask for help. Not one to wait for conditions to better themselves, she again applied for a job that required skills she didn't have. She was determined and was swiftly hired. For the next two years, she worked as the Retouch Artist and Illustrator for the Quartermaster Corps Graphic Arts Division at Fort Lee, Virginia, where she soon gained proficiency in detail drawing and the use of an airbrush, the latter wholly unfamiliar to her.

A letter from El's superior, Captain G. J. Frame, dated 7 September 1951 and addressed "To Whom It May Concern," attested to Eleanor's attributes under his employ: "Her work has been of superior quality and character, and she has proved to be one of my most loyal, conscientious, and industrious employees. In this line of work, she displays skill and originality … efficiency, initiative, and dependability. She [has been] … courteous and co-operative and has shown excellent attitude both toward her co-workers and the organization. I believe she will go far in this field." Captain Frame was correct in conjecturing that art would become a major part of El's life. He just left out the part about horses.

Within the next year, Lt. Smith received orders to Bavaria, where he would be assigned to the Quartermaster Corps., engaging in post-war aid during the final years of the Marshall Plan. His assignments included overseeing four Army hotels in Germany; teaching nutrition and food service courses in the USA Quartermaster School in Lenggries, Germany; and overseeing for one summer the Boy Scout and Girl Scout Camps for Army personnel throughout Europe.

El's passport indicated that she did not join Rob in Bremerhaven, Germany, until March 13, 1952. In the months before her departure, she stayed with her parents. They had sold the house in Melrose and moved to Freedom, renting a small house just outside of the village. A blind collie named Bonnie, a cherished addition to El's life, accompanied her to Freedom. That winter, a terrible snowstorm struck the village. El remembered helping her father shovel and shovel and shovel. One night, she let Bonnie out. Usually, the dog made her way back to the house with no trouble, but El believed that on that particular night, Bonnie's sense of smell was diminished because of the heavy snowfall. When Bonnie didn't return, El and her father went out to find her. She had gone down to a creek to get a drink and stepped in with all four feet, which were swiftly frozen in. Mr. Fracker rescued Bonnie and carried her back to the house. "We thawed her out, and she was okay," said El, "but I had been so worried about her." Shortly after the incident, El received notice to depart for Germany.

She was eager for the adventure, but she knew she would miss having her beloved parents in her life. She would miss the fresh seafood, right off the boat in Maine, where her father commuted for his job. She would miss their Melrose neighbor, Mr. Harry Dibbins, the lobster monger, who often supplied them with fresh catches for supper. She would not find in Germany the morning-chilled bottled milk with cream floating on the top that the Frackers received daily in Melrose. She would hold dear the Christmas memory, when El was six and Carolyn two and the Depression was making its mark, of her parents placing small gifts all the way from the top of the stairs to the bottom and on to the Christmas tree, all tied together with a single string. In a game that El said "made Christmas seem bigger," she and her sister were instructed to "follow the string." El had no recollection of the Depression having a significant effect on the family, but perhaps her parents didn't let on. "We never did have a lot of money, but my parents made every Christmas and holiday fun."

El would miss another Melrose neighbor, Mrs. Fuller, who had lived next door to the Frackers and had touched El with her kindness, graciously taking El in when her parents traveled out of the country. El, a college graduate and an employee with the Red Cross in Boston, was certainly able to stay on her own, but she was not one to depreciate even the smallest moments of generosity. "Mrs. Fuller was so nice. She even fed me breakfast."

El would miss her sister, neither girl ever believing they had anything in common but for one brief time. When they were little, a carnival came into town, and together they rode donkeys, El on Lightning and Carolyn on Thunder, or perhaps it was the other way around.

And would El miss horses? She hoped she would not have to. But Germany was waiting, an adventure in a different country with a different culture, and El was fascinated to hold a passport, with all its power, in her hand.

In nearly every photograph of El as a young girl, her wide grin lights up her face and truly makes her eyes sparkle. Her passport picture, as required, was in stark contrast. Her tight lips suggest impatience, her eyes peer blankly, and her shoulders appear rigid. Nowhere in the picture is there a hint of the delight this young woman found in life. An official stamp indicated that regardless of her desires, she would reside overseas until the last months of 1953. "Person upon whom bearer is dependent" was "Lt. Robert K. Smith." Her "Exact Address Abroad" provided not a physically accessible and welcoming street address but a string of cryptic letters, numbers, and abbreviations: 7717EUCOM Q.M. School A>P>O> 407, %P.M. N.Y N.Y. All this stiffness was deceptive. The holder of this particular passport awaited with eagerness an adventure ahead, one that would unfold in a country and culture so different from her own, with new experiences and circumstances. She was fascinated with the power of this tiny notebook, not much different in size from her father's journal, to enrich her own life, especially the pages waiting for visa stamps. And she would not be dependent on anyone.

As El packed for her trip, she received the strangest of requests from her husband: that she "pack a bunch of ammunition" in her suitcase. Surely, he would not need to engage in any standoffs, but, she surmised, a soldier had to be prepared. She asked no questions, received no answers, and thought nothing of squeezing the ammunition into the small space that her many books had not yet consumed. "I wanted my books, and they were all probably horse books. I didn't know if I'd have time to read or not, but I wasn't taking any chances." Both departing the U.S. and arriving in Germany, the ammo-toting El may have been a bit disappointed that "no one checked anything. I got through without anybody finding out that I was hauling all that ammo." Whereas some might have found the situation cause for worry, El said of her adventure, "That was fun."

The trip to Germany was one of many times that El put her animals' comfort and safety before her own. In fact, placing her utmost efforts toward caring for any animal that depended on her had already become her personal creed. Bonnie, she decided, would make the trip as close to first-class comfort as the airlines could provide. El would travel only a few notches above baggage status. "My aristocratic-looking collie, with such a great ruff of hair, deserved a trip as swift and comfortable as I could arrange." She booked a flight for Bonnie, sending her on her way before her own journey even started. Rob would meet Bonnie in Munich.

El's passage was on the USS Washington, which had been a troop ship during World War II. Post-battle days, the government had stripped the ship to its bare bones. "It certainly didn't have any pools or boutiques or activities," El said. "There really wasn't anything to do, but it was what I needed to get from A to B, and that's all I cared about."

At Bremerhaven, El was given a tag, with a number, to pin on her coat. The number told the authorities how to direct disembarking passengers. "That's all they'd say," El recalled. "I couldn't go exploring about. I didn't like that, being told exactly what to do, so I just held the tag in my hand. I guess I wouldn't have made a good military person."

El found her train on her own, settling into a compartment that was, in her estimation, absurdly small. "To sleep, I had to place my legs in a box that went over to the next compartment. So my body was in one compartment, my legs in another. The bed was quite short, and the bathroom was small, like a porta potty. I had to get used to the toilet rocking back and forth and to the toilet paper, which was somewhat like elastic. A challenge during the trip was getting used to the train's constant pattern: go, stop, back up, repeat." Many would grumble about a stripped ship, compressed spaces, stretchy toilet paper, and a rocking, indecisive train. Not Eleanor Fracker Smith. "I just had to laugh the whole way. It was an experience to remember. It was fun."

Hoping that Bonnie had not met with any bad experiences, El was glad and relieved to finally be reunited with the collie. "When I saw her, I realized that she had been scared. She wasn't with her own people, and she had been in a crate. But she did all right, and of course I was proud of her. She had lost weight, though, and I found out that she wouldn't eat during her travels. I vowed right then and there that if I ever had the chance to train dogs, I would make sure to train them to eat for any handler. I would do all I could to ensure the comfort and care of my animals."

The family of three, finally together, traveled to their small, attractive house, named Waldfreiden ("Friendly Wood"), in the town of Bad Heilbrunn, in Bavaria. Once a resort area, the town where the Smiths would live was struggling. El observed that "on the weekends, everyone got out of town. They went to the mountains, and left everything behind, as if they just walked away. It was nearly an exodus, but a good exodus. They even left their woes behind." That, she considered, was not something that would happen in America, leaving everything behind.

The Smiths lived on the top floor of the house; the lower floor was vacant. Flowers grew on the balcony. The door handles were not the round-knobbed kind that El was used to in America. Instead, each was a long, thin bar of a handle. They proved, to El's delight, to be practical. A second collie, Barry (pronounced as "bar e"), purchased after the Smiths' arrival in Germany, soon mastered the handles and was able to open the door that would allow him and his blind companion Bonnie, on whom he doted, to go outside on their own.

The lovely house's property backed up to a mountain, and El soon discovered there were many places to walk, run, and bike. She had had her bike shipped to Germany. It came to practical use in that the Smiths had only one car, a DeSoto, and Rob needed the car every day to get to the military post where he was stationed. If El needed the car, she had to drive Rob to work. On the way, the ever-friendly El always picked up a German boy waiting for the bus. "He and his friends were so courteous. The people in Bavaria were all so pleasant." The Bavarians, she learned, liked having the Americans there. They shared that Bavaria had wanted to secede from Germany and had wanted nothing to do with Hitler.

El was warned about the difficulty of getting a driver's license. According to the grapevine, even some of the colonels could not pass the test, not because of the driving required, but because of the written part of the test. A baffling question appeared on the test, involving all the possible circumstances at cross-roads. The cross-roads were devoid of a light, and the traffic included buses, cows, oxen, humans, and other assorted animals. The test-taker was asked to determine, in given situations, who was to proceed and in what order. This scenario actually happened in reality, with frequent accidents occurring at numerous cross-roads. Luckily, there wasn't much traffic in this southern area—unlike Munich, where drivers were advised by the locals to close their eyes, shove in the accelerator, and go. El easily figured out the logic required to negotiate the intersections and passed the test.

A gardener and a maid were assigned to the Smiths' house, but they didn't stay long. With no gardener, the grass grew, and eventually some workers arrived with a horse and a cow harnessed together to a wagon to cut the grass. El learned that milk cows were being used in harness because few horses remained in the area. Survivors of the war had had to eat their animals. El was saddened but not horrified by this fact of life in the war-torn country. The measures the people took were practical and necessary. After cutting the hay that grew on the Smiths' property, the wagon drivers somehow ran the wagon through the clothesline. Rob had a temper, and it flared, and he demanded they put the posts back up. El, in contrast, sympathized with the people who were becoming her friends, people who were delighted to share with her what she saw as a touch of home: "milk from Denmark, with a lot of cream on top."

Upon arriving in Bavaria, El tried to get a job similar to the one she had held at Ft. Lee, but dependent wives were not allowed to take jobs. Available jobs had to go to the Germans. The gregarious El accepted the circumstances and turned to making friends. The colonel's wife recruited her to be head of a girls' and boys' club for the young military dependents. "I was supposed to teach them how to ski. I didn't know much, so it was like being thrown into a pond to learn to swim." To teach herself how to teach, she borrowed a lesson from horseback riding. "I made myself go up the ski lift. Then I had to get back down. I had no choice. It was pretty much stop and go, but by the time I got to the bottom, I had learned what I needed to teach."

The colonel's wife urged El to continue with the group, which was not unlike the United States' Boy and Girl Scouts. El agreed to help, but only if the other parents became involved. No parent came forward. El, who knew the love and involvement of family and the kindness of adult friends, was astounded that any parent would show a lack of interest in their children's development. The teacher in her must have had a change of heart because notes in a later resumé indicate that she "taught crafts at a Boy Scout Camp in Germany."

In Bavaria, the gregarious El and the charming Rob made numerous friends with whom they skied and shared meals. El particularly remembered a Swiss woman named Doris, who gave El gifts of wonderful Swiss candy. Once, El and Rob, both strong and athletically adventurous, took the tram to the Jungfrau, one of the main summits of the Bernese Alps. They required the assistance of a guide to make their way down the mountain. "Boy, I needed it," El said of the snowplow ski maneuver, calling it "her savior" on the mountain, which offered many icy angles and turns. As they made their way down the mountain, Doris's husband, a member of the Swiss Air Force, flew his squadron plane low to gesture a greeting to these new American friends. The Smiths' guide was irate, fuming and shouting that the stunt could have caused an avalanche. It did not, but El was rather delighted by such a unique—albeit reckless—show of friendship.

As they neared the bottom of the Jungfrau, El and Rob had to remove their skis and climb a ladder to the next slope. The descent was narrow and twisting, like luge driving, El recalled, with many crevasses. "I think I snowplowed all the way. So did Rob." She would not, however, have missed that experience for the world. Despite the extreme danger and risks—or perhaps because of them—the trip was, according to El, "a highlight, an exciting adventure and a real challenge. I enjoyed all of it, as well as the amazing hello from high on a mountain!"

The treacherous Jungfrau did not daunt El's newfound enjoyment of skiing. In fact, she became quite the daredevil. Nebelhorn, German for "fog," was never free of fog. In the Allgau Alps of Germany, Nebelhorn rose to 7,297 feet. El took the hills fast and shot down the steep slopes, going, as she was told after a run, 50 miles per hour. "It was exhilarating until my skis lost their parallel position. One ski tipped one way or the other, and I fell hard. It took two days to get my stomach back to where it belonged." Her father and grandfather taught her that no experience was without a lesson. "I learned a lesson that applied to life—that if you felt you were going too fast, you probably couldn't handle it."

One unique incident occurred on the Zugspitze, the highest mountain in Germany, at 9,718 feet. Its name, from "Zugbahnen," translates to "avalanche paths." El was descending the mountain when she spied a policeman sitting on a snowbank. As she passed him, he required that she show him her passport, which she knew to always carry with her. He stamped her passport, and she went on, realizing that high on the mountain, she had just passed from Bavaria, Germany into Tyrol, Austria. She was much more impressed with having skied from one country to another than having made her way through treacherous avalanche paths.

Skiing, a novelty, took up most of El's time in Bavaria. She admitted that she had very little time for all the reading she had packed in her suitcase alongside Rob's requested ammunition. Soon, though, another interest, known well to some of the actors in her ancestry, presented itself to the young woman who would never tire of new adventures. The interest was wood carving. "I had always been interested in wood. I loved wood. In Germany, there were many carvers. The one who taught me had been a former SS captain. I don't remember how I learned about him. He had returned to Bavaria, to his folks, once he got out of the SS." Wood carving, like painting, became one of El's lifelong hobbies. Her favorite subject and her specialty? Horses.

The wood carver often invited El to dinner. The meals included berries and other ingredients, cooked in a great pot. "It was a sort of dumpling," El remembered, "with bread that rose on the top. It was so good. These meals were special to me, regardless of this man's past. I was breaking bread with a German family. A man, his mother and father, all together, with me."

El soon discovered that a common practice existed in the military community. The dependents, all of whom shopped in the commissary, were given allotments on certain items, for example 12 cartons of cigarettes per month. They bought up cigarettes, cocoa, and coffee till they reached the allotment level and then used these commodities to trade with the Germans. El traded for dishes, crystal, and carvings. And borrowed horses.

El had been determined to learn German so that she could better immerse herself in the experiences waiting for her. Frustrated by trying to use a book to learn the language, El turned to the maid, before the maid departed. "I had trouble thinking in the language because all the verbs come at the end. Our maid sat down with me and taught me the names of things I had to work with, like 'table' and 'stove.' And then she went with me in the car to farms, where I could talk to proprietors to rent a horse to ride. I found one and paid for the rental in cigarettes, cocoa, and coffee. After I paid, the owners simply said, 'There's the saddle,' and left me free to ride."

El was ecstatic that she had traded for a horse, but she quickly discovered that she faced two immediate obstacles. "I brought out the horse and groomed him. I reached for the saddle, which was sitting on a wooden structure, and quickly realized it was a doghouse and that inside was a German Shepherd with her pups. A huge German Shepherd, I realized, when it stepped out of the house, going 'grrrrrr.'" El was not afraid. The dog opened its mouth, pinched El on her calf with its teeth, and then went back inside the doghouse. El never had any more trouble with the dog. She may not have mastered German, but she had indeed learned the language of the German Shepherd. "The dog was teaching me a lesson. If I didn't pay attention to the lesson and learn it, if I stepped over her bounds, I would be in trouble. I learned it, and she didn't bother me again." The second obstacle was this: The horse knew only German. Luckily, they both knew body language. And they both knew "Halten Sie!"

Despite the language barrier, life in Germany was easy for the young military wife. El spent her days with her dogs, hobbies, and pleasant friendships. She traveled to Italy, Austria, France, Belgium, Switzerland, and Holland. Characteristically, she took advantage of all that was offered. She missed her family but was content to write them long and detailed letters of her experiences. Sometimes she imagined staying longer in Germany, finding the country and the people wonderful.

She had an unshakeable feeling, though, "that I wanted to accomplish something. I wanted to get home, to get going with my life. In Germany, as wonderful as it was, I felt kind of stalled, like I was sitting in limbo. I couldn't do what I wanted, so far away from home." She pushed these ideas to the back of her mind, but horses and the West would not stay there. When the orders came through for Lt. Robert K. Smith to return to the United States, El was not the least bit unhappy. El's final passport visa was stamped November 1953.

Honorably discharged from service, Rob entered MIT to complete a Master's degree in the field of food science and chemistry. El returned to the work force, securing a job as a file clerk at MIT. She was shortly "rescued" by the head of the Alumni Association, who found out that El was "outdoorsy." She soon had a team of six people working under her, as they prepared the large MIT-published roster of MIT alumni. All revisions were El's responsibility, and of course, all the content had to be correct to the letter. She often had to take work home with her, but she found the job fun, partly because of the precision involved and partly because her boss held a position in the Appalachian Trail Association and asked her to handle all his correspondence with the association. She worked in the Alumni Association office until the early summer of 1956.

His degree earned, Rob shared with El that he had been awarded an assistantship to teach and take courses toward a doctorate in chemistry at the University of Wyoming in Laramie. El knew that if she agreed to go with Rob, she would leave behind her loving and supportive family and the familiarity of the two small towns she called home. The passion was too great, though, and the pull too strong. She wanted the West, and she wanted lots of horses. "I told Rob that Wyoming was fine with me."

In late August of 1956, El and Rob loaded up their car "and possibly a trailer," El recollected, "since we had an awful lot of stuff," including two collies, one kapok-stuffed coat, a pair of snowshoes, El's bike, and her grandfather's refitted wooden "Old Maine" canoe. They headed west along U.S. Route 30. With that, quite suddenly, El's unrelenting dream to spend a life out west, surrounded by lots of horses, became a practical reality.

Just Up Route 230

Chapter 6

It was Monday, September 3rd. A light snow had just started to fall when El and Rob Smith stopped on U.S. Route 30, not yet "old Route 30," just as the two-lane gravel-and-oil trans-American road leveled out from its steep descent. The couple had made the arduous climb from Cheyenne over the wind-whipped summit of the Laramie Range, where the highest point of the transcontinental route, named the Lincoln Highway, marked an elevation of 8,640 feet.

From where the couple stopped, they could see to the west the Laramie Valley, where the town of Laramie, which by then was calling itself a city, was nestled. At an elevation of 7,220 feet, it was a dry and windy place. Bland, blocky houses crowded around the downtown area, dusted heavily with soot from the trains that rumbled through daily. All the trees were gnarly cottonwoods, and they were lacking. Bleak, brown grass and a brittle sage-scratched prairie spread out in all directions and forever. The late summer palette of browns was interrupted only once, by a large plot of green that El mistook for a meadow. It was part of the University of Wyoming's land. Called Prexy's Pasture, this grazing section in the center of the campus was still on the books as the location where horses were to be hobbled while their owners attended or taught classes.

If El felt a wave of homesickness for family and familiarity, she didn't let on. If the dry, chilly, stinging wind on her face made her suddenly long for the green grass, trees, rolling lawns, and northeast humidity of Melrose, Massachusetts, elevation 95 feet, and Freedom, New Hampshire, elevation 439 feet, she said not a word.

She was worried, though. "I came here for lots of horses, and I knew I couldn't have them in that compressed town. It wasn't what I wanted at all." She shaded her eyes and peered further across the valley, her view made hazy by the swirls of horizontally blowing snow. Jelm Mountain, Sheep Mountain, and the Snowy Range Mountains rose in the distance. Offices were surely closed in town, for the young couple had arrived on Labor Day. On Tuesday, then, El would see about a place to live, up near those mountains. The couple spent the night at the Snowy Range Motel, near the bridge over the railroad tracks to the west side of Laramie. The townspeople, El and Rob discovered, were friendly.

At the university's Agricultural Extension Office, El was told of the immediate availability of a small, rustic cabin on Sodergreen Ranch, just a stone's throw from the Big Laramie River. The cabin squatted near a big house and a huge old barn, all of which were owned by the Lewis family of the Lewis Ranch. El and Rob could rent the cabin for a month until the house became available for rent. El did not hesitate to sign the papers and was instructed to "head southwest from here just up Route 230 for twenty-three miles, go past Sodergreen Lake on your right, and then turn left at the first entrance you come to." El might have missed the lake, with nary a landmark nor the greenery customarily surrounding northeastern lakes, but she held the keys to the cabin, and although a total newcomer to the vast country of endless prairie and few signs, she already sensed where her home was. "The whole vista was primitive, and that's what I had longed for. I loved all the woods, the fall colors, the wooden bridge, and being out in the country. I belonged." She and Rob, with her collies, the small and athletic Barry and the elegant, full-ruffed Bonnie, made themselves at home in the cabin on Sodergreen Ranch in short order. Even blind Bonnie adapted quickly enough to lead the German-born Barry about the place as if she had lived there forever.

The towering barn stood to the west of the house, which faced west. Just south of the house and barn flowed the Big Laramie River, its origin in the mountains of northern Colorado. The old barn had once been a way station for the stagecoach that had brought vacationers and those eager to fish the mountain streams. Out front of the house was an oversized, circular, graveled area. In days past, it had served as an easy turnabout for the stagecoaches' teams of horses.

The ranch structures had been hand-built in 1878 by Swedish homesteader Oscar Sodergreen, who had lived on the property with his wife and their daughters Cora, Sonny, and Susan. Thick, tall pine trees had been felled and planed into heavy timbers, and stout boards were connected with dovetail joints. All the work had been done by hand, and no nails were used. In the barn, El found an old adze, Mr. Sodergreen's carved initials visible on the handle. Adzes and hand saws, craftsmanship and brute strength, and the determination to create a home on the lone prairie had been responsible for these sturdy and functional buildings.

In her book *Just Beyond Harmony*, Gaydell Collier described the tiny, four-room cabin that briefly was home to the Smiths. "Framed by a thickness of large cottonwoods … it looked overgrown and abandoned, but also snug and permanent. … [It] looked square, and the roof sloped up on all four sides to the center chimney. … [An] enclosed porch ran the width of the front. … Wild roses ran rampant … and the burbling sound of gentle water lent a cheerful aura."[38] It was a long path from the primitive house to the privy; the kitchen was equipped with only an old, enameled cookstove and a hand-pump; and there was no running water. El never uttered an unkind word about the cabin. It was perfect. She was sure, however, that the ranch begged for horses, lots of them. And if there were horses to be had, El would find them.

El soon made the acquaintance of John Gorman, who was at the time Assistant Professor of Animal Sciences at UW and had authored the book *Western Horses*. He took El on as a student of Western riding and, after only a few classes, was talked into letting his affable, energetic, pony-tailed yet highly practical student from the Northeast "borrow two horses, one for me and one for Rob." El appreciated Dr. Gorman's instruction but found it interesting that much of the information was familiar to her. "I did learn, though, how to put roses correctly down the draft horses' manes for parades." At the end of the class, El returned the horses and set out to find her own.

Even before her search began, El was confronted with what she saw as a critical decision: to buy a saddle and continue to cook on the massive cast iron stove that was primarily designed only to heat the big house, to which she and Rob had now moved, or to buy a new electric stove. "Most people might choose modern, but that old stove gave off lots of heat. It was a big old thing with a place for mittens. You had to keep feeding it and cleaning up after it, but I loved it. It was better than electricity. It was practical. Besides, I needed a saddle more than I needed to cook on any fancy new stove."

The horse purchases imminent, El chose slick fork saddles, from the SIMCO company out of Tennessee, for herself and for Rob. His cost $85, and hers $75. "My golly," El said of her purchase, "they were expensive saddles, but they were nice." She wanted only what was best for her first horses in the West. A slick fork saddle, which looked like a typical Western saddle, featured no knee rolls. It also lacked carving on the flexible fenders, allowing for more comfort for the rider. A light saddle, its seat was fairly flat, and there was very little slope from the pommel (the swell in front of the seat) to the cantle (the swell behind the seat). The reddish leather was of high quality. Most importantly, the saddle was designed to sit well on, and conform to, almost any horse. Thus, El didn't have to deal with too wide or too narrow a gullet (the underside/backbone of the saddle). The saddles were easy to clean, with just the use of saddle soap and Lexol. "That didn't mean we didn't have to take care of the saddles. Saddles must be treated with care. In transporting, showing, or roping, no rider should ever want to throw them on the ground or just toss them in the back of a pickup where the motion of the truck will rub and wear away the leather. If they're taken care of, they'll always look like new. The leather will last forever. I still have Rob's."

Rob's older sister and her husband worked a cattle ranch in Bozeman, Montana. She said she had a Thoroughbred named Ranger for Rob. El made the trip to Bozeman by herself. With Barry and Bonnie as companions, she drove through unfamiliar and unforgiving territory, pulling an empty wooden one-horse trailer, to fetch the horse who, she assessed, "turned out to be not so great at racing." The trip with what El assessed as an "adequate" trailer was not without its adventures, but El, daughter of the daring Walter S. Fracker Jr., was ready for the adventures that seemed to always accompany trips.

"Before I left, a woman asked for a ride as far as Douglas, Wyoming. She had a little brat with her, who kept throwing things out the window. I was happy when I could leave that woman and her child behind. Then a terrible storm hit at the pass into Bozeman. At one point, I had to find a place for Barry and Bonnie to relieve themselves, so I got off on the side of the road. The storm was so bad, I had to keep the dogs on their leashes. I had just decided to sleep there till morning, since I couldn't see a thing, when a big rig with bright lights passed, and I knew I could follow it into Bozeman. I took off." This newcomer to the west had intuitively and decisively picked up a practice known well to old-timers and seasoned travelers of the West: When visibility doesn't exist, get behind a trucker.

El bought Prince, an American Saddlebred, from a Colorado State University student. Advertised for sale in the Laramie newspaper as a five-gaited horse, Prince turned out, according to El, to be a three-gaited horse. "He loved to jump. He loved it so much that he would jump by himself." She described him as "a wonderful, gentle, nice horse even though he was high-spirited." He was trained for steer roping but soon became accustomed to El's use of him in everything from instruction to Jubilee Day parades. "I had to teach him how to be comfortable with the flag. I'd never done that before. So I put a blanket on a pole and rode him around and around the pasture. He did everything right. The neighbors thought I had lost all my marbles."

Training Ranger, the Thoroughbred, was El's job. Rob's connection to horses went only as far as his love for El. He was intrigued by the West and by horses, and even learned, under El's tutelage, how to properly care for and shoe a horse. Dealing with quirks and stubbornness and reversing any poor training, though, was best left up to El.

Ranger was not without his challenges, and El was not without her love for any opportunity that involved horse and rider training. Once, after taking Ranger on a morning-long trail ride parallel to the Big Laramie River, El turned Ranger for home, at a walk. Ignoring El's cue, Ranger took charge and bolted toward home and hay at a gallop, displaying an equine behavior known as being barn-sour. Barn-sour behavior wouldn't do, not in any of El's horses!

"I would call what I did intuition," she said. "I wouldn't call it knowledge back then. Every time he got it into his head to bolt, I started turning him round and round and round, in tighter circles, to slow him and make him mind my leg and body cues, to show him who was boss. Evidently that was the right thing to do. I kept it up nearly all day, as long as it took us to get back home at a walk. He never bolted again, and I was pleased that he and I had learned a lesson."

El and Rob had patiently counted the days till they moved into the big house. It was admittedly large for one couple, with two stories and an attic, seventeen large rooms in all, but El was already brainstorming how she could use the space to fit her dreams. The house looked west, toward the barn. Through the entry and to the south was a bathroom, a pantry, and a kitchen adjacent to a spacious living room. Just outside the kitchen was the water pump house, with the pump precariously perched on a sewing machine. Through the entry and to the left, or north, was an equally roomy dining area, and just beyond, a bedroom. A sunny living room, a craft room, and the stairs to the bedrooms were to the back and north of the house. Those who had ever stayed upstairs in any of the five or six rooms depicted the house as a drafty place. When the wind blew through those big rooms, the guests feared the roof would come off.

Even the pups had their own room. One can't manage on the Western prairie without a healthy dose of cleverness, and El was clever, working with what she had on hand. When El's German Shepherd, Minx, had her litters, El placed her and her pups in a back room that served, when there were no litters, as a second living room, complete with ping-pong table. El altered the low single window in the room to provide easy access to the outdoors and then constructed a pen in the outdoor space below the window. When the pups needed to be put out, El conveniently dropped them out the window. From the pen, she could plop them back inside.

As happens in many small towns in Wyoming, even before the Smiths had settled in the big house, their circle of friends began to grow. On a particularly windy afternoon, El chose to ride her bike farther up Route 230 to the Jelm Post Office, a small, isolated wooden building just off the main road. She referred to her exhausting push up the road and into the characteristically ferocious wind as "resistance training." Her plan included, in proper New England fashion, a visit with the kindly postmistress, Phoebe MacDougall.

As El was preparing to leave, Margaret Johnson strolled into the post office. Margaret and Everett Johnson, married in 1947, lived just west of El and Rob, on the ranch that had been owned and worked by Everett's parents, Wes and Geil Johnson, and had been settled by Everett's grandparents and great uncle in 1879. When Margaret learned of El's plan to ride her bike the three-and-one-half miles back home, she responded in ranch-friendly fashion by lifting El's bike into her car trunk and stating, "I am going to take you home." Thus began the close friendship between the Johnsons and the Smiths. Margaret's daughter, Joyce, described El and Rob as "part of the family, nothing less." El didn't see Margaret "as a mother figure in any way. She was a mentor and a dear friend.

She helped me with so many things, including introducing me to the families who would become part of our lives."

El made a particular impression on the young Joyce. Horse-crazy herself, Joyce fell in love with El. "I idolized her. She had so much knowledge, especially about horses. And she had that strong New England accent. She told us that she'd spent several years overseas with her husband Rob, and so I was convinced that hers was an overseas accent, probably German."

With no television, Joyce looked forward to neighborhood get-togethers of plentiful food and conversation, especially those with El and Rob. "Some evenings, we'd go down to their place, which was so wonderful with all its big rooms, and El would always have a cake ready. Despite later stories of El's dependence on Bisquick for cooking, these were homemade cakes, although she might have baked them ahead and then frozen them."

What Joyce and El soon held in common was their love of the big barn. "Close to 100 years old," said Joyce, "that barn was my favorite place in the whole world to play, starting when I was five or six years old. As you entered, to the left were the five or six stoutly built and wide horse stalls, open in the back, with no gate, and a feeder in the front. When the guests went to the big house for their lunches, the stagecoach teams, of two horses each, were led to the barn, with all their harnesses still on. They went right to their own stalls and were then tied with their halters. They were hungry and nickered in anticipation of the hay that would be put down to their mangers from the hay mow above."

The Johnsons spread the news that there were newcomers to the area, and El and Rob Smith were absorbed into the community. Fall picnics drew large and amiable crowds, and when winter descended in full force, skating parties were held on the canal that carried water from the Big Laramie River to Sodergreen Lake, on the other side of Route 230. This same canal was where, in the summers, El paddled her beloved grandfather's canoe.

As friendships developed, the Wyoming wind became responsible for triggering a significant change in El's life. Back east, where breezes blew, a name could afford to be shortened to a single soft staccato, such as "El." El's new friends, who in daily practice bellowed into the wind's blast, knew that even the slightest bit of additional weight to a name, if only in syllables, was a necessity under the big sky and over the vast prairie. Without discussing it among themselves, El's new friends began to call her "Ellie."

Ellie and Rob settled in the big house just after Rob began his teaching assistantship and doctoral coursework in the University of Wyoming Chemistry Department. It was October, and although the vibrantly colored maples of New England were not to be seen, the trees and brush came alive with autumn's bloom, described as "so beautiful" by Joyce, "with the red fringe of the willows and the yellow cottonwood leaves above. And there were those bountiful lavender lilac bushes surrounding the house, certainly planted by a previous dweller."

Ellie, as farsighted and shrewd as her mother taught her to be, had known that unless she wanted to work down in Laramie, away from the ranch she had immediately loved, she might eventually have to find some sort of work in the little town of Harmony, just a few miles down Route 230. She embraced learning and could not dismiss the notion of teaching young people. Perhaps Harmony's one-room schoolhouse, for grades 1 through 8, would have her. In the early fall of 1956 she enrolled in teacher certification classes at the University of Wyoming. For the next two years, she sailed through applied and advanced art courses and history of Wyoming, as well as Education courses in teaching language arts, social studies, science, and arithmetic. "Perhaps," as far as Ellie Smith was always concerned, was merely the precursor to "Definitely." Teaching certification could be a ticket to Ellie's dream: a ranch with lots of horses.

Holidays, weekends, and summers were free, though, during the five semesters Ellie studied to become a teacher. All around her was the beauty of the foothills of the Snowy Range. All around was a new way of life and new experiences to be had. Not one to sit around and wonder, Ellie greeted each day as full of joy and adventure. And into nearly a year of those days marched Rosemary McIntosh.

Rosemary remembered "exactly when Ellie and I had our fun together. It was from September 1957 to June 5, 1958. It was a very small part of her life, but it was some of the best months of mine." Rosemary's husband was a student in Animal Husbandry, in the College of Agriculture at UW. After living in the Ivinson Apartments on Ivinson Street in Laramie, Rosemary and Bob jumped at the chance, at $25 per month, to move into the cabin that the Smiths had vacated for the big house.

"The cabin may have had only an outhouse," Rosemary said, "but at least it had the pump for water, which was a fortunate feature." Bob had also been a farrier at the UT Bar Ranch in Glendevie, Colorado, so he knew horses. However, he didn't know chemistry, so Rob offered to tutor him at night, in the cabin's kitchen. "That's how Ellie and I met," Rosemary said, "over chemistry."

Rosemary worked in the Ag Building as a typist and secretary for seven Ag Research scientists. She and Bob took turns driving to the university with Rob, just to save gas. Bob was on the GI bill, making $105 per month, $25 of which he gave to Rob. "They weren't rich," recalled Rosemary, "but they were happy together. Rob had a great sense of humor. We all had a lot of fun together. We mostly talked and did things around the ranch. It was good that they found the property up Route 230. Ellie would not have been happy in the town, with just Second and Grand streets and scattered gas stations, nothing to the left or to the right except for the university. Laramie was layered with cinders that spewed from the smokestacks of trains that rumbled through daily." Old-timers would tell of the drugstore, which had had a chair set up specifically for taking painful cinders out of people's eyes.

When Rosemary's husband graduated in June of 1958, they moved to another ranch, but Rosemary and Ellie had made sure that every day prior was filled with fun. What Rosemary loved most about Ellie "was her sense of humor. We would laugh at anything, especially the harshness of living out there in Wyoming. It was an adventure, and Ellie was just beginning her life as a horsewoman in the West. She'd been an English rider till then, and she encouraged me—all Western, old Western saddle, tall Western horse—to ride English. She loved trail riding, and when it warmed up on winter weekend days, we rode up Jelm Mountain to a vast view. Ellie and her plans fit into that vastness. She came here knowledgeable about horses and just picked up more knowledge and more horses."

The McIntosh and Smith families often ate meals together in the big kitchen. Ellie liked to cook, but, according to Rosemary, she was dependent on Bisquick. "I always thought she might add something to it so that it didn't taste like toilet paper. But she didn't."

Rosemary also had a bit of trouble with Ellie's dogs. "They were beautiful, but one of them would always come up and pee on my shoes. And she was always boiling elk bones for those dogs. I can still smell that awful smell after sixty-seven years. But, damn, I loved her. She was like an older sister. We loved to talk, and Bob was always saying, 'Talk faster or tell shorter stories.'"

Stories that Rosemary and Ellie vividly remember lay claim to the fact that neither of these energetic and animated women, immigrants to the West, were content to sit on the sidelines as mere observers of this new world of theirs. Theirs was a desire to immerse themselves in that different and wondrous land, to learn and live every aspect of it, fully and delightedly.

As one story goes, an old trapper named Walt Smith set beaver traps along the Laramie River bank. Ellie and Rosemary, fascinated with his trade, begged to go along on one of his trap checks. Despite the stinky smell of trap scent and nearly 50 pounds of dead, wet beaver, Ellie and Rosemary eagerly agreed when Walt suggested they haul his catch of the day back to the ranch. Stumbling and laughing, clinging to each other so they wouldn't fall flat, the two friends lugged their load across the dam and one-eighth of a mile back home. The beaver's head, like an off-kilter pendulum, butted them in their backs as the tail whacked their legs. Rosemary "bet Walt was laughing all the way behind us. And darned if we weren't too, even as we pulled the tub in front of the woodstove and took bath after bath."

Just before their Thanksgiving together, Ellie bought two white geese, which took over the yard, like watch dogs. The problem was how to catch them and get them into the pen she had built. Bob offered to rope them, but how might one rope a goose? Bob climbed on his horse, uncoiled his rope, and began chasing one of the geese. Ellie and Rosemary followed in Ellie's old Willys jeep until the bird jumped in the river. Bob and his horse charged right after, into the cold river and directly into a river hole. Bob's hat got soaking wet. So did Bob. So did the horse. The horse bobbed up and got onto land, as did Bob, with his hat. Rosemary recalled that it was a new hat, now ruined. Bob, however, was victorious. Shivering uncontrollably in the cold, he had the goose roped. Ellie wasted no time. She grabbed it, pulled the goose's neck up the arm of the kapok-stuffed coat she had brought from back east, and somehow secured the coat to the jeep's gear shift, which came up from the floor of the vehicle. It was up to Ellie then to figure out how to kill, boil, and pluck a goose. "It was the toughest goose the four of us ever ate," she said, "and we had a blizzard of goose feathers for a long time, but at least we had a bird for Thanksgiving. And we got to see how a goose is roped, although Bob never offered to do that again."

Life up Route 230 was not without its hardships. The Smiths' home had no conveniences but for roofs, walls, and the big stove. If work was to be done, it was up to the Smiths to do it, however difficult, unless they called on their caring neighbors, who themselves were living long-day, long-week lives. When Ellie and Rob decided it would be important to have a television in the big house, they mastered a means to climb up onto the towering house, the roof of which was steeply built to prevent snow from piling on it. Figuring that the house had two stories, an attic, and eight-foot-high ceilings on both floors, the roof was, in Ellie's estimation, "high off the ground." From their risky perches, they ran wire from one end of the peak to the other to secure the antennae. It was Ellie's job to scoot the entire spine of the roof, and she was scared. "But you can't not do something if it needs to be done, just because you're afraid," Ellie believed, and so she inched her way along, making several trips, making sure to never look down. "I soon got a bit braver and started crawling on all fours rather than sitting. And, you know, the view was beautiful from up there—the vast meadows, the wooden bridge, the copse of trees, the meadow, the river, and the old but stout buildings. Everything everywhere was beautiful."

All could not be perfect, however. From up that high, the beauty obscured the enormous mosquito swarms of the spring and early summer. Then there were the winters. When she eventually acquired horses, Ellie had no need to haul water to the animals in the summer because the river flowed through their corral. However, in the winter she had to cut the ice, which formed on the river at least five inches thick, so that the horses might drink. "Sometimes I had to use the adze to cut through the thick ice, and when I was done, I came inside the house looking like an iceberg. My wet clothes were stiff, my joints were stiff, and I stiff-wobbled instead of walked. My situation was not good for forward motion, and I was forced to take only small steps. Iced up in my many layers of clothes, I looked like and felt like a snowman."

The dangers of winter gave way in the mid and late summers to another menace: lightning. Ellie recalled that one summer day, she and Rob hauled their Laycox horse trailer over to Cheyenne to pick up a mare and foal. The trailer was ideal for safe and comfortable travel because its design allowed the foal to move freely near his mother, who was tied. The trip was an enjoyable one, but after returning in the afternoon to the ranch and taking care of the mare and foal, they entered the house and knew something was wrong. In the dining room were signs of a lightning strike. After investigating, they determined that the lightning had hit the transformer, which was outside the house but close to it. They then discovered the path of the lightning inside the house: bursting through the electrical outlets in the dining room and traveling along the wainscoting and farther up the wall. The floor itself was charcoaled. Ellie could not believe, and was thankful to God, that the old house hadn't burned down.

Wild animals were also a frequent menace. Looking out the back window of the house, Ellie once saw "a very long and bushy tail going through the back yard." She had no idea how long the huge cat, its species prone to attack, might lurk about, but she did know that it was time to let her dogs out to relieve themselves and have a bit of a run, and she was impatient. Her animals came first. She grabbed the only means of protection in the house, an ax, and headed out just ahead of the dogs. "I couldn't be afraid of the mountain lion because I was concerned for the dogs. When I let them out, their hackles were up and I was ready with the ax, but we never saw it." However, when she told her father the tale, he immediately sent out, through the mail, his .25-35 saddle rifle, complete with scabbard for use on horseback.

Critters inside were as bad as those outside. "Rats!" Ellie said. "Can you believe it? Rats that were able to get between the logs in the kitchen and behind the wall boards? You could hear them running in there, about waist high. The cats were so intrigued." Not one to shudder at any task, Ellie, with Rob's help, cut through the wallboard, and the cats got the rats. "It's strange how they eat all but the tail," she reflected, without an ounce of squeamishness. Because they didn't want to bother the Lewis family, since they paid so little for rent, Ellie and Rob mixed up cement to fill the big hole they had made, cleaned up the mess, and got everything back to order. Nothing daunting, just routine life in the wilds of the West. Ellie wouldn't trade these "routines" for the world.

Life just up Route 230 was incredibly different from that of Melrose and Freedom. It offered daily lessons that might try a person to the edge. Success was in attitude. Living there and loving it required ingenuity, strength of character and body, a desire to learn, and an incredible sense of humor, optimism, fearlessness, and determination, all of which Eleanor Smith possessed.

Rosemary presented this sentiment in more personal terms. "Ellie was young, gregarious, loving, savvy, smarter than all get-out. But what was most important for her story is that she was eager to get something going on her own. And of course she did."

Getting Something Going

Chapter 7

BARRY AND BONNIE WERE NOT JUST DOGS. THEY WERE ELLIE'S LOYAL companions. Of course, they had their moments of mischievousness, but for the most part, they bore an uncanny knack for reading Ellie, for understanding what she needed and wanted from them. Ellie had the knack as well. She could read her two sweet collies. She loved them and never raised a hand or her voice, with the exception of beckoning them from danger. She was empathetic, sensing their needs and fulfilling them even before her own. She knew that patience, kindness, and caring, as well as consistent and clear requests, would plant the seed of trust and eager obedience in her animals. Love, Ellie knew, could move mountains, or in her case, a very large dog. From love, mixed with innate skill and pedigreed acumen, it was a short distance to recognizing that she could breed and sell dogs to responsible and loving owners. She could then stay on the ranch, work with her animals, and not have to go into Laramie for a job. That's what she did.

"I loved my collies, but it was German Shepherds that I wanted to own and work with as far back as I can remember," Ellie said. "I'd describe them as helpful dogs. You really had to train them, but once bonded, they would do anything for you." Minx and Derry were the first of the loyal and loved Shepherds at Sodergreen Ranch. Minx, a bitch, was sold to Ellie by a family that had been in Germany in the Air Force. With a German pedigree, Minx was a true German Shepherd, "a better pedigree," Ellie explained, "than most dogs in the States." Derry, the sire, was from Arizona, sight unseen except for pictures. The breeder had sent him on a plane, in a crate, to Laramie. Before Ellie could get to the small regional airport, the plane landed, and the crate was unloaded to the tarmac in the dead of a Wyoming winter. Luckily, Ellie was not long in getting there, and "oh, my, I was really, really angry at Derry's treatment." She bundled the German Shepherd into the airport to officially claim him and then bundled him to her car. Settling him on the front seat for the trip to the Sodergreen ranch, she noted that "he acted as if he had always been my dog."

The first time Ellie bred Minx to Derry, "Minx had a litter of 14. She was the smartest female I'd ever known. She knew what to do. While seven ate, seven slept, and I didn't have to do anything. She did it all. And she didn't even lose much weight, although I did feed her five meals a day." The pups were beautiful, sound, and healthy, and after inoculations and vet checks, were sold only to people of whom Ellie approved.

It was because of Minx's intelligence and sensible disposition that Ellie felt confident using her for breeding purposes. She had no interest in bringing into the world a litter of dogs that might exhibit shy or aggressive behavior or that lacked the intelligence that German Shepherds were proven to have. Ellie acted on principles. Her creed, when dealing with her dogs, was one of love and respect for the natural world and for the breed, but her praise for the Shepherds came with a sensible caveat. "German Shepherds can be too aggressive, too dangerous. Some can have a temperament close to that of a wolf. A good disposition is everything, and that comes with good breeding. I was once given a German Shepherd, but the dog hated everyone, including me. I kept her but wasn't about to breed her." There was nothing naïve about Ellie as a dog breeder. Right along with her delight in these animals came her insight.

Sometimes delight was the only part of the game. When Ellie acquired Devil, a small version of a Shepherd, she decided he would not be used for breeding purposes because he lacked registration papers. He would stay on the ranch because he came with a personality and antics that made him, despite not being on the payroll, one of the most beloved. "He was the smartest dog in the world," Ellie boasted. She didn't bother to train him. Born on a neighboring ranch, Devil seemed to know from day one what was expected of him. "He was always busy," Ellie said. "He did things for himself, things that I didn't quite understand as anything but sheer pleasure. He'd go down to the river and catch bubbles in the water by jumping on them. He also fished out pebbles from under the water to make little cairns along the bank." Once Ellie watched him as he proudly carried around a long stick. When he tried to make it through a gate, which was only a foot and a half wide, the long stick stopped him. He dropped the stick, stood staring at it for a moment, and then grabbed one end of it and easily dragged it through the gate, trotting proudly as if announcing that dog ingenuity and ranch life were one and the same.

As if that story wasn't enough of an opportunity for Ellie to brag, she remembered the time when Minx was in heat and she took Devil instead to a dog training class. "He'd never had any training, but he did everything right. He went through every single task. I asked if I could bring him to the upper-level companionship class. Again, he did everything absolutely perfectly, every obstacle, every command." Nearly ten years later, it was Devil who rode shotgun when Ellie drove from Wyoming to Freedom, New Hampshire, for the summertime memorial service for her mother and father, who had both died in the winter of 1975. Devil was not welcomed in the big house called Acorn, so Ellie chose to bunk with her very smart friend in her RV.

Nearly every avenue in Ellie's life was paved with books, and dog training was no exception, but Ellie also thought it wise to take advantage of the Laramie Kennel Club. She attended club meetings with her new friend Gay Collier, who, with her husband and four children, had moved into the cabin that Rosemary and Bob McIntosh had vacated when they became caretakers of a ranch in northwest Wyoming. When the pups from the latest litter turned six months old, Ellie and Gay each took one of them to a formal class.

"Here's what we did," Ellie said, as if involved in delightful intrigue. "We decided to take the class twice. The first time, we learned a few of the obedience instructions, but we were there mainly for us and our dogs to socialize. It's important for a dog to learn to get along with people and other animals, to become gregarious, like horses in a herd." The second time Ellie and Gay enrolled their dogs in the class, however, they were there to learn the important basic commands, such as to sit and to stay. "At that class," Ellie said, "we and our dogs had to step up and do it right. It was all about demonstration. You can't learn everything by the book. You've got to see what is being done." The two-class approach did the trick. Ellie's German Shepherds performed well, both during class and in the final evaluation. Ellie humbly took little credit. "German Shepherds are a wonderful breed. They're really smart, so mine did really well." The German Shepherds might have been thinking the same about their gentle and caring handler.

While in Germany, Ellie grew interested in animal nutrition. Stationed close to the Austrian border was a United States military canine unit, which patrolled for illegal crossings and contraband. She knew that dogs were good animals for this kind of work. Their ability to track and to smell was greater than most humans realized. As was typical, Ellie made her way over to the canine unit to observe and ask questions sparked by her curiosity and interest. She soon discovered that the canine unit handlers were feeding their dogs only once a day. Ellie reached into her supply of book-reading information to corroborate her notion that nutrition is lessened if a dog is fed only one meal. Never mind that she held no stature with the good veterinarians who took care of the animals' injuries. Never mind that she lacked formal training in veterinary work. Her concern was only for the dogs when, most politely but emphatically, she informed one of the vets that it was better for a dog's nutrition if it was fed twice a day. She was upset to be told that the canine units in Germany were allotted only so much food for the dogs, an allotment that definitely wasn't enough. As Ellie confronted the veterinarian that day, a principle was taking shape inside her, one she would carry all her life: "Any animal entrusted to my care will, without exception and with the utmost of respect, receive the best of care despite any obstacle."

Breeding German Shepherds brought in money and satisfied, to some extent, Ellie's need to be surrounded by animals. However, the ache in her heart remained: to have horses, lots of them. "That was why I had come west."

It was just before Rosemary and Bob McIntosh left the cabin at the Sodergreen Ranch to become ranch caretakers elsewhere that Bob did something that in other circumstances could be considered less than monumental. He told Ellie about a horse, born in 1952, that was for sale, cheap, on the UT Bar Ranch up the Big Laramie River, in Colorado. The horse was in poor condition, having been fed the same food as cows. According to the owner, the horse, named Khizan, was an active stud, or stallion, for a dude ranch and wasn't used for any other purpose.

Eleanor Smith saw more. "He was a black-bay stallion with white markings, a papered Arabian. I was never so excited in my life. I had never seen anything so majestic, so beautiful. I honestly didn't know I was going to breed Arabians until I found Khizan. I bought him and immediately set to work on his health."

The four-year-old stood only fourteen hands, two inches (or fifty-eight inches tall at his withers) and was very thin. Ellie started right in with proper, nutritious horse feed, and it wasn't long before he gained stature, up to 15.1 hands (sixty-one inches tall). He had white feet, which are notorious for being weak, but his were strong. Ellie made sure that they would stay that way by applying a mixture of equal parts of bacon grease, Neatsfoot oil, and pine tar, the latter holding the mixture onto the hoof. This home-made, tried-and-true recipe had been given to her by a farrier at Estes Park, Colorado.

Khizan quickly showed an aptitude for endurance, as is common to the Arabian horse breed. Every day, the young Joyce Johnson watched in fascination as Ellie "took Khizan up and down a high, steep hill just south of the ranch and across the river to muscle him up and wear him down a bit. Ellie couldn't wear him out. We never saw anything like it."

Ellie started taking Khizan to horse shows at Estes Park, but the show horse in Khizan was a lot to handle. Ellie found it necessary, before any class, to run him on the racetrack. "We went out early before showing him in his class. I raced him around, trying to get that energy out of him. He was a horse who wanted to get going. He didn't do well in Pleasure classes, where you want a quiet, laid-back horse. He wanted to move."

When Ellie first showed Khizan in conformation classes, the judge told her that her horse was in the best condition of any horse in the class. The only problem was that he wasn't fat enough. Ellie dove into research on nutrition and the second year, with continued proper diet and a year of racing Khizan up the nearby mountain slope, Khizan was carrying "hard fat." He won Reserve Champion at the 1960 National Estes Park Arabian Horse Show, qualifying him to show at Calgary, Canada, in 1961. There, he placed in the Canadian National Arabians Championship Top Ten Arabian Stallions at Halter. For Ellie, this was a pivotal point in her life and in what was fast becoming her career. It would be good, as well as essential, she realized, to show her well-maintained horses and have them place and receive awards. Likewise, she knew that people would now notice Khizan and would want to breed to him. She was pleased that after all her care, "Khizan finally looked healthy and fit. You have to remember that Arabian horses were bred for endurance. Khizan looked like he could do the work of endurance. He was beautiful. His silhouette was correct and smooth. He showed a smooth line from his poll (between the ears) to his withers (the swell on the backbone just below the neck) and to his croup (the swell above the hip and thigh). He had big jowls and nostrils, the Arabian head, and a high tail and flat croup. Because of his ancestry, he was a horse of good disposition, willing in task and easy to handle. The bottom line was that I now had the interest of those who wanted to breed their mares."

The stud fees came in handy, to say the least. It was because of Calgary and Khizan that Ellie decided she could go full-time at the ranch. As an interesting aside, the Calgary experience resulted, not surprisingly, in Ellie's success as a writer. In 1964, she published five articles on horsemanship for *Arabian Horse News*. Owner, breeder, handler, writer. Was there anything she couldn't do when it came to horses? No.

Out of the limelight, Khizan was an all-around champion in his own right. As grand as he was in the show ring, he was equally utilitarian on the ranch, especially when gates needed to be opened or bridges needed to be crossed. He was willing and able to complete any task asked of him. It was all a matter of mutual trust, according to Ellie.

Riding on Khizan, Ellie sensed that her freedom was complete. Because she loved him, and because exercise was part of good equine care, she rode Khizan every day, and they learned together how to thrive on the land. Once, during her first year at the ranch, Ellie rode Khizan across the highway to Sheep Mountain, her lunch packed for an enjoyably long day. Soon, the horse and rider spied a herd of animals in the distance. Ellie thought they were cattle but soon realized they were mountain elk. The curious horse and rider kept looking, the rider assuming that they were watching at a safe distance. The elk, however, alerted to the scent of unfamiliar human and horse, took off, gathering together and gaining momentum. Ellie marveled that they crashed effortlessly through ranch wire fencing. Even though she was upset that she and Khizan had spooked the herd and made them run, and concerned about the fence damage, she couldn't help but feel elation at the sudden sighting of wildlife running free and wild. "I've never lost that feeling," she said. "It is an amazing sight. And often, you can only see that on a horse."

Another door of equine opportunity soon opened for Ellie. Two mares became available to her. Joyce Johnson was delighted with this addition to the herd that had begun with Ranger, the big bay, and Joyce's favorite mount Prince, the smooth Saddlebred with an aptitude for cattle work. Spending time with the two new mares, Joyce decided that the tall Tammy was an "easy going sweetheart." On the other hand, the registered Arabian filly named Kataffa "always seemed to have her ears back, as if they were on wrong. There were times when she was definitely not happy—a grump, in fact."

Born in 1958 and purchased in Lander, Wyoming, Kataffa had been a late foal in the season, a fact interestingly attributed to a stallion who had made an unsupervised trek one night over his fence, which had been buried in packed snowdrifts. What most impressed Ellie about the filly was that "she fit in well with Khizan. Katie, as I called her, followed Khizan everywhere. He wasn't afraid of anything, and clearly neither was Katie. When Khizan walked into water, she did as well, and that was unusual. Fillies aren't supposed to follow a stallion around, but she did. Add that to her sound disposition and that she loved to get hugs, and I was ecstatic to own her." Khizan and Kataffa were from the very breeding that Ellie knew she wanted for her own foals for sale. When her stallion and favorite mare became her show horses at Estes Park, Colorado, she couldn't have been more pleased.

Khizan was sire to another wonderful addition to Ellie's growing herd. El Khilet, born in 1961, became, when gelded, Ellie's favorite school mount, especially when Ellie gave a demonstration in dressage—the precise cavalry-born movements asked by a rider to improve a horse's suppleness, balance, cadence, and obedience. At Estes Park, El Khilet showed in dressage, jumping, and trail riding, and was then nominated to show in the Arabian Canadian National Champions Top Ten Halter Champions in Calgary.

A doctor in Salt Lake City owned an Arabian stallion named Fasaab. The 16-year-old horse was out of shape and flabby, and the doctor couldn't take care of him anymore. He decided to sell Fasaab at a low price. Ellie Smith decided to buy the black stallion.

In examining the horse and his pedigree, Ellie said that she was "thrilled to death." Fasaab was by Fadl and out of Bint Bint Sabbah. He was a straight Egyptian stallion, one of three brothers imported by Babson Farm in Illinois. Ellie offered a 2-year-old colt for the horse, the deal was accepted, and the broker soon arrived at the Sodergreen Ranch with the pure black horse. Ellie was "almost in tears when that horse stepped from the trailer. He was everything I wanted in a stallion." Her joy was short-lived because the broker soon wanted to sell back the colt. It frightened Ellie that Fasaab might be suddenly sold to someone else. "Some guy down the road would have paid all kinds of money, and even though we had Rob's income and my money from selling pups, we didn't have that kind of money. I was scared to death that I might lose that beautiful horse."

The ending to the story was a happy one. Ellie was able to keep Fasaab, who soon topped "happy" with "remarkable." After working with Fasaab, Ellie developed a keen desire to show Fasaab in the Costume class at Estes Park. Khizan showed well, but it was Fasaab who seemed to delight in being in the limelight. He would be perfect for Ellie's grand plan. Ellie admitted to Margaret Johnson and a neighbor, Dorothy Orton, that she hated sewing—"I'm really not good at it. At all. That's it."—but needed an elaborate costume. Neither of the two experienced seamstresses flinched when Ellie explained that she needed "a Bedouin costume, for me and for Fasaab." The two women agreed to sew whatever Ellie needed. Loose-fitting pants and a flowing blouse were quickly designed and created. That was the easy part.

Ellie also needed a cape, stressing that the costume's flair and drama were important to the judges. The cape had to be flashy. The seamstresses turned a substantial bolt of rich scarlet material into a long, billowing cape that would cover Fasaab to his croup and down almost to his hocks. Ellie knew that the cape wasn't authentic to the Bedouins of the desert, "but I wanted it to be stunning. I wanted the judges to be impressed. Back then, showy stuff was popular. Bedouin-realistic desert colors were not popular, although my pants and blouse underneath and my veil and headdress were tan, like the desert."

Stunning, according to Ellie and her seamstresses, required something more than just the flare and color of the cape. It required something that, according to Ellie, made the cape actually flash. That something was mirrors. Ellie had no idea where the women found them or what their original purpose was, but the tiny square mirrors attached with adhesive to long strips of paper were perfect for a Bedouin costume that had to catch the attention of judges and spectators alike. Margaret and Dorothy, with Ellie's help, assumed the task of cutting out sections of the little mirrors and pasting them as unique multi-shaped designs all over Ellie's cape and Fasaab's tack. Mirrors adorned his breast collar, and covered his bridle between his ears and over onto his forehead. Even the stirrups were covered with mirrors. With the slightest of movements, the mirrors reflected light, causing the flash Ellie had hoped for. "Oh, my," Ellie reminisced, "we used an awful lot of mirrors."

Ellie requested as well that there be tassels, many tassels. She envisioned tassels "that waved in the wind from Fasaab's back and his croup. I wanted the tassels and the flashing mirrors and the billowing cape and my blowsy blouse to look like we were blowing in the wind through the desert. I wanted to get the people's attention. I wanted people to look at me, even though they couldn't tell if I were a veiled woman or man. I wanted them to look at my horse. I suppose it was an ego thing. I guess I wanted to show off, to give it my all. But gosh, people who go to a show want a show, and I was determined to give them one!" Costume, horse, and rider were soon ready to perform.

The Costume class called for a walk, trot, canter, and hand gallop, which is a faster and flashier canter. Entering the ring on Fasaab, Ellie gathered the end of the cape with her right hand and held it high in the air, as if the cape were floating away from the rider. "No one had ever done this," she excitedly recalled. "I think I might have started some trend."

After some time, Ellie realized she was heading into a predicament. "I remember that I wasn't scared, and I knew I had to make it through the class, for me and for Fasaab." Ellie was riding with a cavalry saddle, which was open but narrow in the gullet. Fasaab wasn't narrow, so the saddle perched without fitting down over the horse's broad withers. As Ellie and Fasaab dazzled the spectators, the saddle started moving to the right. "I didn't want to go down with Fasaab, in case he stumbled and fell, so I shook my feet out of the stirrups and kept going. The saddle was soon on Fasaab's side. Everything was going sideways. I kept wiggling to move me to where I should be, and the whole time, one of my hands was on the reins and one was still holding out the cape. It could have been a catastrophe, but Fasaab, even though he sensed that my body was giving him a wrong signal, never lost his footing and never lost his rhythm."

Ellie and Fasaab made it through the hand gallop. They even took second place, although Ellie wondered if the judge awarded them a second-place ribbon because Ellie stayed on the horse and Fasaab maintained his beat. After the show, Fasaab was surely lavished with a long brushing and a good meal.

"And this," Ellie said, "was the same horse who, in the Cheyenne Frontier Days parade, threw up his head at one point, probably showing off to the mares, and managed to toss off his bridle. I jumped from the saddle, slipped the bridle back on, and re-mounted. Fasaab and I never broke cadence. He was certainly the showman. He loved being on stage."

Fasaab and Khizan showed their worth on the ranch as well. Both horses knew the difference between working alongside the ranch mares and breeding the mares. They never acted up around the mares, and they never confused their roles, even though the showman Fasaab was often described by Ellie as "stallion-ish."

Although the Costume class dilemma and Fasaab's launching of his bridle into the air could have resulted in injury or disaster, they did not. In both situations, Ellie and Fasaab never lost their established and understood synchrony. Ellie's meticulous training certainly played a part. There was something else, though. As the situations were developing, Ellie, without any degree of mental or verbal articulation, knew in her heart what she needed to communicate to her horse. Fasaab sensed the message. Had anyone been aware of the quick, intuitive dialogue that passed between Ellie and her horse in the ring that day, this might have been the conversation they heard: "I trust you. And I trust you. I know you.

And I know you. This is not just about me. No, it's about us. I know what you're thinking. Likewise. I know you care. I care too." Horse and rider were as one.

How did this ability to create synchrony with her horses develop? Some might say it was the result of the young child's sitting amidst a horse's hooves at the age of four. It surely came as well from groundwork, grooming, learning, and loving. It came from catching the horse, caring for his or her needs, mucking the stable, measuring out the grain, engaging in words-and-nicker conversation. It came from gentleness and firmness. It came from respect. It came from losing one's heart and listening. From feeling and sensing. From living among them. As partnership first, ownership second.

Ellie's philosophy had crystallized. It motivated her in training, breeding, and caring for her horses. It would guide her every time a person came to her and said, "Teach me how to ride. How to *really* ride." The philosophy was this: Know your horse, and it shall follow, as the day the night, that your horse will know you.

Fasaab and Ellie had their moment under the lights, and Ellie returned to the task of searching for "lots of horses." She was looking mostly for mares, to be used for breeding to Khizan since she needed breeding stock. She soon purchased three mares from a horse dealer, considering herself lucky since horse dealers weren't always trustworthy people and a buyer never knew what he or she might get. Ellie knew her horses, so there was very little about luck in the purchases. She wanted sensible horses and knew how to spot them. The little Grey Girl fit the bill. So did an amazingly fast trotter, when motivated, named "No Name" because no one could agree on a proper name for her. According to Lynn Hornby, a young girl who hailed from a ranch in Arlington, Wyoming, and eventually became one of Ellie's Western instructors, the gentle No Name appeared to have been "put together by a committee. It didn't help that her bottom lip was always hanging out." The third horse's name has been forgotten, but without exception, if she became one of the Sodergreen horses, she had the makings of a good and sensible horse.

Daisy, an eventual purchase out of Walden, in the North Park of Colorado, looked like she had curly-hair horse breeding. Her specialty was running barrels and jumping. Lynn Hornby discovered one of Daisy's delightful quirks: "She loved to jump. She would actually point at something and then jump it." Daisy, a large, red mare, was known as well for taking care of all the foals. Even on trail rides, she shared her milk.

As her herd grew, Ellie was becoming what Joyce Johnson described as "a horse magnet, especially as people got to know her and what she stood for in the horse world." Joyce saw the expanding herd as "quite a bunch, unique, different, all with their own personalities." She watched them through the day with a child's love, and at feeding time, she eagerly anticipated the sound of their hooves on the boards of the old barn. "The clip-clop was so distinct, and the barn was filled with the smell of hay and horses hungry for their meal. That smell, that sound, would always be there, in that barn."

Hay was provided to Ellie by the Johnsons. Ellie and Rob, on Khizan and Ranger respectively, paid the family for their generosity by helping in the summers with the Johnson Ranch cattle drives. The families along Route 230 lived, as Joyce remembered, with the belief that "we all looked after each other," and Ellie and Rob had no trouble fitting into that community's lifestyle. Joyce joined the drive, riding Prince. She admired her new friend from the East, dressed in sturdy clothes, her hair pulled back in a ponytail, her face alight with a smile, looking like she could do this hard work all day, as long as she had a horse and dear friends. "You couldn't hide Ellie's love of people and horses," Joyce said. "It was going to come out. Under a ten-ton brick of cement, it was still going to come out."

I Had This Teacher in Wyoming

Chapter 8

On the 16th of June, 1958, Eleanor Smith signed a contract to begin teaching, on the 2nd of September, grades one through four, at Harmony Elementary School, a rural school near Sodergreen Ranch. Rob's salary and the money Ellie was making from breeding and selling Arabian horses and German Shepherd pups was not enough. Working even a small ranch required money they did not have. An old poster that hangs in the home of many a ranch family shows a worn and weary fellow feeding his animals and lamenting to the viewer of the poster, "If somebody gave me a million dollars, I'd keep ranching till it was all gone."

Ellie could have easily found a job working in Laramie for the county, but her love of people drew her to seek a job where she could be free, animated, and creative throughout the day: that of teaching young people. She honestly didn't think she would be hired at an elementary school, grades one through eight, even though she had spent quite a bit of time earning her teaching certification. "Then, I was just trying to figure out how to live." The school district was impressed and offered Mrs. Smith $320 per month.

Harmony Elementary School opened in a log building in 1905. Given the name because of its proximity to Harmony Church just across the road, the building was replaced by a brick structure in 1953.[39] Two large schoolrooms made up the first floor. The basement housed a large kitchen, a large multipurpose room, a gymnasium, and an auditorium with a small stage at one end. A teacherage by the original log structure was moved to the new site but never used. Living quarters existed for the bus driver. The 1958-59 teaching staff consisted of Mary Blumfelt and Eleanor Smith, the 1959-60 teaching staff consisted of Margaret Blount and Eleanor Smith, and Dixie Barnhart and Eleanor Smith were the teachers in 1960–61.[40]

It suited Ellie that the school, eighteen miles from Laramie, was only about eight miles from the Sodergreen Ranch, just off Route 230 to the south, on the Lewis River Road. She wouldn't be that far from the ranch and the animals who had stolen her heart. Besides, she would have time before and after school, and summers, holidays and weekends, to work with her pups and her horses.

The school district clerk whose signature appeared on Ellie's contract was Everett Johnson, Margaret Johnson's husband. Ellie taught children from the neighboring homes and ranches. Their parents became Ellie's friends. "Through the school," Ellie said, "we had fun neighborhood parties and birthdays. I got to know and enjoy these families that were part of the school and community." In particular, she remembered the evening skating parties on the canal that flowed into Sodergreen Lake. "We had cocoa, bonfires, and marshmallows. Everyone came, the kids, their parents, and their friends. Word about the parties would spread at school, or the families would call each other on their home phones."

In her book *Just Beyond Harmony*, Gaydell Collier, whose children attended Harmony Elementary School, described enrollment of children or hiring of teachers as "official assimilation into the Harmony Community."[41] Parents, friends, teachers, students, and nearly every other living soul in the community were, according to Ellie, drawn into nearly every function provided by the school.

Ellie quickly became friends with the Beidlemans, who lived near the school. Emma Beidleman was the school cook and had an outstanding reputation for her bakery delights and "from scratch" recipes. She served hot meals, no sandwiches. She worked out of and offered her meals in the school's basement lunchroom, which also served, as is often the case in rural Wyoming schools, as the gym, meeting room, and crafts area. A bit of a disciplinarian, Emma made sure the children knew the rules, and they were smart enough to obey them.

Chuck Beidleman was an all-around fix-it man. He also drove the bus, which began as a "short bus," then gave way to a 1956 Chevy Station Wagon, only to be replaced by a rather unreliable International Travel-all, and finally a Chevy Suburban. When picking up all the kids from the ranches and taking them home after school, he was known to drive fast on the county roads, but he safely delivered the children right to the doors of their homes. Ellie herself sometimes rode the school bus because "I was always having some problems with my Willys Jeep. But one time the bus got stuck in a snowbank along the river road as we were heading home. We had to wait for a rancher to come along and help us get out. We could have been scared, but the children and I decided to make it a fun time. We sang songs, that sort of thing. We thought of it as just a little adventure in a snowbank. It helped that Mr. Beidleman was the nicest person."

Ellie delighted in the freedom provided by the rural school. Her love for and talent in art spilled over into the classroom; the children were treated to art projects nearly every day. One popular project involved making papier mâché animals. The smaller children couldn't make the requisite knots in the project, so Ellie pitched right in and helped them. "We were in the big inside gym in the basement, where the school did all the big projects. All that glue. All that paste. It was wonderful." Ellie's class size numbered only seven or eight pupils, and the older children helped the younger ones, "but still, I tied a lot of knots that day, the knots forming the skeletons of the animals. I went home with the sorest hands and had blisters the next day."

The art project lasted over a couple of weeks, "and the children and I got so much out of it. I learned a lot about teaching and planning from having to do things for them. That was important, my learning as they learned. And of course every project I created always had something to do with animals, even mice. We had so much fun."

To Ellie's delight, the other teacher, who taught grades five through eight, didn't like to go out for recess. The athletic and energetic Ellie, never minding the winter cold, found herself with double recesses. "I loved racing, basketball, and baseball. Just not football. I loved going out with the kids to play games. I became 'the recess girl.'"

Ellie's fondness for her students did nothing but grow. "Most of my pupils were inventive. Most were ranch kids, with chores and a sense of responsibility. They were involved in watering and feeding their animals and chickens and helping their parents harvest crops. These kids wanted to do things. They wanted to be active and wanted to learn. I saw that ranching was a healthy way of bringing up youngsters."

In her third year of teaching, Ellie was moved to grades five through eight. She was delighted that she had some of the students she had taught in the younger classes. Gaining confidence in herself as a teacher, Ellie took on a new project: She expanded the school library. Remembering when she was barred from reading horse books in the fifth grade, she vowed that her students would never be subjected to that same policy. "I believed that kids should read what interests them. I also believed that if you enjoy something, like reading, you can pass that enthusiasm on to the kids. Young people can feel your enjoyment and live on that enthusiasm and become lifelong readers."

To pass on that enthusiasm in reading and all other subjects, Ellie knew that as a teacher, she had to be firm on respect and make herself likeable. "You also have to get to know the children's backgrounds. They're not just images. They're real." She believed as well that "an empathetic crossover" needed to occur in the classroom. "I had to discover and incorporate what my students liked. At the same time, I had to instill in them an enthusiasm for what I liked and what I was teaching. In my classroom, we all taught, and we all learned."

One of Ellie's seventh-grade students was Joyce Johnson, witness to the start of Ellie's horse herd. Joyce went on to become an elementary teacher herself, teaching for 50 years in the small Wyoming town of Buffalo. As a student, Joyce found it fascinating that Mrs. Smith could be both a teacher and a ranch woman. "She was always up at around 4:00 in the morning, even in thirty-degrees-below-zero weather. She'd feed the horses, groom them, and possibly ride. Then, she'd change into her school clothes." The dress code for the teachers at Harmony Elementary School was dresses. Ellie didn't like them, so she compromised by wearing, with her requisite dress, knee socks and functional shoes. "In the evenings," Joyce remembered, "it was the same routine with her horses, after Ellie got into what she called her sensible clothes. She never missed caring for her horses. That responsibility came first, even in the cold. But she was always prepared each day to teach."

It was apparent to young Joyce that Mrs. Smith respected the students' time and never indulged in busy work. Projects that reflected the students' interests were planned instead. Joyce's interest was arts and crafts. "When I finished my work early, she gave me projects I enjoyed. One involved using colored rice to make designs, and I created a butterfly in flight and a flower. Another involved decorating a tray from a colored-pencil drawing of our ranch, which was copied from a slide of the ranch. The tray became a Christmas gift to my parents. I still have it and one of the rice designs. Ellie meant a great deal to me. As a teacher, she was so kind and so inspiring."

As Ellie began her first year of teaching at Harmony Elementary School, in the fall of 1958, Joyce Johnson's older brother, David, entered the third grade. Mrs. Wilkey, his second-grade teacher, should have been his teacher for a second year, but she resigned when her husband left the University of Wyoming. Into that void stepped the energetic, eager, and friendly Mrs. Smith, who would be his teacher for three years and whose determination to succeed with her pupils was as strong, according to David, as that which she displayed toward her dogs and horses. "Both in and out of the classroom," David said, "she lived her creed that when you take a living being into your care, you have no option but to fully care. The job of teaching our class was going to take a pretty talented and committed teacher, and Ellie fit the bill."

In first grade, David reluctantly carried home a note from Mrs. Goetz. She wrote to his parents that "I am happy to have him in my classroom. However, he was very rambunctious, and he didn't come in when the bell rang." David's mom wrote back that this wouldn't be a problem from now on, but when Mrs. Smith, not one to appreciate controlling bells, took him under her wing, he had no problem settling down.

"Mrs. Smith was not a strict disciplinarian," David said. "Somehow her style worked. She had to—and did—maintain a quiet classroom, because her students, depending on their class level, were all doing different things with different outcomes. Her classroom management plan was effective. While she'd be working with the kids in the middle grade, she had the older students mentor the youngest ones." David described this strategy as a type of "interactive dynamic, to which Ellie fit right in." The young Mrs. Smith indeed made sure the students buckled down and did their work. She was not a taskmaster. She gently but repeatedly required her students to do their best. She kept them busy and, most importantly, intrigued. She went beyond rote, blending the creative with the basics. For example, in fifth grade, David delighted in the word game of finding synonyms to strengthen prose. "Gusty wind" became "sudden blast of wind." A revolt became an uprising, and a criminal could be caught, apprehended, or arrested.

A teaching technique that Mrs. Smith used, and the students all enjoyed, was the incorporation of a special notebook. David's dad helped him cut out the plywood cover for his notebook, and David used his wood burner to create, on the cover, a cloud design and the inscription: Current Events, David Johnson, Grade 5, 1961. "We had to fill our notebooks with current events from the year. I enjoyed the project so much that I can still remember that my March 16, 1961 entry was taken from an article in the *Laramie Boomerang*, the county newspaper. It was about the thirteen jurors who would serve in the murder trial of Joseph Corbett Junior, who murdered Joseph Coors."

David was hard pressed to think of anything he didn't like about his third-, fourth-, and fifth-grade teacher. "There was one thing, though. She fit right in with all of us in the community, but sometimes what she said was puzzling. I couldn't, for example, figure out what she meant when she said 'Asiar' and 'ca.' But soon I figured out her accent, and all was okay, especially since John F. Kennedy had just been elected as our country's president and he said 'Asia' and 'car' the same way."

According to David Johnson, Mrs. Smith was not only clever but also creative. "She was also a caring teacher who could sometimes be one of us." If a student had a problem or was hurting, Mrs. Smith would hold and talk to the student. Once during a school event, David threw a softball a bit too hard and fast. It broke a window. "Mrs. Smith didn't reprimand me. Instead, she coached me through the apology."

David reminisced that life on a ranch is mostly about the survival of the ranch. "There is little room for emotion. Ellie, outside of the classroom, knew how to touch us emotionally. She was like a second mother figure. We had many stresses in our ranch life, and Ellie was always there for everyone, without any baggage. She was living out her dream and encouraging us to do so as well. When there were obstacles, when she was told she couldn't achieve something, she told us that her response was, 'Just watch me.' She stepped out of the strictures that women had to live within in those days. I'd like to think she was never restrained from anything."

At the school, there was a sense of freedom. David and his classmates, with the teachers, "went for walks and hikes, often to the Big Laramie River. We'd be tossing rocks and getting into discussions with our teachers, about nature or anything. At recess, the teachers were always with us, standing out in the cold while baseballs and snowballs were thrown. They were with us all day long, even at lunch. I don't remember any punishments at the school because there just wasn't any bad behavior. There were only clear and upheld consequences for poor behavior. We understood the rules, and everyone respected them and each other." It was no wonder that Ellie fit in.

Some young people might have felt queasy about having their teacher living next door, but David and his little sister thought it was grand. David remembered that Ellie was as joyful as a kid when she joined the Johnson Ranch cattle drives, when she was working with and caring for her horses, and when she was with her friends, old and young alike. The young David watched as "everyone morphed together at family gatherings. We just became Ellie's family. She was my teacher, but she was also my friend. She was Mrs. Smith and Ellie."

David, however, was not into horses, preferring instead "something that stayed put when the ignition was turned off." He took note of Ellie and Rob's "big old white and burgundy Dodge Power Wagon," but he found especially intriguing the 1961 Plymouth "with glued-in push-button drive and a little square of a steering wheel."

Despite his disinterest in horses, David found it intriguing that Mrs. Smith could draw a parallel between herding a bunch of cows and teaching in a classroom. To understand and be successful in the craft of moving cattle, Mrs. Smith, as both horsewoman and classroom teacher, explained that "you have to get in the head of a cow, just as you do for a horse. You have to ask yourself what one cow might do or is doing. Then, you have to determine what the other cows might do. You have to observe, study, and be ready. You have to know where everyone else is, while you're focusing on what is around you. You have to be confident. You have to trust yourself and your horse."

Moving cattle was a community event and celebration, drawing together various families. Geil Johnson, David's grandmother, made cinnamon rolls for everyone for the lunch break. Sometimes she carried the rolls to the riders, and sometimes the riders came back to her house. Often, afterwards, everyone congregated at the Johnsons' house. Ellie remembered that it was always a fun get-together. "Just a fun group that hadn't seen each other for a few weeks. We didn't play games, but instead we caught up on news, how everyone was getting along, the weather, the horses." It was a talk fest, and there was always good food. Ellie admitted that she was not "the greatest cook in the world. If I took something, it was often a cake, and it probably was a cake that Emma Beidleman made."

In remembering those years at Harmony Elementary School with Mrs. Smith, and the wonderful memories of Ellie at the ranch, David was adamant in giving full credit to this cherished woman, probably not for her cakes, but indeed for inspiring both his vocation and his avocation. Mrs. Smith had made her students memorize and recite poems. In recalling the opening lines of a poem by Robert Frost—*My little horse must think it queer / to stop without a farmhouse near*—David shared that "the exercise of memorizing and reciting poems helped me learn to think poetically. I started to think in poetry, and to this day I love poetry." Mrs. Smith also taught David to write legible cursive. "She taught the Palmer method of cursive writing. She let us all go at our own pace in learning it. In learning all our subjects, for that matter. I was blessed to have her." Ellie also encouraged imagination. "There were no restrictions on what we would write," David said. "I soon worked on the school newspaper, *The Harmony Hilltop Herald*. Ellie as well inspired me to do this."

David's career path took him to the John Hancock Investment Firm, which involves extensive documentation and signatures on deals up to $150 million. "They always turned to me to do the writing because of my penmanship. Once, I had to sign my name, over and over, onto sets of documents. Ellie would have been proud of my legible signature, but probably not when my hand eventually grew tired and I resorted to signing only my initials."

A published writer of essays, short stories, and poetry, David attributed his creativity and love of writing to Ellie. One of his short stories involves a young man inspired to follow his dream by his female rural schoolteacher.

There is something to be remembered about Eleanor Fracker Smith's years in a small schoolhouse in a rural setting. She grew up near the bustling city of Boston, attended the urban Boston University, and was a counselor at what she described as "elite country club-like camps." Somehow, this city girl, without hesitation, grew right into loving and being loved by a community of ranch people working through hard times. To David Johnson, that she fit in so well is remarkable. "It's like a slice of Americana. There, in the high finance world of New York, I am explaining to all these people who appreciate my penmanship and work and talent that, well, I had this teacher in Wyoming, see, …"

Sodergreen Horsemanship School

Chapter 9

One evening in 1961, two sisters, nine-year-old Deb Matthew and her older sister Linda, were posed a question by their father, Air Force Major Harry L. Matthew. Major Matthew was enrolled, with fellow officers, in engineering courses at the University of Wyoming, as part of the Air Force Institute of Technology (AFIT) program. At that time, the UW Engineering Department was so reputable that the Air Force sent 100 officers and 100 enlisted men to get engineering degrees there.

Major Matthew's question was this: Would his girls like to take private horseback riding lessons? Horse-crazy as they already were, they both were utterly beside themselves to learn that a young woman named Eleanor Smith had been teaching some of the other Air Force children in Laramie since about 1958, and Deb and Linda were welcome to join the lessons that this woman was offering at her ranch. Looking back on four years of private lessons with Ellie, Deb saw their instructor as nothing less than extraordinary. "Ellie made a huge impact on my sister's and my life, and of course it was great fun that we met kids from all over as excited about taking riding lessons as we were."

"News traveled fast in Laramie," Ellie remembered, "and word got around. These parents wanted their children to experience horseback riding while in Wyoming, and I was delighted to provide that experience. I just gathered up all of my Boston University years' reading, my experiences at camp, my teaching at Harmony Elementary, all that I was learning in buying horses, training horses, taking care of horses, and loving horses. It all came together as if it were a bloom on a flower. I have to say it was kind of fun to be teaching like that, and I'll admit that I did need the money. Oh, and north of us, out in a huge meadow, I was able to fashion a riding ring. I finally had a ring. You can't get the mechanics of horsemanship, you can't even get started, if you don't have a ring."

The parents who had approached Ellie early on wanted her to give their youngsters "a feel of the Old West." Ellie was determined as well to give the students a feel for every aspect of horsemanship, including English riding. By the time Deb and Linda met her, Ellie had established herself in the English show ring at Estes Park, Colorado, where her beloved, dashing, and dramatic Arabian horse, Khizan, was included as a National Top Ten Arabian Stallion. She showed Khizan as well at the prestigious Calgary Stampede fairgrounds in Canada. It was Khizan's narrative, "as told to the writer Fran Farrell," that was published as "My Canadian Capers" in the October 1961 issue of *The Arabian Horse News*. The whimsical article, with illustrations by El Smith, secured some level of publicity for Khizan's owner, and it didn't hurt that on page 15 of the same issue, photographs of two wooden horses carved by Eleanor F. Smith of Laramie, Wyoming, were featured. What came from the article, cleverly portrayed as Khizan's supposed first-person, or first-horse, account, is a clear indication of Eleanor's depth of understanding of the care, training, and love necessary to transport a horse from the quietude of the Snowy Range foothills to the clamorous atmosphere of a large, professional show ring. Fran Farrell knew how to sell her good friend Eleanor and Eleanor's good horse Khizan.

As the Harmony Elementary School calendar flipped from 1960 to 1961, Ellie knew that she had gained much from her years of teaching youngsters the basics of reading, writing, math, science, art, and sportsmanship. Likewise, her years of working with horses had fed the confidence she needed to take a huge leap, without looking back, into a major endeavor. She knew it came with many risks, the most critical being that she would be primarily dependent on horses for her livelihood. Her life among horses had started with a risk: a four-year-old girl sitting in the strike zone of the hooves of a cantankerous equine. She had blindly, unwittingly trusted the animal. She would trust now. All would come together. Private lessons would continue for a time, but there would be something new just up Route 230. In the summer of 1961, Eleanor Smith formally opened the Sodergreen Horsemanship School. She submitted her resignation to the Albany County School District and started the design sketches for her school's brochure.

Khizan's noble profile graced the cover of the brochure, which advertised a June to August in-residence summer school for young girls, ages 10 to 19. Ellie had debated four, six, or eight weeks, but with input from the Air Force parents, she settled on the latter, from June 20 to August 14. From her background in art design, Ellie knew the brochure had to be informative in detail and significant in size. It had to be a keepsake as well. In later summers, she switched to open pamphlets that could be mailed for less postage, but in these first years, every decision she made had to be related to the salability and growing reputation of the program.

As a writer, Ellie was skilled in enticement. The introduction, five paragraphs on the first inner page, could have recruited the wariest of potential students.

It told the reader that the instruction provided by the school "could not be acquired in most summer camps" and was all about "teaching our girls as much as possible about horses and promoting their love for and interest in them." It cleverly lured West-romantic parents who would be charmed by this part of "historical, picturesque Wyoming, [where] inhabitants of the ranch once heard the jingle of harness as the Walden Stage Line wended its way up the valley, and big game hunters stopped at the ranch to taste the delicious Swedish food served by Mrs. Sodergreen." Citing the beauty of Jelm Mountain, the abundance of wildlife, and the "cool, dry climate," the introduction ensured, with mention of crafts and other activities, that more than just horsemanship would be part of the fascinating summer adventure. All for $700, plus home cooked meals and boarding in the big house or a small nearby cabin.

The remaining pages of the brochure reflected the thoroughness of the catalogues from the summer camps, Winnemont and Merrymeeting, where Ellie had been a camper and a camp counselor respectively. Considering parents her prime readers, Ellie made sure to answer every question imaginable, from details of a typical day to health issues at high altitude as well as personnel and ranch facilities, necessary clothing, and the actuality of transportation. Ellie's brochure, however, was different from the Winnemont and Merrymeeting brochures in one significant way. The New England camp brochures provided brief paragraphs about the horsemanship experience, indicating that the young rider would be assigned to a saddled and bridled horse, mount the horse, ride in a line on a trail ride, and then dismount and walk away. In stark contrast, Ellie used a full section of her brochure, titled "Our Program," to describe what educators would call immersion learning and what horse-crazy youngsters would call eating, sleeping, and breathing horses. Ellie's only prerequisite was "an interest in horses and a desire for learning the many facets in the business and enjoyment of horses."

Breadth and depth made the school unique. For eight full weeks, morning, noon, and night, the girls' lives would revolve around horses. Western equitation was taught alongside English. Handling one's own mount was given the same attention as preparing for the show ring. Well-trained older horses were aids in instruction, as were foals. Bareback riding, mounted drills, the cavalry style of training and riding known as dressage, games, and trail rides all blended into a day that also urged observation of the surrounding world. Learning took place in the saddle as well as, in Ellie's words, "from the ground up." Learning horse psychology was as important as learning to lead, longe,[42] and use voice commands. Drawing and painting of horses was a craft, as were trail-riding, fishing, and outdoor cookery. Sprinkled throughout the printed information were Ellie's tiny line drawings of frolicking, thick-maned horses on dainty legs, all looking eager for riders. Throughout the text were words that hinted at joy and enjoyment. One could only assume that the director and instructor of the school was a woman whose eyes sparkled when she laughed, which was often.

That first summer, the small staff was suited to the anticipated school enrollment, capped at fifteen girls. Ellie enlisted her husband Rob, on whom she had become dependent as her horses' farrier, to help with many behind-the-scenes tasks. Joyce Johnson, who reveled in the idea that there was a riding instructor "just next door," was always ready to help with any chore necessary. Emma Beidleman, renowned for the Harmony Elementary School lunches that satisfied both students and drop-by community folk, signed on as Sodergreen Horsemanship School's cook. Ellie described her as a wonderful cook, and not just because she made her own noodles. "Emma promised that on Saturdays, she would prepare for each Sunday breakfast one of her specialties: a huge horseshoe of baked dough, filled with all kinds of citrus and berries, like a stollen."

A young university student from Canada joined Ellie that first year, doing much of the horse feeding and odd jobs as they occurred. For some of his tasks, Marvin needed a horse, so Ellie chose El Khilet for him to ride. Marvin was an asset to the school, but he caused Ellie a bit of extra work at the session's end. Marvin had a stiff right leg, and as a result of his summer partnership with El Khilet, the horse was no longer responsive to leg aids on his right side. Ellie, "working my right leg an awful lot that late August," had to re-train El Khilet to be equally sensitive to leg aids on both sides. Marvin was remembered as a hard worker.

That first summer, and into the mid '60s, Ellie was assisted at the school by the most amiable and level-headed equine staff. They included the brood mares Grey Girl, Kataffa (Ellie's beloved "Katie"), No Name, and Tammilass (Tammy). Dixie, a retired veteran pack horse who came with the reputation of being "a pistol," was given to Ellie by Anna Dunlavy of the Broken Bridle Ranch just east of Laramie. According to Ellie, "Dixie was one of my favorites. She was old, but she loved to run and jump. I didn't really buy her. She just came to me." Prince was a regular in the classes, but Ranger and the stallion Khizan were reserved for more experienced riders. Joyce's horse, the reliable-for-everything Pickle, was ridden as well by other students. Ellie rode the gelding El Khilet to provide in-the-saddle demonstrations for the students, and students gaining experience would later select El Khilet as their horse of choice. The stallion Fasaab would be reserved during lessons for admiration only.

Ellie made sure that advertisements for the school "were placed in all the big horse magazines, including *Horse Lovers*, *Western Horseman*, *Horse Illustrated*, and all the Arabian horse magazines. As soon as I was contacted, by phone or letter, I sent a brochure by mail to those interested. That's how we did things back then."

Only one student enrolled in the Summer 1961 session of the Sodergreen Horsemanship School, which was the only school of its kind in Wyoming until its closure in 2001. Ellie had no recollection of the student's name, but she remembered her as "the sweet little girl who was allergic to hay and sage," the latter growing in abundance on untamed prairie. She was also allergic to horses. "I had to take her into town every week," Ellie said, "for her allergy shots. But she had a good time, and she was able to do everything." Ellie took her time with the little girl, gave her a healthy dose of trust and confidence-building, and helped her to realize, as Ellie had learned as a young girl, that you can do anything if you set your mind to it. Ellie also learned an important lesson in education that summer: Even if you have only one student, you must teach as if you're teaching the world.

Later that year, the handsome and charming Rob, who had provided Ellie support and assistance with the school, who had seemingly settled into ranch life and rural community, who had professed to loving Ellie, shattered her world. He met another woman, and he and Ellie chose to divorce. At the time, Ellie thought she had failed. "It came out of the blue and probably wasn't just Rob. Both of us had to be blamed. I wondered at first if there was something I lacked. I was so focused on my horses and my business that I wondered if I had neglected parts of my marriage. But eventually, the whole situation made me dig in more. I realized quickly that I had to support myself and my classes, school, dogs, and horses. I also realized that they were all there to help me. After a while, I started thinking about what I had to do. I feared I might have to sell some of my horses, and that was the impetus for me to continue breeding and training. I started to think optimistically—that I could do it if I wanted to do it, and that all would work out for the best in the long run. But I have to admit, it was difficult to keep everything on the high side when I was constantly worried about finances."

In retrospect, Ellie convinced herself that the marriage probably wouldn't have lasted long. "Rob was gregarious, and people liked him, but he wasn't without a streak of egotism. He was what I would call a 'white glove' person. He wanted the furniture dusted, and he wanted things in place. I didn't do those things. I was too much of a free-thinker and doer, and I admit that when I had the time, I wanted it with the horses and dogs. The army was a good match for Rob, but it wasn't for me. Oh, we were both athletic and loved the outdoors, but he had his own ways of doing things, and I didn't want to be pushed into a corner. I started doing what I wanted to do without saying anything." She also recognized that Rob, from a military family, had in his blood the urge to "move, move, move." Ellie, instead, "had found home and wanted to stay there."

Ellie may have seemed without emotion in describing the dissolution of her marriage. Rosemary McIntosh, however, saw her beloved friend in raw pain. "It just hurt Ellie so terribly when Rob had that affair. It was a horrible time. If you can understand, her heart was truly, and I mean truly, broken. Not only that, but she knew, and I knew, that being on her own would be a serious venture."

For fear that she might be asked to move out of the big house, Ellie told only a few close friends that she and Rob had broken up. For a time, on his days off from teaching, Rob drove up to the ranch to help with necessary work and repairs. Ellie described their new relationship in one word: "amicable." In a few months, Rob took a job as Dean of Men at Ohio State University. He left Ellie the Dodge Power Wagon and the red and white Plymouth station wagon, saying he'd have no need of such vehicles. Word spread that Ellie was a single woman, but nothing really changed. She had earned the unspoken trust and love of those who knew her.

She had also won the hearts of the two horse-crazy students Deb and Linda Matthew, whose parents had given them the gift of Saturday private riding lessons. It was these Saturdays that the girls remembered most intimately.

Deb shared that their lessons were "in the winters, and Dad drove us from Laramie to the ranch in his '58 Cadillac, the only car we had. It was not a car that blends in with a rustic ranch setting. We got to stay overnight with Ellie in that big house. A huge pipe from the enormous stove in the kitchen heated the upstairs. It was still chilly on that second floor, but Ellie had lots of covers. As soon as we got up in the morning, we ran down to the kitchen. Even the cold was a happy memory for us because we just loved Ellie. We'd do any chores, just to be around her. And my favorite meal still is one she used to make us: peas from a can, boiled hot dogs, or ones heated on the stove, and toast with butter. Her hot chocolate was made and served at any time.[43] And if we had a dessert, it had to involve chocolate. And of course, after working hard all day, we had ice cream before bed."

The girls' parents grew close to Ellie as well. Deb didn't remember if her parents actually followed through on any paperwork, but they told their daughters that if anything ever happened to them, they had arranged that Deb and Linda would go to Ellie. "I didn't want my parents to die or anything," Deb said, "but I remember thinking, well, that's just great."

In the early years of Sodergreen Horsemanship School, Ellie took everything she had learned throughout her life thus far and channeled it into philosophy and techniques for training both horse and rider. Nothing was passive; all was active and positive as she researched and crafted a curriculum that would bring her young students fully into the world of horses. She was focused. She was driven. Rosemary McIntosh described her dear friend as "dead serious. Ellie had a passion for understanding and taking care of everything horsemanship. In no way would you ever see her cut corners or mistreat a horse or rider. She was born that way, loving the world of horses and horse lovers."

Ellie asked herself constantly, "What more?" and answered those questions through the curricula she began designing. "Lesson plans and lectures were something new in the West," she said. "So much that was taught on ranches was done in the corral, the task or lesson started in the morning and learned by the afternoon, usually out of necessity during the hard and constant work on a ranch. In a way, I was feeling my way around. I was actually learning from the students as much as they were learning from me. It was through the Air Force kids that I discovered the value of lesson plans and of listening to my students. They had good ideas and comments, and they had goals. With every group of new students, I asked their goals. I asked what they do, how they do things, where they're from, what they wanted. Talking to my students every session resulted in a more well-rounded program."

Deb and Linda Matthew would not have thought for a minute that Ellie was feeling her way around as an instructor. Although they would not enroll in the horsemanship school until 1966, they saw emerging, through their private lessons, the Ellie whose students would eventually come in large numbers from all over the United States as well as South America, Canada, and England.

Deb insisted that "Ellie was fearless in all things pertaining to horses. Her knowledge was working knowledge. She gathered all these different breeds, even accepting the challenge of nurturing injured or neglected horses back to health. She took those walking wounded and turned them into superb school horses, all with unique personalities and different physical characteristics. She was even soon experienced in all the local grasses and savvy in knowing the weather."

From the beginning, Deb and Linda recognized Ellie's school as unique. Tripping over each other to share memories, they explained that they learned everything: Eastern tack, Western tack, ailments, care and feeding, equipment, even breeding. There were lectures, discussions, and of course hands-on time. There were tests and homework, which Ellie always graded. After every demonstration, Ellie provided handouts of all that she had lectured on. Each student also had to prepare and decorate a notebook, which would be a collection of all the materials Ellie gave the students to learn and what they learned on their own. Reminiscent of the Harmony Elementary School current events notebooks, the covers were wood; each student painted a design and then covered it with varnish. Deb remembered decorating hers with a picture of an Arabian horse. The students also had to present formal oral reports, including ones on books from Ellie's library, which was filled with all manner of equine reading, fiction or nonfiction. No student was ever reprimanded for reading too much about horses.

"It scared me," Deb said, "giving reports. But Ellie taught us and challenged us. She knew we all could do it. Just like with riding, she simply said, in her kind voice, 'Do it.' And we did it."

What Linda Matthew took from these early days with Ellie were "critical skills. We learned more than just riding. We learned about the care and treatment of animals. Ellie taught us the responsibility and accountability that we would need to work successfully around and with animals. Our experiences were hands-off and hands-on. We even learned a great deal about how to live and work with others. In fact, a lot of the material she taught us would apply to raising children, such as having a consistent schedule. Ellie taught us that kids, dogs, and horses are happiest on a schedule with no surprises and lots of love."

When the sisters stayed over with Ellie, they got up at 4:30 for chores, the animals' needs always coming first, with no exceptions. The memory of the dark, early, chilly mornings lingered with Linda. "I never forgot opening the stalls, putting the feed in for the horses, and listening to their hooves thunder as they headed into their stalls, each one knowing his or her own special place."

From Ellie, Linda learned empathy, confidence, and especially how to face fears. "Ellie used to put me on Ranger during those Saturday lessons. Ranger was prone to running away with the rider. I always cautiously and nervously asked Ellie how Ranger was feeling that day. Regardless of his mood, though, I had to do it, and I wanted to do it. Ellie gave me Ranger because I was afraid, and she worked me through my fear. As a result, I learned the value of practice, improvement, consistency, and self-confidence. I learned how to use reward and punishment that was in no way demeaning to horse and rider. I must have gotten over my fears with Ranger because it wasn't long before I went from him to the stallion Khizan, who in his prime was a handful. When our family returned to Laramie in 1966 and Deb and I were in the Sodergreen Horsemanship School, Ellie asked me to teach some of the Western riding sessions. That was a compliment never forgotten."

As the school developed, Joyce Johnson saw Ellie as a trail blazer. "Most of the people training in Wyoming didn't know her method of teaching. My dad had told me I had to learn to work with a horse so that I didn't get hurt, so Ellie taught me early on how to longe a horse. She taught all of her students that it was essential to both training and safety. No one else was out there using longe lines. Most folks didn't know what a longe line was. Ellie stressed that the emphasis should be on ground work with the horse, before getting in the saddle, for the rider's safety as well as the horse's. She taught me how to properly groom, saddle, and bridle the horse. She taught me dressage—how to teach the horse voice commands, and how to use my body to communicate with the horse. She was teaching dressage, and nobody even knew what dressage meant. I was so lucky to have her next door, and to learn everything English. Ellie even picked out and ordered my first English saddle, after I did enough chores at my ranch to buy it. Ellie was just that way."

Joyce always remembered Ellie as a kind and generous instructor. "She bent over backward to help anyone who needed help. I couldn't be in the school because I had to help with haying, so Ellie would tell me what time the class was heading up to the ring, which was in a big grassy park east of my family's ranch house. I'd ride up quickly on my little black horse, Pickle, and meet them there for the riding part of the class. Then I'd quickly ride home and help to get lunch ready for everyone on the hay crew. Ellie borrowed horses and tack from my family, and I'd help clean the tack before the school opened in the summer, just so that I could meet the class at the ring and have a lesson from Ellie."

Joyce loved that Ellie talked about the horses just as she might talk about people. Ellie knew each horse's personality and needs as well as each student's. She used this knowledge to effectively match horse and rider. "For the benefit of the horses, Ellie always made sure the students took good care of the horses' tack, saddles, and blankets, and cleaned up the barn afterwards. She kept everything in the barn all oiled and conditioned. Afterwards, when the horses were comfortable in their corral, she'd stand outside that wonderful barn and tell stories, mostly about horses."

Every Sunday, Ellie would take the girls into Laramie, for church and laundry, counting the group before they left town so as not to lose a single cherished student. Packed into Ellie's 1961 red and white Plymouth station wagon with power steering and push-button drive, the girls were having the time of their lives.

Joyce believed that Ellie was also having the time of her life. "I could not remember a time when Ellie dwelled on the negative. She was always smiling, always laughing. She had a feel for people and, as a result, introduced natural horsemanship: desensitizing, exercising common respect, easing into, reinforcing, and eventually taking your horse into the show ring."

Deb Matthew was amazed that Ellie always had so much work to do. "But there was joy in it all. Ellie was having so much fun. Just to see her with her horses and dogs was a joy. She loved to play with her animals. And she loved people. It was heaven to hear Ellie's laugh. And remember, Linda? Remember how every morning, Ellie would hold her long hair over a tea kettle of steaming water on the stove? Every morning. That was how she got her curls going in dry old Wyoming. Then she'd pull her hair into a beautiful ponytail. Ellie was beautiful. And, you know, she was worried after Rob left. But she taught us that, like her, we could take care of everything if we needed to. Her philosophy for us was 'Nobody ever said we couldn't, so we just did.' That was Ellie's way."

So I Just Did

Chapter 10

"Being attracted to someone," Ellie reflected, "is a natural thing. I don't think anybody really knows why they marry someone, so I will say that it's just one of those things we all do. If we're willing to commit, we have to feel for them a lot. If we feel for them, we have to focus on them. I was attracted to Rob. He was good-looking and smart. He was interested in animals, and like me he wanted to go west. I admit that was the factor that attracted me the most. But when he wasn't loyal, the focus was gone. We were married thirteen years.

"Would I say that Rob was my ticket to Wyoming? I would say so. I don't know if I could have done it on my own. Looking back, though, I accomplished more in the next five years than the whole time I was married. All the things I did, so many said I couldn't do, so I just did. A good friend offered to set up a Laramie bank account for me, with several thousand dollars to draw from. I didn't argue so as not to hurt her feelings, but I never thought of that money. I was determined to depend on myself, on my abilities, and on my horses and German Shepherds."

Even though Ellie continued her dog breeding business, Khizan helped Ellie more than she thought to imagine. Winning an award at the 1961 Calgary National, which placed him in the National Champion Top 10, pushed Eleanor Smith's name into the world of horse showing, and especially horse breeding. Khizan proved through his performances that he was not only beautiful but also a level-headed stallion of sensible temperament. He would be sought after for breeding purposes, and Ellie would receive the stud fees. She could depend on this.

Ellie, though, was a realist. In 1961, she had planned out her life but realized that training and breeding and private lessons were not going to cover the costs for the second and subsequent sessions of Sodergreen Horsemanship School. Even if she increased the existing tuition fee of $700 and could depend on full enrollment—at least 15 girls—she couldn't shake the idea that the business venture was risky. As loving and loyal as they were, her horses required care, vet visits, tack purchase and repair, and feed. Horses were expensive. And Ellie owned, as she had dreamed as a young girl, lots of them. She would also have, for eight weeks of the summer, a group of exuberant, energetic, and growing young girls, who would hike, have pillow fights, and use up vast amounts of calories riding, caring for, and loving and learning about horses. Such young girls would eat a lot, and their needs, albeit sensible ones, could tip any budget.

Ellie refused to consider taking a job that took her from Sodergreen. She wanted nothing to do with a job that absorbed her time to plan and develop the horsemanship school's curriculum. Ellie could not take a job that filled the summer or prevented her from being physically active. On August 9, 1961, after much thought, Ellie submitted an application to the Albany County Public School System for substitute teaching during the regular school year. She was hired. Then, on August 27, 1962, Eleanor F. Smith signed a contract with School District 12, Albany County, to teach in Fox Park, in the Medicine Bow Range. Her assignment would be grades five through eight, for one school year, for the sum of $4,600.

For Ellie, teaching at Fox Park, more a village than a town, more or less west of Jelm Mountain, was an entirely different experience from her years at Harmony Elementary School. To be honest, she felt she was doing little good. The students were nomadic, from Missouri and other points east, as their parents followed the logging business. Most of the students were unfamiliar with and uneasy about the forests of the western mountains. For the transient families, education was a low priority as they sought the critical seasonal jobs.

Ellie recalled one family in which the father and mother had little, if any, education. The son had lost significant schooling because the family moved around constantly. He, like others Ellie taught, had no cohesive education. In fact, the parents did not seem pleased that their child was still attending school at the age of fourteen. Ellie tried but was unable to get to know the parents because they shied from her and the classroom. "Their son was a good boy," she said. "He couldn't read well or do the other fifth grade work, but he was a whizz in mathematics." She began to work with him, but then he was absent for quite a few days. Ellie sent a note to the family, and someone responded in writing with the brief sentiments of the boy's mother. The note simply stated that the mother was lonesome and wanted her boy at home to keep her company. Ellie thought about the situation and decided she would not give up. She ordered books for the boy, "special books that had more mature stories that the boy might enjoy and yet were easy to read." Soon after, the family was gone.

Ellie called the experience a wakeup call for her. Because of her own background, she never realized that some children are not encouraged to learn, and some just never get the chance. "It made me think about giving opportunities and never giving up on young people. I took my time and went

Ellie with Bonnie.

Khizan.

Ellie working with a young horse outside the old barn.

Minx and Derry, Ellie's prize breeding pair.

Ellie on Khizan, with Sheep Mountain in the background.

Ellie on Khizan, Champion, English Pleasure Class, Estes Park, Colorado.

1961 Sodergreen Horsemanship School brochure, featuring Khizan in a sketch by Ellie. Over the years, Ellie designed and drew all the school brochures.

Ellie on Fasaab, Cheyenne Frontier Days parade.

Opening exercises.

Fasaab.

Ellie's students showing at Estes Park Showmanship class.

Kataffa during the Estes Park All Arabian Show

Kataffa, Ellie's beloved brood mare, as shown in the 1961 brochure.

Anna and Don Dunlavy, owners of Broken Bridle Ranch, Laramie, Wyoming.

Photo courtesy of Linda Dunlavy Johnson.

Ellie's first new truck,
a blue Dodge, ordered
and paid for by Ellie.

Bill and Ellie on their wedding day, August 29, 1966.

The Oscar Sodergreen family. A daughter relinquished to Ellie the professional use of the surname.

Undated photo courtesy of the *Laramie Boomerang.*

A more recent Sodergreen Ranch sign. Designed and painted by Ellie, built by Bill, sometimes blown over by the Wyoming wind.

The cabin for the girls attending the Sodergreen Horsemanship School, built at low cost by Bill and his dad, uncle, and son Carl.

The school's new indoor riding arena and outdoor ring, Ellie's dream come true.

The new Sodergreen Ranch, surrounded by the vast Wyoming prairie. Mary O'Hara's Remount Ranch was just behind Saddleback Mountain, to the north.

A swelling Goose Creek before the spring floods, bane and blessing to Bill's hay meadows.

over all the material I had already taught in Harmony. In Harmony, there was cohesive family life, and there were animals, which can anchor young people. I pulled what I thought I could usc to tcach these young people at Fox Park. The families were good people, but their lives were unstable. It was a great challenge to try to teach, but I did the best I could for my students."

In addition to the instructional challenges, Fox Park offered a harsher climate than the one Ellie was used to. The mountain village sat at a higher elevation, and the snowplows ran constantly in the winter to keep the roads open. Ellie could have stayed at the teacherage in Fox Park, but she declined because, as would be her life mantra, "I had to get home to feed." She navigated the wintry roads in her big Dodge Power Wagon and took measures every day to make sure it started when she was ready to head home after school. "I parked it outside the window at the back of the school. I put a heat lamp upside down in a big kettle that had been my grandmother's and positioned the kettle under the front of the station wagon. Then I plugged in the heat lamp by running the cord inside through the window. Fox Park can be a chilly place, and I didn't want to have to be there overnight."

Concerned about finances, on April 2, 1963, Eleanor F. Smith again submitted a teaching application to Albany County, this time for a position in Art Education at Laramie High School or Junior High School, or in the Elementary grades five, six, or four (her order of preference), or at a rural school. But then, word spread about the Sodergreen Horsemanship School through a series of articles in *Arabian Horse News*. Ellie did not follow through on the teaching application.

It was through her success with Khizan, in showing and breeding, as well as the popularity of the October 1961 publication in *Arabian Horse News* of Khizan's story, "My Canadian Capers," that Ellie decided she could make her own contributions to horse magazines and build her reputation and the school's. Since fifth grade, she had been compiling material for ownership, care, and training of horses. She had learned so much from setting up the Sodergreen Horsemanship School, and she could bank on her natural acumen in and affinity for anything equine.

Her teachers at Melrose High School would have been pleased. In April 1964, Eleanor F. Smith published, in the *Arabian Horse News*, the first of five impeccably crafted and thorough articles, "the first," according to the matter just below her byline, "in a series on the training of the horse." The series was titled "Is It—Magic?" The articles were derived from the compilation of notes she had made throughout her short lifetime of training. The impetus for the articles was the result of her extensive study of books that dealt only with "almost finished" horses.

The first article, titled "Part I—General Conditions of Training," included the author's stylized and informative sketches; a brief biography, complete with a photo of Khizan and Ellie, she in ponytail and signature red lipstick; and an introduction of Eleanor F. Smith as "Arabian owner, breeder, exhibitor and trainer at Sodergreen Ranch, Laramie, Wyoming." She was mentioned as well as "riding instructor and [director] of the Sodergreen Horsemanship School." Quite characteristic of the humble Ellie, she asked for and was granted a disclaimer for her readers: "Eleanor has requested the *NEWS* to point out particularly that the methods and techniques set forth in her articles are those she has found most satisfactory for her own use—however, this is not to be taken as meaning that they are the ONLY ones or the BEST ones."

In a picturesque, lively, and second-person account, Ellie set out to convince the reader that "hard work, common sense, patience and especially love" are the essence of training, the goal of which is to establish mutual trust and enjoyment. The author's tone was intentional, placing reasonable but thorough responsibility on the trainer, encouraging him or her to learn about and understand the horse. She slid in horse psychology without intimidating the reader. She offered an empathetic ear and encouragement. She was generous with scenarios and solutions. From size of bit to size of arena, from purpose of lessons to environment of the stall, the kind and caring author left nothing out.

In the May 1964 *Arabian Horse News* issue, which included a separate photo of Eleanor and Khizan taking a jump in perfect form, Eleanor returned, in "Part II—Foal Training," with the same caring voice and thorough methodology. Featured were pictures of foals by Ellie's Khizan. A strength of this installment was that Ellie, who was not a mother, knew exactly how to deal, lovingly and firmly and respectfully, with foals, be they obedient or not so. Words or phrases like "repetition, patience, one step at a time, building trust, and knowing the foal" all suggested that success was ensured if the trainer put the needs of the animal first.

The June/July 1964 issue walked the trainer through the practice of longeing a horse. It was, the author stated, "a part of what we call 'ground training' and is a phase of training that is beneficial to the horse mentally and physically." When the article "Part III—Longeing" was written, ground training (heavily dependent on longeing) was rare, if nonexistent, in many Western training arenas. Yet Eleanor wrote of it as critical to the training of any horse.

In the August 1964 issue, Eleanor expanded the rider's world with detailed discussion and instruction in the fourth installment, "Suppling Exercises, Collected Gaits, Driving and Other Ground Work." The rider's work on the ground with a horse was clearly the key to success in every other aspect of horsemanship. The fifth and final installment, "Part V—Saddle Training," was nearly doubled in length, taking the rider through fifteen days of layered instruction, which nearly any educator would have concurred is essential to learning. One step was fully described, and the second was then built upon it.

Photos were included for illustration and demonstration. The lessons extended beyond the basics to gaits and eventual trail training and training for show.

These articles were not just for the reader. They were for Eleanor as well. They solidified and crystallized her teaching beliefs, philosophy, and methods. They convinced her that she was on the right track to developing a program of excellent horsemanship practice and practicality. It is no wonder that the series of articles formed the basis for the three books on horsemanship that Eleanor, with Gaydell Collier, would eventually write and publish in 1974, 1979, and 1986. Did Ellie receive payment for the five articles? "No," she said, "advertising was payment enough."

In the summer of 1962, the Sodergreen Horsemanship School's enrollment grew to 12 girls. Six of the girls roomed in the upstairs bedroom of the big house, and six filled a second cabin on the property. Lynn Hornby, who declared that she grew up on horses, had become Ellie's afternoon assistant. Ellie remembered Lynn as "one of those ranch girls who quickly figured out how to do things." Lynn easily caught on to instruction, and when Ellie taught English in the mornings, Lynn taught Western riding in the afternoons. There was one small problem: Lynn insisted on bringing her goat named Enchiladas to the school. The stories are varied, but in Ellie's version, she insisted that the goat be tied because during feeding time, the unneutered animal would charge a person to get to the feed, causing that person to have to ward him off with a pitchfork. The goat chewed through his rope, and the end of the story was that Ellie had to sit on the goat—"a horrible, stinky animal that chased the other animals and peed in the horses' hay"—while he was being castrated. Enchiladas was then allowed to stay. The practical Ellie thought that fair.

Lynn started riding lessons with Ellie at the age of 15. She wanted to learn to ride English. Ellie soon had her working with a young Arabian mare and then asked Lynn to teach the school's Western lessons for two years. "How much fun can that be," Lynn whooped. "I thought I had died and gone to heaven."

Lynn remembered that, in the early mornings, before training work began, Emma Beidleman served a substantial breakfast. "Ellie worked on a tight budget," Lynn recalled, "so Emma cooked frugally. She made the best meals and the most beautiful chocolate peanut butter cakes. She always had a bowl of rhubarb sauce around, even though she had to talk some of the girls into eating it, and she used a lot of rice with milk and cheese for the meals. She was a delightful person, pretty basic, but very creative. She was tall and stocky and always wore a house dress and her hair braided and pinned up. She had a wonderful accent and was a good listener and a good friend. She fit right in with Ellie's school philosophy."

Deb Matthew, who with her sister Linda attended Ellie's school in 1966 and 1967, attested to Emma's wondrous cooking. "All her dinners for the school were good, but I remember most the smell of cinnamon, and Emma sprinkling the raisins in dough, folding the dough over, and then rolling the dough out. Like an expert, she baked that bread in Ellie's black wood-burning stove, and the whole house smelled wonderful!"

Ellie was soon taking her schoolgirls to Estes Park, advertised as "The Center of the Arabian Horse Population of the U.S.," with shows and competitions every July 3rd, 4th, and 5th. She drove the pickup and horse trailer, and Lynn, pulling the camper trailer, drove Ellie's red and white push-button-drive station wagon filled with a load of girls. It was a shared story among the girls that Ellie, on more than one occasion while driving, "positioned her big flat-head screwdriver on the reverse button, and whacked the screwdriver with her hammer." Striking the reverse button in such a fashion was the only way that Ellie or anyone else could get the old car into any other gear.

Ellie wryly spoke of the drive up the narrow Thompson River Road, which climbed dramatically to Estes Park, as "fun and games." The canyon was known for occasional violent flooding, "but our problem," Ellie said, "was the station wagon. It kept overheating during the trip up the canyon, and the girls had to climb down to the river to get water to fill the radiator." The girls saw the task as great fun.

Lynn recounted that "at Estes Park, Ellie rented a cabin for all the students. Emma cooked and sent our food along. Ellie easily got to know all the horse owners and went right up to them, and we eventually did too, to ask if they would let us show their horses, even the gentle Arabians. Ellie had become a respected and trusted figure at this Colorado horse show. With the training and self-assurance she had given us, we showed those horses well. It was an amazing experience. Many of the girls had never been out of the city, and they were excited. Horses sustained Ellie. She lived for her horses and was living her dream. Her joy wore off on all of us."

When the gelding El Khilet developed bad habits, Ellie, seeing an opportunity for Lynn to grow as a trainer, turned El Khilet over to her. "She knew I could do it," Lynn said, "and he earned a ribbon in Western Pleasure." Lynn gained confidence and went on to participate with the University of Wyoming rodeo team as a barrel racer. She later became a horsemanship instructor, "all because of Ellie. She gave me a good foundation and she wanted all her students to have a good foundation. She wasn't in this business for herself. She was a patient and careful teacher, explaining different techniques to the girls, especially those who had never been around horses."

In describing Ellie, Lynn implied attractiveness with an equal amount of practicality. "Ellie told me her mother didn't approve of her wearing heavy gabardine pants, but that's what she wore. That's what was best for the Wyoming weather and for teaching her classes. She often wore a plain but pretty button-down shirt, and always, in the winter, her thick, warm jacket that she made at a factory during the war. And who can forget that ponytail with the barrettes and that smile of hers?"

Even though she didn't like cooking, Ellie often pitched in to prepare meals. "Her specialty," Lynn said, "was French toast, with a little sugar in the batter to brown the toast. She'd let the dogs clean the skillets, and then she'd wash them, of course, with plenty of soap."

Lynn recalled that Ellie always found a lesson in everything. "I had a corner room upstairs. One time a bat tried to get out of the attic, where at least a hundred of them lived. The girls were all screaming, but I just slammed a door hard to keep it from coming into the room. Ellie ran upstairs, thinking I had fallen out of bed and broken my leg. She was that concerned about us. But she was also concerned about the bat. 'Behave yourselves,' she said to all of us, 'This is not the end of the world. That baby bat is more frightened than you!' She was always helping us see the animal's perspective."

In the back of the big house, a table was set up just off the large dining room and the sunny living room as a crafts room for the school. The girls worked there on designing and assembling their required notebooks, which grew in cherished content—handouts, lecture notes, completed tests, articles, and pictures—and would never be forgotten or given away.

The dining room, with its big table, was used for lectures, lessons, and meals. For every meal, the table was set to provide a formal yet relaxed atmosphere. Just off the kitchen was a single bathroom. Because the water was supplied by a well, bathing time was brief. The upstairs of the big house had only a chemical toilet. The girls didn't seem to mind these less-than-luxurious accommodations because Ellie had a way of making everything a wondrous adventure. She was every girl's ideal sister, best friend, and even mom—whether in the riding ring, on the trail, at Estes Park, or in the evenings, when all gathered in pajamas and drank hot chocolate.

As one of the young girls who traveled with Ellie every July to Estes Park, Joyce Johnson marveled at how Ellie kept the girls together and safe. "The girls' chores and activities were all lined out. Each had a job, and everyone knew what everyone else was doing. There was a lot to keep busy with, when preparing for the halter class. Ellie didn't believe in tight rules, but the kids knew to help her with feeding, grooming, and cleaning tack. They knew to shine their boots and have their riding outfits ready. And, of course, the horses, whether they were ours or the ones loaned to us for the competitions, had to be washed and brushed to a shine. We had to know how to lead them with their halters and how to make them look good. It took hours to prepare, and we loved it."

The judges at Estes Park tended to prefer the horses from the large ranches. Ellie's students were delighted that Khizan, a horse from a small ranch, placed in English, Western, dressage, and other competitions. "That just showed," said Joyce, "what Ellie could do with her horses."

As the girls watched competition after competition, show after show, Ellie, in quiet but constant narration, taught them all about training for the show ring. "In your mind," she began, "you have to say and be centered on 'I am going to win this.'" She stressed that a rider had to block out the yelling, the distractions, and the band playing. The rider needed, as well, to remember that the horse hadn't been in the ring for probably a year, and that Wyoming horses often were not used to all the noise and chaos of competition. It was good practice for the rider to familiarize her horse with the new surroundings by making use of any morning practice allowed. Just as important was where a rider stabled or tied her horse. Doors and drafts and heated areas were not wise choices. Places close to other horses or commotion of any level could be problematic. The key, as Ellie always taught, was for the rider to know her horse. Ellie reminded her girls, for example, that "Fasaab was an ego trip at shows. Khizan was not."

Ellie shared with her rapt audience that horses were unpredictable and could act up unexpectedly. The fear could spread, so a rider had to be ready for anything that could go wrong. It was important for the rider to ask herself, "How could I make a mess of this?" and it was equally important for her to ask, "How will I deal with it?"

"In the ring," Ellie explained, "you must stand out somehow. It's important that the judges notice you. But you can't be ostentatious. Try to give the horse as few aids as possible and be as subtle as you can. You don't want the judge to see what you're trying to do. It's all in lots of training, and it's all in trust and respect between the horse and the rider. Your horse knows you care for him and that his best interest is at heart. Don't ever question that. And for goodness' sake, practice ring generalship. Watch the others, watch where you're going, and look ahead. You don't want to crash into someone."

Regarding the horses that owners eagerly loaned the girls for showing at Estes Park, Ellie reminded her riders that it is "an awful lot to ask a strange horse to trust a strange rider during a class." Her advice was to "just ride the best you can." She encouraged the girls to ask questions of the owners before the show, but she said that the rest would be luck. But not quite. "The horse knows when someone knows what they're doing and is firm and clear in what they are asking of the horse. The horse will have immediate trust, as if an innate feeling kicks in."

Ellie was delighted to be with her girls at Estes as they watched both men and women, young and old, compete in the many trials and events. She appreciated that horsemanship competition was for everyone; there were no men's teams or women's teams. Anyone with training could enter any show. She had observed over the years that "now men compete in dressage and barrel racing and women compete in polo and roping" and expressed the wish "that all sports were that way—that you qualify, enter, compete, and say 'I did it,' whether you won or lost."

When the excitement of Estes was over for a summer, Lynn Hornby remembered that equally enjoyable were the trail rides and overnight campouts. Generalship, which involves the awareness of what is happening in a riding area and the respect for all riders, was expected on the trail, just as it was in the show ring. Proper riding skills were to be practiced as well. The hours in the country were relaxing, with the feeling of freedom that Ellie believed could be found only on a horse. Bedrolls, sleeping bags, and equipment were lugged up Sheep Mountain to the north or Jelm Mountain to the south. The girls learned to hobble their horses in the big meadows where grass grew to the horses' knees. The evening setting involved bonfires, marshmallows, hot chocolate, and according to some, snipe hunts, which the girls insisted were instigated by Ellie.

Participants delighted in all manner of escapades, including one ride up to the watch tower on Jelm Mountain, which involved riding home at dusk past scary-looking cows. On another trip, up Sheep Mountain, Deb Matthew swore she had hobbled her horse Pancho for the night, but Pancho took a nocturnal walk down to the ranch without, mysteriously, destroying a fence wire or post. The searching girls, however, had to cut through fences, re-mend them, and even use keys to open gates. To get back to the ranch, Deb rode double with another girl, and Ellie lugged Deb's big Western saddle on her own horse, but no one was upset. The memory would be one of fun, adventure, and a lesson or two. And of course, there were the trips to the Snowy Range Mountain peaks so that the girls could play in the lingering snow on the cool summer days.

Ellie even made the hard work enjoyable. There were few admonitions and never a hint that failure could take the place of success. Yet there was scholarship in Ellie's summer program. The Sodergreen Horsemanship School taught English and Western classes as well as dressage, jumping, showing and from-the-ground-up care. Ellie demonstrated, through her own thorough instruction, the value of riding a horse correctly and forming a partnership with one's horse. She was committed to teaching well, so well that no committed student would leave at the session's end being less than darn good. Every student knew she had learned something valuable, whether she was returning to her family's ranch or to the East Coast. As far as Ellie was concerned, every skill she taught was going to be of value to any sort of horse lover. And word was getting around.

Flavoring People's Lives

Chapter 11

THROUGH THE EARLY SUMMERS OF SODERGREEN HORSEMANSHIP SCHOOL, Ellie's philosophy, techniques, and application were developing and solidifying. As an instructor, she had accumulated and answered the why's and how's. This is not to say that she was complacent. To the contrary, she believed that she learned something every day, from both her horses and her riders.

The tenets of her philosophy were driven by her belief that nothing was good for the rider unless it was good for the horse. The relationship was synergistic. The rider had to feel the horse, mentally and physically, and the horse had to be given constant, clear signals for trust.

To Ellie, ground work was essential. Students couldn't possibly know their lesson horse unless they had groomed, saddled, and bridled the animal. Ground work included correctly haltering and safely tying the horse, currying and brushing the animal, and checking his mouth and hooves to ensure good condition. Exercises in suppleness were often included, as were longeing sessions for review and relaxation. Ground work helped the rider to know the horse and the horse to know the rider. Ellie insisted that "the longer you are with the horse on the ground and before and after the ride, the more you and your horse enjoy and understand each other. Just getting on, riding, and getting off doesn't teach you anything."

A great deal of discipline was needed to prepare her riders and their horses for pleasure riding or the show ring. Ellie honored discipline, but she also believed that, as an instructor, she had to show enthusiasm, "even though I was teaching to a receptive audience that wanted to be there. Enthusiasm breeds enthusiasm, as does humor. If they were loving the lesson, they automatically wanted to do well, and I knew I was getting through to them."

To make her classes as interesting as possible, Ellie made sure to adjust her teaching to the individual students. She quickly learned their backgrounds, where they came from, and their physical and mental plusses and minuses. Her students came from different areas of the country and the world. They spoke of different foods, geographies, ideals, and even saddle types. "They learned from me," Ellie said, "but I learned so much from them as well.

"The individual is key," Ellie maintained. "Every horse is an individual, just like every rider. I had to bring out the individual in both the horse and the rider. I had to identify it and work with it, and then turn it into a team. Along with that was inventiveness, for me and for the students. We learned that if one thing didn't work, we had to discard it, but then we had to try to find something that would work. All this was challenging but worth it."

Something that Ellie admitted she had to learn was patience. "Patience involves thinking first, doing things slowly, and not jumping in too fast. Doing all that was at first hard for me, but laughter helped, and so did enthusiasm and optimism. I learned to look on the good side and learn from the bad. That was part of patience."

Although she had gleaned ideas about structuring her school from her years at Merrymeeting, Ellie soon learned the best school schedule from her students and, of course, the equine staff. The students rose at 7:30 in the morning and had breakfast at 8:00. Inspection of their rooms occurred soon after. The girls then readied themselves for their morning lecture, which focused on topics ranging from horse conformation to tack, feeding, care, and stable management.

Dismissed from lecture time, the eager girls headed to their assigned horses, which they haltered, groomed, and tied at assigned areas. As part of ground work, each girl was taught to gently encourage the horse to raise his or her leg for hoof inspection and cleaning. Horses were saddled and bridled with gentleness and respect. After longeing their horses, the students correctly mounted and headed to the ring in the meadow, where instruction began with exercises and warmups, all in the saddle. Ellie then had the students walk or trot their horses, all the while demonstrating and instructing, and gently but firmly correcting posture, rein work, and body and leg aids.

Break time, lunch, and rest led into the afternoon, when the girls saddled up for trail riding and Western instruction. Leisure time and activities, followed by dinner, preceded preparations for the next day. Ellie knew to be flexible. An interesting guest, the weather, or an unanticipated situation could shift or change what was planned. The girls willingly followed the gently imposed schedule. Ellie could not remember ever having a disciplinary problem. She remembered well how respect and courtesy were politely enforced at Harmony Elementary School and used similar techniques with her horsemanship students. She explained her rules and made sure she anticipated problems so that she could quell a worrisome situation before it arose. She showed respect for the girls, making sure she corrected the error, not the girl.

Ellie believed that learning to ride included time away from work with the horses. Time was needed to just have fun, as she once had, cantering Sammy while she shot arrows at hay bales. "I had small horse shows at the end of the summer school. One event that would be frowned upon today but that the girls loved was the burlap sack race, which involved two to a team. One rider dallied a rope, which meant she draped it around the saddle horn without knotting it. The other team member got on her stomach on a sack tied to the rope. The teams raced to the line, went over the line, and switched roles. The first team to return to the starting point was the winner. Nobody got killed and the girls had a great time, even though most of them lost the buttons on their blouses. I guess you could say it was a wild thing, but the horses had as much fun as the girls."

Ellie intended to make the experience of the West indelible and enjoyable for her students. If any of her helpers or friends had a talent, they were encouraged to teach or entertain. Helpers Lynn Hornby, Lana Brokaw, Danelle Schmidt, and Kirsten Springer often taught Western riding in the afternoons, adding their own experiences and knowledge to the lessons. Ellie's friend, Gay Collier, taught guitar lessons and sang. Ellie recruited anyone with an interest in just about anything. All manner of learning, be it about the local environment or southeastern Wyoming history, went on during the chilly but lovely summer evenings at Sodergreen Ranch.

"When all was said and done," Ellie maintained, "for a school, it all came down to the basics. Teaching what was basic was key. How to translate those basics to any student was an important goal of mine. Determining what was necessary and what was unnecessary was important. It was about setting a strong and permanent foundation.

"And of course," she added, "you have to teach in a ring. I had to see the students, everything that they were doing on and for the horse, at all times. I finally had the ring I had wanted even before I realized I wanted to teach. It was a huge, grassy meadow, but it was still a ring, my ring."

Ellie was resolute in how she trained her school horses. "I did things quietly. I didn't believe in riding the buck out of the horse. I worked around the horse until he was receptive. The biggest part of training was working on the ground—working with the horse's head, making the horse supple, and longeing. So much is longeing. I trained in steps, adding something new to what the horse had already learned. I never jumped too quickly to something new. Everything had to be gradual and gentle."

Ellie trained in a way so that the horse didn't know that he was being trained. Her goal was to have the horse happy with the rider and willing to help and perform what the rider wanted. She was firm and consistent in her requests of the horse, but not to the point where the horse became bored. "I did different things in different ways to make it interesting for the horse. If a horse had bad habits or was mishandled, I'd sublimate the bad and add on the good in layers. I always rewarded the horse with a pat or with my voice. I talked a lot to my horses, and never saw them as mechanical. Horses are more human than you think. Just like a parent would do for their children, I kept my training sessions short and made one point per session. I learned a lot of this from the old horseman at Camp Merrymeeting. He was a horse whisperer before all the horse whisperers who are making all the money. Maybe what I do is horse whispering. I don't know."

A pet peeve of Ellie's was hearing that a problem was the horse's fault. "That seemed to be the case at the first camp I worked for, people always blaming the horse. That just didn't make sense to me. A horse works fine if you know what to do. It's better to try something than to just lay blame. And a trainer has to remember that horses, like youngsters, have short attention spans. You can't go over and over the same old thing. If the horse is getting what you're asking of him, then add something new. Build on what the horse knows, even if it's just to go in a different direction in the arena. And when you finally get on the horse, if he doesn't do what you want, you probably didn't do it correctly on the ground. Ground work is everything. You just have to keep working till your horse decides to listen to you."

Ellie was adamant "that training sessions be happy sessions. You shouldn't use force. You should only use your voice and petting. You want the horse to think, 'Oh, this is fun. She's giving me a lot of attention.' If you don't do this, they may respond negatively." She admitted that there were some horses she didn't like, but then quickly retracted her statement. "I like all horses, but some give you trouble. They couldn't care less about you and would rather be alone. Training and respect will work, but the training will just take longer."

Deb Matthew never saw Ellie get rough with a horse. "Ellie took a couple of months to train a horse. She trained in a gentle, slow, thoughtful way, especially when she started longeing the horse. If the horse was naughty, you could hear the command in Ellie's voice, but that was it. Maybe there was an occasional 'Quit that!' or a smack on the neck, but never in anger."

Ellie's early training techniques were not from any book. She made things up as needed, adjusting for both the horse and the rider. For example, when she first got Khizan, he was always looking around for other horses. He didn't watch what he was doing or where he was going. Next to the Big Laramie River, where the marsh dried up, were dried mud hummocks. "You had to really watch where you were going," Ellie said, "or you'd fall on your face. So I started leading Khizan through the hummocks while I walked beside him. I did this for a long time and finally, he started watching where he was going. You just have to see what's going on with a horse and then do what you can do to help."

Ellie was irritated that some people professed to be able to train in two days. "It was fine if it worked for them. But when I was going to train a horse, I had to have the horse for three months. I trained step by step, for English, Western, and trail. One step at a time. It all had to be gradual because it took time to learn well."

Lynn Hornby, who followed Ellie as a student and then as a teacher out at the nearby Dunlavys' ranch, said that everything she did was inspired by Ellie's teaching and training. "I taught from May till the weather turned bad. I leased horses to teach. I taught kids and adults, anyone, always conscientious about how Ellie would teach them. She could teach anyone and any horse. In fact, not too many people knew that she housebroke Khizan. Ellie would lead him to the door of the barn and wait a few minutes. He would do his thing, and then Ellie would lead him back into the barn. I don't think there was a horse she couldn't train. I don't think there was anything she couldn't get a horse to do. She just took all the time that was needed and didn't let anything get past her."

You couldn't put anything past Anna Dunlavy, either, whose ranch lay just east of Laramie. She'd hear about it sooner or later. As co-owner, with her husband Don, of Broken Bridle Ranch, established with that name in 1956, she was a staunch believer in training both horses and riders well. Less than "well" was not acceptable. "Well" was the only way you could get anything done, according to Anna, either on a ranch or in the 4-H horse program which she directed and was totally committed to. There was no sense in doing something wrong on or with a horse. That just wasn't part of Anna's scenario. If you didn't know what you were doing, she often said, you might as well just stay off the horse. An excellent rider herself, Anna was practical, savvy, and sensible. She knew horses, and she knew people. When she placed a horse with a potential buyer, neither party ever regretted her decision. She also knew genuine when she saw it. The more she heard of Eleanor Prince, the more Eleanor was "yep, uh huh" genuine.

Anna taught Western pleasure riding as well as rodeo event riding. She was an integral part of 4-H and state and county fair competitions. She trained, bred, and sold the best of horses. In fact, she could train just about anything on two or four legs. Her pet raccoon, antelope, and owl were testimony to the fact. Had she more time, friends said, she might have been able to teach them to talk.

Anna Dunlavy could read the mind of a horse and his rider, and those who knew her insisted she could predict the short- and long-term outcomes of that partnership. She was one of very few in southeast Wyoming who held to the value of ground-up training, and she had a strong inkling, when she heard about Ellie Prince, that English and dressage could become an integral enhancement to Western riding.

Word continued to get around about what Ellie was doing. Anna Dunlavy thought about it and said, "Well, yeah, uh-huh, that's good." She knew a superb teacher and horsewoman as well as a superb horse. When she finally met Ellie, the horsewoman from the East fit Anna's bill. After a few introductory conversations, the two women settled on Saturdays as a good day for Ellie to teach dressage lessons at Broken Bridle Ranch. According to Anna, dressage was a style of riding foreign to most Wyoming ranch kids. Anna took on the responsibility of enrollment for the class, and as gregarious, well-known, and loved as she was throughout the county, it wasn't surprising that on the first day, Ellie had a full house—or, as the case was, an outdoor arena full of young people eager to learn about dressage.

It's probably safe to say that El Khilet was Ellie's partner in most of her instruction. The gelded, dapple-gray Arabian was Ellie's choice in demonstration from the saddle. He was her jumper and her dressage horse, and he and his owner were excited that they were going to teach the youngsters some new skills.

Ellie settled in to teach at the Dunlavys' ranch during the summer and autumn Saturdays of 1964 to 1966. Anna had easily recruited a number of students, including her own children. Linda Dunlavy, the oldest daughter and a near look-alike friend to Deb Matthew, was in junior high school at the time. "Mom didn't ask us if we wanted to take the lessons. She just told us that's what we'd be doing. She didn't care that my baby brother Danny whined that he would miss Saturday cartoons. Mom was raising Morgans back then, so I rode three of them, King's Dawn, King's Giggles, and Hamilton Dome. My younger sister Lisa rode Miniway, one of mom's other Morgans. Our younger brother Lourie rode Miss Hacking, a chestnut Quarter horse, and our little brother Danny, who was seven at the time, rode Crockett, an Appaloosa gelding."

For two years, Linda showed with King's Dawn, a chestnut mare with a flaxen tail. King's Dawn was high point mare in English and hunt seat for two years in the Rocky Mountain Region. "All because of Ellie," Linda said. "Ellie taught me English and influenced me to continue. She was a big contributor to my awards. I even rode other folks' Quarter horses, so that they could earn points under English tack and I could ride English."

Linda believed that Ellie's thorough English instruction made her unique in the west. "People just didn't do English. But it's important. I later taught English in 4-H and at Eastern Wyoming College in Torrington and used all of Ellie's techniques, with a touch of Anna, of course. I sometimes had forty in my class. English was becoming popular. Before all this, there was just 4-H, Western lessons and gymkhana, and moving cattle. You know, ranch riding. This, of course, was important, but Ellie opened up the pleasure and skill of English riding, at least for Albany County, if not for Wyoming."

Ellie fashioned the Saturday lessons after her horsemanship classes at Sodergreen Ranch. Besides instruction, there were exercises and warmups. Classes were held up in the ranch's roping arena, which, for the purpose of lesson focus or as windbreak, was surrounded with tall, solid railroad ties and wide, wooden panels.

Linda was sure that Ellie didn't leave anything out of her lessons. "She taught us so many of the intricacies of dressage. She taught pivoting on the haunches, posting on the correct diagonal, and loping on correct leads. She taught safety and cavalletti, head set and hunt seat. She even taught how to pass each other in the ring. And when she chose to ride Khizan to demonstrate, it was poetry in motion. You couldn't take your eyes off that pair."

Linda loved that Ellie often stayed at the Dunlavy ranch after the day's class was over. "I remember her beautiful hair, with frizzies of curl around her face. She was always happy, always joyful. Her cheeks were naturally rosy." Linda remembered that Ellie could be stern. She worked the class hard, and there was intensity in her instruction, but there was always laughter during the class. "Ellie taught us that life is fun, that horses are fun and beautiful, but that riding also requires respect for the horses. I carried Ellie's attitude into my own teaching experiences of 21 years and 4 years as a school principal. She taught that teaching doesn't always have to be serious, and you don't have to be the taskmaster. She taught that there was a lighter side in everything.

"Mom and Ellie appreciated each other," Linda said. "Mom was a taskmaster, but like Ellie, she was welcoming, and she loved people and horses. Mom contrasted well to Ellie's playfulness. Mom did the organizing, and Ellie did the teaching. Whether she was providing classes, or competitions, or games, Mom loved to provide riding opportunities that were good for horses and riders. She loved bringing in the students and the teachers, especially Ellie."

Anna even invited, via Ellie and a relative of Lynn Hiatt's, a cavalry officer stationed at Ft. Robinson, Nebraska, to introduce Ellie's students and possibly Anna's 4-H kids to the benefits of cavalry riding, which was the precursor to dressage. The Ft. Robinson cavalry might have once been a supplier to local ranchers who bought the cavalry's remount mares, as did the fictitious ranch owner, Rob McLaughlin, in the novel *My Friend Flicka.*

Linda appreciated that her mom worked hard with Ellie to help many people learn more about horses and riding. "That was Mom's purpose in life, to better the lives of people by pairing them with horses. That was the similarity between Mom and Ellie. Mom said they were flavoring people's lives through horses. That's what they loved to do. Mom was a pilot trained in the WASPs (Women's Air Service Pilots) to eventually transport the jets in World War II back and forth. Ellie started a renowned school of horsemanship on her own. Those two were powerful women, forces out here in the West."

At the foot of Jelm Mountain, across the Laramie Valley from the Broken Bridle Ranch, Sodergreen Horsemanship School was growing, as was Ellie's reputation and her vision for the school. In 1958, Gaydell Collier moved with her family from Vermont into the cabin that Rosemary and Bill McIntosh had recently vacated. A writer herself, Gay read the five articles Ellie had published in *Arabian Horse News* and insisted that Ellie expand the articles into a book on basic horsemanship. Gay would edit. About the same time, a widower from Windsor, Vermont, Bill Prince, gathered his two sons and one daughter and drove to Wyoming to be with old friends who once lived on a neighboring Windsor farm. A bigger ranch would soon be a matter of necessity for Eleanor Prince.

Family, Inherited

Chapter 12

In the mid-60s, Ellie finished her terms as Harmony School school board member, president of the Arabian Horse Club of Wyoming, and president of and instructor at the Laramie American Kennel Club. Sire Derry and bitch Minx, renowned for her excellent care of a fourteen pup litter, continued to put forth beautiful and desirable German Shepherds. Gay Collier, raised on Long Island and the daughter of a reputable artist, huddled in the evenings with Ellie to outline the chapters of a book that Ellie planned to title "Basic Horsemanship." Sensible school horses continued to find Ellie, the stallions were proving their fine lineage, and the Sodergreen Horsemanship School enrollment climbed significantly with each unfolding summer.

Up in Wood's Landing, Gay and Roy Collier's closest friend and long-time New England neighbor, Bill Prince, was living in a trailer with his teenage son Carleton, felling logs in Fox Park for a salary and dealing with grief. His two younger children, Lynn and her little brother George, remained in New England with Bill's parents. Bill's wife, Corinne, had been killed a few years earlier in a horse-riding accident at their small family farm in Windsor, Vermont. George had witnessed the fatal accident when he was only three years old. The grieving family needed a fresh start, and just up Route 230 seemed to be the place for it. In Windsor, Bill had logged, raised beef and dairy cows, and helped his then-neighbors Gay and Roy with the many chores at their place. It was only neighborly that Gay and Roy, living in the small cabin near Ellie's house, would help Bill get settled in Wyoming.

When Gay did another neighborly thing and introduced Bill Prince to their neighbor with the new powder-blue Dodge pickup, Ellie Smith saw much to like in Bill Prince. He wasn't crazy about dogs, although a dog had traveled west with him, but Ellie appreciated that in the mornings, before Bill went to work, Bill and Carl, as he preferred to be called, came by to help Ellie with chores. Ellie enjoyed Bill's sense of humor, especially his jokes. "He wasn't handsome," she said, "but he was physically attractive, a big, rugged guy." She also admired his strength, his vast knowledge of farming, and his love of reading. "Bill went only through eighth grade," Ellie explained, "but he read voraciously, especially nonfiction and biographies. You could say that he was self-taught in so many subjects. And of course, besides farming and logging in Vermont, he had also worked at the Goodyear Tire and Rubber Factory and in machine shops." Ellie was quick to notice that both Bill and his son "had a good work ethic. They were good people to be around. And we all liked the same thing—animals."

According to Ellie, what Bill didn't like and what was probably the worst thing about living on the Big Laramie River was mosquitoes. Back then, there was no spraying for these blood-thirsty swarms. The mosquitoes were so horrible at the ranch that Ellie bought woolsacks used to gather shorn sheep fleece and made nearly full-body coverings for her horses from them. "I made a cut from one end of the long part and then fitted the long part over the horse, securing what was the open end of the sack around the horse's neck. I secured that open end with lacing. Then I pulled and tightened the created pocket at the sack's bottom over the horse's hindquarters. The sacks were thick enough to keep the mosquitoes off." These woolsacks, purchased for only one to five dollars apiece, became a critical part of Ellie's horse care during the mosquito months.

Mosquitoes were so bad that if anyone placed their hand on a horse's neck, a bloody imprint would result. Bill created a get-up for making it through the haze of mosquitoes while he did his chores: winter coat, heavy gloves, thick boots, hat, and mosquito net over hat and head. If he had to work on an outside project, a car, or a truck, a smudge pot was the additional accessory. The mosquitoes lurked in bulk in the tall hay, and before it was cut, the horses suffered the most. After the hay had been cut and put up, life, especially in the evenings, was somewhat better for both horses and humans.

Mosquitoes aside, there was much to appreciate in this new Western world, and on Monday, August 29th, 1966, Eleanor Fracker Smith and William Raymond Prince were married. Neither went in for all the trappings of a wedding, so the ceremony was simple, with the Albany County Justice of the Peace officiating. Bill's gift to Ellie was practical and, in her estimation, wonderful. "He gave me a big, sturdy metal horse gate. It was lovely."

Bill supplemented his income as a logger by cutting firewood to sell in Laramie. Ellie recalled that this money was usually spent for groceries. She kept a little book with their customers' names, and it wasn't long before these customers became friends. One of them was the agent at Laramie's Farmers Insurance, who would prove in future years to be of utmost assistance to the Princes.

Bill realized that if he was going to make any kind of money as a logger in Wyoming, he would need to work for himself. Thus, he would need the logging truck that he had left behind in Vermont. He had made the trip east after he and Ellie married, to gather daughter Lynn and son George, so he thought little of making the trip again. Besides, what he really wanted to retrieve from his parents' farm, on which sat the partially finished house he and Corinne had planned to someday live in, was his 1904 McCormick tractor. Roy Collier offered to travel with Bill, and Ellie insisted that Bill drive her reliable blue Dodge.

The logging truck loomed high with the tractor and odd pieces of family furniture, and Bill set out on the return trip to Wyoming. He feared that the sometimes-unreliable logging truck might give him some trouble, so the plan was for Roy to follow Bill in Ellie's truck, to help Bill with repairs if necessary. Repairs were indeed necessary during that long stretch between Vermont and Iowa, and Roy proved to be all-the-time unreliable. He woke up each morning long after Bill had left and followed too far behind, his absence during the repairs aggravating to Bill. Eventually the logging truck broke down and couldn't be fixed. A helpful farmer in Iowa offered to let Bill stow the logging truck at his farm. He even offered some tools. Bill knew that what he needed for repairs was back in Wyoming, so he thanked the farmer, left the truck, and headed west in Ellie's pickup, with a nonchalant Roy riding shotgun. On the return trip to Iowa, by bus, Bill had his reliable son Carl with him. The logging truck repaired, they headed for home. There would be no permanent return to New England for Bill and his new family. For the rest of his life, though, as a landowner immersed in the constant complications and frustrations of Wyoming ranching, when Bill talked of home, he was imagining Windsor, Vermont.

When asked if she ever wanted to have her own children, Ellie's response, after a long pause, was, "Well, yes and no. Children would have been nice, but I had so much to do." Yet it had become an obvious matter of fact that Ellie loved and nurtured any living creature placed in her care, no exceptions. She set out to do what she could to create quality time with Bill's children, absorbing them into the world she had established for herself, one that involved the love of horses.

Trail riding was a significant part of Ellie's school curriculum. It also became a way for Ellie to introduce her new family to the beautiful land that surrounded them and, of course, to the joy of days on horseback. As a string of excited students and Bill's sons and daughter mounted up, Bill set out for Sheep Mountain in the old brown 4-wheel-drive Dodge carryall, loaded with sleeping bags, drinking water, and assorted other provisions including slippers and cameras.

These trips were icing on the cake for the students as well as for Ellie's new family. She made sure that the rides were adventurous and fun. The route took the school's riders and the Prince family up Route 230 to Fox Creek and then south to north along the high ridges of Sheep Mountain. From that vantage point, the riders could see forever into the wide valleys and high hills that stretched out from the mountain's base. They could see nearly to the small town of Centennial, situated on Route 130, the only town between Laramie and the Snowy Range peaks.

Streams were frequent on Sheep Mountain's summit, and one such lovely stream posed a problem. It had to be crossed to get to the designated camp for the night. Eight-year-old George was riding Ranger, who, regardless of the number of times he had crossed a creek, saw the water and stalled in fear until he realized he could jump it. With an overly enthusiastic leap, Ranger cleared the stream with room to spare. George, as Ellie remembered, "shot about five feet above the horse but managed to land in the saddle when he came back down. We later thought of the moment as comical, but it could have been a disaster. I was proud of George. He did just fine."

In the midst of thick pine trees, the party made their camp for the night. Before any other activity occurred, the horses were grained and cared for. All slept well in the chilly night air of a Wyoming summer, lulled to rest by the pines' occasional whispers, the sweet nickers of the horses, and the occasional settling stomp of a hoof. In the morning, an experience of a lifetime tucked into the riders' memories, the group turned toward home.

For Ellie, marriage would bring its changes, but she and Bill, from the first, chose to be open and honest with each other. Because of the circumstances of his wife's death, Bill shared that he was leery of Ellie's animals. Ellie told him that horses were her focus and that she was not, in any way, going to alter what was most significant in her life: her animals, her school, and her goals. Bill said that would be fine. He would not interfere with her work with her horses. Ellie agreed that she would not interfere with Bill's raising his children.

It was impossible, though, for Ellie not to grow fond of the children. Although she respected that Bill alone was to raise and discipline his sons and daughter, Ellie could not help but be drawn into their lives. In fact, Rosemary McIntosh observed that Ellie's gentle manner might have been a balance to Bill's strict ways with the children. "Ellie worked at keeping her distance from the kids, as if she were restraining herself. I always wondered if she had really wanted to have kids, since she always seemed to be wanting to show her loving side to them. It was foreign to her nature not to be open and loving, a big adjustment for her. This was a hard time for Ellie."

Ellie gradually discovered that she and Carl shared a similar work ethic and liked the same things, which, of course, included animals, especially horses. When Carl, who she described as a likable, self-sufficient, and inquisitive teenager, expressed an interest in learning to drive something more than a tractor, Ellie jumped at the chance to help teach him. Bill agreed to the arrangement but insisted that Carl take his lessons in Ellie's Dodge Power Wagon. Bill wouldn't trust any other brand but a Dodge. Ellie loved that vehicle as well, the growing joke between the two of them that each married just to keep the Power Wagon "in the family."

Behind the wheel, Carl headed out east on Route 230 in the Dodge. Nearing the few buildings that constituted the town proper of Harmony, Carl somehow hit the gas instead of the brake, and according to Ellie, they roared into Harmony Station, Carl scared to death. Bill decided that Carl had learned quite a bit about driving from the incident, and he granted Carl permission to use the family's Dodge Dart station wagon to drive to and from Laramie High School.

Sad memories had accompanied Carl to Wyoming, but in reminiscing, he indicated that life at Sodergreen Ranch was pretty ideal for a teenage boy. "I remember that June of 1965, Dad meeting Ellie, the green of Jelm Mountain, and the water standing in the fields, from irrigating. Before I had to enroll at Laramie Senior High School, we explored ghost towns, saw the Rawah Mountains in Colorado, went on picnics up the Snowy Range and on the Laramie River, and hiked Jelm Mountain." Carl spent a good deal of time helping Ellie with the ranch while Bill worked at the Fox Park sawmill. In turn, Ellie taught Carl the basics of horsemanship as he rode on Ranger, Red, or Mouse. She took him to the Estes Park Horse Show and to dog shows. Carl even contributed to the herd by buying Goldie from a neighbor, Mr. Phillips. Goldie fit in well and soon became a favorite mount of Carl's dad.

Carl recalled that he was on the University of Wyoming campus on one of the last days of August in 1966, waiting for a ride home with Margaret Johnson. "My dad and Ellie swung by to let me know they'd just been to the Justice of the Peace. It wasn't long after they married that my dad and Ellie went back to Vermont to bring George and Lynn out to Wyoming."

"I was twelve or thirteen, going into eighth grade," shared Lynn, "when Dad drove back to get me and George. I was scared of leaving my home, my grandparents, and my friends, but Wyoming, with its horses, was exciting. The ranch was big, and there were a lot of horses. Everything was different from what I'd experienced in New England."

Lynn credited Ellie with making her and her brothers feel welcome. "She was super friendly and outgoing. There was a lot to do on the ranch, and she kept us busy with chores and new things to do with the horses and dogs. We fed the horses and cleaned out their corral. We fed and played with the dogs. We went to horse shows and dog shows. Everything was horse-related or ranch-related. She didn't do any girl things with me, and I never called her 'Mom,' but I thought of her as a mom. And that was great."

Lynn recalled that every summer, her dad took the kids back to Vermont to visit his parents. "Ellie couldn't go because one of them always had to be at the ranch. It was fun to go back, but I was getting used to Wyoming, where there was so much more to do. I was making friends at Harmony School, which was a much more relaxed setting than I was used to, and the teachers were all nice." In the summers, Lynn enjoyed being a part of Ellie's horsemanship school and remembered that she loved all the horses. "And Ellie was such a good teacher, even when I was having so much trouble trying to figure out how to make my horse take the proper lead during a canter. She never scolded or yelled. She worked hard to figure out how to help all of us. Riding was just a good feeling, a free feeling. Especially out there with Ellie, in Wyoming."

It was during one of her early Wyoming summers, during a family drive and hike up to the summit of Jelm Mountain, about ten years before the University of Wyoming assumed the operation of the newly built Wyoming Infrared Observatory, that Lynn received an honor she never forgot. "When we got to the lookout tower, the forest ranger, a woman who might have been Native American and who might have been named Charlie, gave me the materials to fill out to become an Honorary Squirrel, probably because I had climbed up that steep mountain. Somewhere I still have all the paperwork that says I am an official Honorary Squirrel."

In the spring of 1963, ten years after Walter and Maxine Fracker had moved permanently to Freedom, New Hampshire, they made a cross-country trip in their 1963 Blue Chevy Impala to visit their daughter. After Ellie and Bill were married, Ellie's parents again visited Sodergreen Ranch, in the fall or early winter of 1966, to meet the family Ellie had inherited. Ellie's fond memories of their visit included the late-night spotlighting excursions. Ellie, Bill, Carl, and Walter Fracker Jr., who Carl remembered as "a neat old guy who snuck cigarettes when Ellie's mom wasn't looking," piled into the old carryall and headed out onto the Lewis' ranch prairie, where they had been invited to hunt the rabbits that were overrunning the ranch. Ellie drove, but not because she lacked marksmanship. To the contrary, her aim was as excellent as her eyesight, at 20/20.

Ellie did not believe in killing for the sake of killing, "but these rabbits were like rodents, plentiful and destructive. We were overrun. They were doing a lot of damage to the ground, and they were bothering the hay by eating the grass roots. We made use of the animals, selling the hides in West Laramie, at McConnell's, for 35 cents. After the shoot and the sales, we went home for hot chocolate."

Whereas Ellie's father was exuberant about his daughter's new life, Ellie's mother was worried about her daughter's choices. She feared that someday Ellie might come to her senses and realize that what she had was not really what she wanted. Although Maxine Griffith did not grow up in the opulence of her parents-in-law, Mr. and Mrs. Walter Fracker Sr., she took advantage of her new station in marriage, became a member of the Freedom Club of Boston, and was elected its President in 1945. She was also in the inner circles of the Freedom Community Club, the Freedom Historical Society, the Church Society of the First Christian Church, and the Effingham Women's Club. It was this societal life that Mrs. Fracker wished upon her daughter.

Deb Matthew, who met the Frackers on one of their trips west, wondered if Ellie's mother "thought that Ellie could have chosen another way of life. She couldn't understand that the path Ellie had chosen was what made Ellie happy.

Ellie's mom was horrified by all the hard work her daughter was doing and worried that Ellie might not be able to manage it. Interestingly, Ellie was really a lot like her mom: successful at business, resourceful, able to juggle all her responsibilities, and just accepting what came by if she truly couldn't change it."

Maxine Griffith's genealogy revealed that Ellie and her mother's lives were woven together with other common threads. Maxine's ancestry can be traced back to the 1700s, with the records of John Grimes Jr. clearly exposing the thread of working the land and working with animals. At Grimes' death, items that were sold to pay the farmer's debts included a yearling heifer and a hog. The items he bequeathed to his wife, Tryphena Razey Grimes, included a horse, a pair of oxen, a cow and calf, most of John's farming equipment, a horse wagon, and a harness. He bestowed as well to his wife "the use of all my estate, both real and personal" for "her natural life." The Grimes' daughter and Maxine Griffith's direct ancestor, Mahalah, who married the established farmer Samuel Griffith, was bequeathed the "equal shares of John [Grimes]'s remaining estate" upon the death of Tryphena.[44]

Thus emerged a second thread. Not only was Mr. Grimes, of Cheshire County in what would become New Hampshire, an established farmer, but the family recognized the women as those who could skillfully run or become involved in a business. Maxine Griffith's mother, after her divorce from Charles Griffith, obtained, in the mid-1950s, a clerk position at the Fanny Farmer Candy Shop in Boston. Maxine herself, at the age of 19, became a bookkeeper at a bank in the Boston metropolitan area.[45]

Despite their differing opinions, Ellie doted on her mother when her parents visited. She knew how harsh the land could be on those not acclimated to it and worried that her mother seemed to have little stamina for the high altitude. Ellie's plan one day was to take her parents through the small town of Centennial and on up to the magnificent Snowy Range peaks. But Maxine was having trouble breathing, and Ellie, highly concerned, decided she should travel no further. Care was most important for those Ellie loved, so the family stayed in the town and had a hearty meal at the Old Corral Steakhouse.

It wasn't long before Sodergreen Ranch, once the reality of Ellie's dream, seemed too small. It had served Ellie well. It was where she became an integral part of a rural Wyoming community and realized and implemented her plans for a school. It was where she accumulated lots of horses and dogs, where memories were made, and where Ellie felt free and strong. However, she determined that "we just had too many horses for the old place. And we wanted and needed to buy a place of our own." She and Bill started looking for property with ample acreage and a reliable well.

Carl remembered that in the winter of '66-'67, his dad and Ellie found what they thought was an ideal place, 30 miles east of Laramie, on Harriman Road, just off Interstate 80. "It was a really beautiful place. Ellie and my dad wanted to buy it, but the owners' granddaughter talked her parents out of selling. Dad and Ellie were disappointed, but they weren't the type to give up. They kept looking."

That spring, Carl spent his days helping his dad fix fences and clean up buildings and pastures at the ranch they were renting. That fall, he was given permission by the Albany County School District to drive to Laramie—as long as he paid for his own fuel and secured his own transportation—to finish his last year of high school. That fall, Lynn would start school in Cheyenne and George would attend Willadsen, a rural school on Harriman Road, because another ranch had come up for sale, also on Harriman Road, just off I-80, between Cheyenne and Laramie. The Princes decided they could afford it, and they bought it.

Ticks and Old Wood

Chapter 13

Wyoming winters are long and the temperatures bitter. In the 1960s, long before the drought that eventually settled in the Western states, snow was plentiful. Incessant, strong winds gave birth to blizzards, the resulting drifts obliterating fences and roads and sometimes burying all but the tips of roofs or the leeward sides of ranch buildings. Work on the new place, purchased in 1967, as well as the gradual moving in, would have to wait till at least May 1968. The work confronting the Prince family before they could settle in would cast a new and unbelievable dimension on the term "spring cleaning."

When they first inspected their new ranch, Ellie's immediate reaction was that the land and the buildings were "all a junkyard." Buildings were in ruin, and the barn held evidence of nearly ninety head of dead sheep. There may have been electricity, but there was no telephone service. The Princes didn't feel overwhelmed by all the labor they faced. According to Ellie, "we didn't have frustrations then, and we knew how to do things. We'd get all the jobs done, doing most of the work ourselves. What was most important was that we now owned this ranch, and Bill and I were paying for it together."

As they toiled to ready the place for occupation, the Princes soon realized that one job was of imminently critical importance: the establishment of telephone service. The development of Ellie's horsemanship school was dependent on it. So too, she quickly discovered, would be the safety of her beloved animals.

Although Ellie had chosen to cease her dog breeding business when the family moved to the new Sodergreen, she brought, from the old Sodergreen ranch, seven six-month-old pups, hoping to sell them soon to good homes. Bill and Ellie devised a pen for the pups, but one night—German Shepherds being diggers—the pups escaped. Without a phone to call their few neighbors to alert them to a lost litter of domestic pups, Ellie set out alone in her station wagon to find them. "I drove all over the place, even across the road to the land where the Air Force Base's missile silos were housed. It was there that I finally found them, all on the road, tired, their feet worn. I got them home safely and got their pen fixed, but I had been so afraid the whole time that if people saw them, they would think the pups were from one of the packs of wolves in the area and shoot them. There was no longer any question that I needed a phone."

Unable to afford to have service put in by a company, Ellie and Bill decided they could do most of the work themselves. "Bill and I got the big poles from Laramie and used our logging truck to transport them. A lot of holes had to be blasted for the poles, so we arranged for workers at the nearby I-80 quarry to come down and set off dynamite. After the initial blasts, Bill and I finished digging the holes. We had to climb and descend hills, we had to go through a low-lying hay meadow, and when we had to turn a corner, more holes were needed for stabilization." The hay meadow at the bottom of the hill did them no favors. Because the meadow was sub-irrigated, the holes filled up with water as soon as they were dug. There was nothing Bill or Ellie could do. They couldn't lean the pole against anything to stabilize it, so they just shoved in the pole and let it wave around. "A guy with spurs on his heels managed to climb up that pole," Ellie said, "and somehow attached the glass insulators while the pole just waved in the breeze. As if the wobbly poles weren't enough of a problem, there were old wood shacks down that hill. It was a junk yard of a place with rotted wood scattered all over. There were ticks everywhere because of that wood, and soon they were all over us. All this was hard work, but we knew we could get to the final pole, near I-80, and we did."

The job still wasn't finished. Ellie and Bill had to string the phone wires from pole to pole. "The wire," Ellie explained, "was fed out from two huge spools in the back end of a type of trailer. Bill drove the tractor which pulled the trailer, and I fed out the wire. When he had to go downhill, the spools started going around to the point of unraveling. I just couldn't hold them, so we switched places. The only problem was that I was not the greatest tractor driver, and Bill wasn't the greatest teacher. I couldn't come right out just then and tell him I didn't know how to run a tractor after he'd made the assumption that I could. I did my best, trying to keep that tractor from going too fast and worrying that I would tip the whole rig over. I kept my foot on the brake rather than use the gear. That was not a good thing. The tractor just skidded downhill faster, but somehow, I got it under control."

When the job was finally finished, the telephone company representative in charge of the project, furious that the Princes had taken so long to complete the work, approached Ellie and "started cussing out me and Bill because we'd been so slow in getting the job done. I just stood there, but Bill came over and the two of them got into it with words. The man stomped off to his truck, and Bill followed. He was so mad that he grabbed the fellow's door handle and somehow yanked it off. He did a good job of reaming out the fellow for reaming me out. I thought Bill made some good points."

In retrospect, Ellie believed that she and Bill were "dumb-dumbs" to have taken on the project. "But we had to do it. We had to have the phone to run the school. We had to figure out how we could get phone service without spending much money, and necessity is the mother of invention, right? But I will never forget how scary it was going down that hill on that tractor."

Whereas the phone line project was scary, other tasks on the property were downright gruesome, signaling animal neglect. Cattle, sheep, and horse carcasses were strewn over the property. According to Don Carroll, a friend of Bill's from the small town of Buford, nine miles west on I-80 from the turnoff to Harriman Road, nearly 900 sheep had once been on the ranch. The owner of a Ford tractor with a front-end loader, Don offered, in neighborly fashion, to use his tractor to help Bill, whose own tractor was equipped with only a sweeper for hay. They worked together to rid the west barn of five feet of hardened, packed sheep manure. The manure was mixed with dead carcasses, needles, and syringes. Ellie described the job as "awful, terrible, and upsetting. It's a wonder we survived all this stuff."

Even more upsetting was the earlier discovery of a horse that was still alive but could not get up. When Ellie and Bill found him, Ellie was shocked "that he had done his best to graze around his body. All around him were signs of a desperate attempt to feed. He had even tried to eat roots. There was no water for him. For three days, we tried to give him water and hay, tried to make him comfortable, but eventually we had to put him down. We were still in the process of buying the place so we couldn't move anything off, including the horse. It was horrible."

When the ranch was finally habitable, it was time to say goodbye to the Big Laramie River, the big house and old barn, and the Johnsons. It might have been tearful, but in Wyoming no one blanches at driving great distances for a cup of coffee and conversation, so there was only need of a simple "We'll see you soon." It was time to gather the dogs and trailer the horses for the trip down Route 230, across the Laramie Valley, up Sherman Hill to the south turnoff that was Harriman Road, a distance of about sixty miles, and then two miles to the ranch's lane. Ellie had planned ahead for one more item to carry with her: the permanent name for her new ranch.

Ellie pursued a meeting with the daughters of Oscar Sodergreen, who had built, on the property she was leaving, the big house and majestic barn. The sisters' names were Cora, Sonny, and Susan. Ellie learned that one sister had died and another had moved to New Mexico. The remaining sister, Mrs. Chamberlain (probably Susan), remained in Laramie, where she had attended the University of Wyoming when it was housed in one building, Old Main. Ellie had found, under the stairs in the big house, old math books that had belonged to the sisters, and her ostensible purpose for the meeting was to return them before she left the big house. However, Ellie harbored a second purpose for the meeting. She wanted to receive from Mrs. Chamberlain permission to use the name "Sodergreen Horsemanship School" for the school that she intended to continue just off Harriman Road. Mrs. Chamberlain, who believed that she and her sisters had given more care and responsible attention to the ranch than the men-folk had, saw it as her right to give her permission to this young business woman.

Bill built their new ranch's first sign from stout wood. Photographs found at the ranch suggest that the first sign adhered to, at least in part, the following description. It measured about six feet in height by about four feet in length. On a background of white wood, Ellie created the design. At the top of the sign, an arch of calligraphic letters spelled out "Sodergreen." At the bottom center was the single word "Prince," also in calligraphy. On either side of this single word were identical, rearing black Arabian horses. Looming large in the center of the sign was a cameo framing of the profiled head of a gray horse against a blue background, an homage to Khizan. Etched in black strokes within the cameo frame were the words "International Arabian Horse Association." To secure the sign against the oft-roaring winds, Bill weighted the sign with metal piping and braced the bottom of it on large moss rocks from the ranch. The sign was placed just inside the ranch's main gate, off Harriman Road. The place was beginning to look like home.

Ellie and Bill came to their new home with little money for the repairs and projects that were necessary. They had no income from property sales to put toward their mortgage. Bill had built his house on his parents' Vermont property, and Ellie had only rented at the old Sodergreen. They did not qualify for a Farm Home Administration loan for the house and buildings in those first years of ownership. Ellie had income from her lessons, and Bill had income from his logging work. In other words, they were not well off financially. To put down money for the purchase of the ranch, Ellie sold the crystal and place settings she had bought in Germany when she lived there with her first husband, Rob. She explained that such luxury items were easy to purchase after the war. She bought crystal goblets, glasses, and a setting for twelve of various items—altogether, about 100 pieces. There were plates, saucers, and teacups in cobalt blue with gold trim. "I didn't buy them because I thought I would use such finery. I bought them because I was thinking ahead, as an investment. I was wise to do so."

When money was desperately needed for one of the early mortgage payments, as hard as it was for Ellie, she took two horses to sell in Aberdeen, South Dakota. "I had Minx and Barry with me for safety and companionship, and also for comfort. Oh, that was a hard trip, so hard for me to take the horses to a sale, but selling the three-year-old gelding and a yearling was the only way we could make our payment." Ellie, Bill, and Carl also hired on to drive the bus routes that served the nearby rural Willadsen School. Sadly, according to the Princes' current FHA agent, there could be no loan for the indoor riding arena that Ellie knew she would need if she were to expand her classes.

Two tiny miracles occurred in those first difficult years. First, the FHA agent who was adamant that Bill and Ellie did not qualify for a loan relocated to Washington, D.C. The kind-hearted agent who took his place worked within the requirements to create an exception so that a loan for the arena could go through. Second, Bill acquired a herd of Polled Herefords.

In that first year of ownership of the ranch, Bill and Ellie took on critical renovations despite a miniscule budget. Specifically, they had to complete two building projects in order for the school to open the next summer. The first was the cabin that would house the first group of Sodergreen Horsemanship School students. Bill came from a family of woodworkers, and soon his father, his uncle Albert, and Albert's wife arrived from Vermont to build a structure south of the house that would evermore be known as the bunkhouse. In addition to Ellie's bus route money, ingenious carpentry methods stretched the store of available and affordable lumber. Sections of logs were wedge-cut lengthwise and, with the bark side out, attached to 4 x 8 sheets of plywood. The final product for the outside of the bunkhouse looked like an attractive wall of logs. The framing and the roof were made sturdy, and the joints snug.

Leslie Turner, who in time bunked in the cabin as both a student and one of Ellie's instructors, recalled that the bunkhouse was "one big room, with a door at the front and a bathroom with tub, toilet, and sink toward the back. Linoleum covered the floor, and sheetrock covered the eight-foot ceiling and the inside walls, which featured windows all around. The bunk beds weren't that great, just a spring form on a frame with a mattress on top, but nobody ever complained. The two overhead lights had pull strings, with fly tape around them, which one of the girls got caught in her hair one night."

The second building project resulted from a structural curiosity. The house had two stories, but there was no flooring in the two upstairs rooms. Likewise, there had obviously never been stair access to the second floor. Ellie had to get up there somehow. She needed to store all that she had accumulated for the school, including her books and the bunk beds that she had gladly taken when the University had announced that they were going to dispose of them. The only immediate solution was a tall ladder at the large second story west window, through which everything miraculously fit.

Bill and his father presumed that much of the upstairs flooring had been removed from the two rooms to build a sheep pen near the west barn. It had been nice tongue-and-groove flooring, but Bill and his father found an inexpensive replacement in plain composite wood, which, according to Ellie, worked just fine. The upstairs walls benefitted from sheetrock. Carl worked alongside his relatives and remembered that they were all "good and clever carpenters."

While these projects were being completed, Ellie stayed at their former home to manage the ranch and teach one last summer school session. When she could, she drove over with the camper trailer in tow. She pitied "the poor house. The windows were broken, there was still food on the table in the kitchen, and birds were flying in and out. We did not want to have any meals in the house at that stage of repairs. So we sat down by the trees, just south of the house where we would eventually put a big picnic table. Right there was a huge cottonwood, with limbs that branched far out and swooped down. Its leaves gave us shimmering shade in the constant sun. It was nice."

Ellie and Bill knew that if they were going to hold on to all that they had acquired, as dilapidated and uninviting as the property presently was, they were going to need successful hay harvests. It had been obvious for a long time that no one had been interested in haying any part of the ranch. In what would become the east and west hay fields, Canadian thistle abounded, and the sheep had brought in all manner of undesired seeds and spread them in the fields via their manure. Horses could eat the tops of thistles for some nutrition, but Ellie and Bill did not want thistle in their hay at all. It wouldn't provide enough nutrition, and it was awful to work with, requiring heavy gloves. Nor did they want the toxic lupine and locoweed, or the invasive cheatgrass. The unwanted plants had to be eliminated.

Ellie was impressed and thankful that Bill knew and loved what he was doing. He worked with what he had, constantly tilling and weeding the fields. On his trail bike, he patrolled the fields constantly, searching for weedy intruders. It took time, but eventually the hayfields were, in Ellie's words, "lovely and healthy."

According to Ellie, who now owned a small trail bike, "my first farm vehicle," Bill needed to constantly check on the horses and the cattle once they were at the ranch and in their grazing areas. "He always took syringes with him. If an animal was down from getting into toxic weeds, especially larkspur, the antidote in the syringe worked like magic. We didn't have to go through government or veterinarian regulations to get what we called the poison to cure the poison. Besides, we were doing everything on a shoestring, so we couldn't afford a vet. In fact, there weren't many vets around. So we did it all ourselves. That's what we always seemed to do."

Haying and Polled Herefords kept Bill busy, as did the never-ending list of repairs and building projects. Huge cottonwoods grew on the ranch, especially along Goose Creek, which flowed from west to east through the property, south of the house and other buildings. Horses, Bill discovered, do not chew on cottonwood; they prefer pine. So, with his chainsaw, Bill trimmed the cottonwoods that were sturdy and felled those that weren't. After sawing the logs into boards, he built solid and safe stalls for the west and east barns and made fittings for the doors in the west barn. Ellie was delighted with the improvement. "My stalls looked nice, and nobody chewed them." Khizan, the stallion, and

El Khilet, the gelding, were moved into the comfortable east barn. Fasaab was contentedly situated in the west barn. It was beginning to feel like home.

Using the FHA loan, Bill and a friend and the friend's son began the work on the indoor arena. "I wanted it wider," Ellie said, "about twenty-five feet, but the building had to conform to FHA regulations, and there was always that shoestring budget, so I made do, even though I knew it would be hard for a large horse with a long stride to canter in there." Ellie maintained that "it was the word 'indoor' that got us the payments, for which we were very grateful. Despite income from the school, though, I still had to continue breeding horses and dogs, Bill had to sell cows, and we had to keep the bus route to keep our ranch going."

Little treasures started to emerge, despite financial woes, Ellie and Bill's having to sleep in the house's old basement, and the constant wind blowing through every joint in the house. The cottonwood-shaded picnic table became a gathering place for family and friends. It was shielded from the wind and warmed by the sun, which was only occasionally blocked by the lovely billows of fast-moving cumulus clouds. The land seemed as endless as the big sky.

Lynn, Ellie's stepdaughter, settled into the bedroom in the northwest corner of the main floor. Stepsons Carl and George slept at the east side of the house, their room separated from their sister's by a long living and dining room. Ellie discovered just how messy boys can be and, never one to scold, simply informed the boys that they were to keep their door shut at all times.

To the north on the property, several indigenous tribes' tipi rings were discovered, and on the west side of the house, a previous owner's bright yellow tea roses, foreign to the area, bloomed in late spring. Carl learned that "the fishing was good in Goose Creek, and in the valley down below, there were beaver and muskrats to trap." That winter, Lynn discovered the fun of skating on the creek.

Noting that "we had our fingers in so many bowls of stuff," Ellie was grateful for her partnership with Bill. "He was so good at taking care of the land. We were suddenly our own bosses."

Ellie was aware that "Bill and I still had to work out some things. I had my dogs, and Bill had acquired chickens from the university. I wasn't crazy about having birds around because they made a big mess. We built an enclosure about halfway up the road to the west barn, one side for the hens and one side for my seven six-month-old pups. But they were very large pups, and they liked to dig. The night before our first Christmas, the pups dug under and got to the chickens. My name was mud. I was in the doghouse. But luckily the dogs weren't."

The move to the new property had been gradual and only fully took place when Ellie and Bill felt assured that all their animals would be comfortable and secure. The brief eastward journey included Minx and her large litter, as well as Derry, Scamper, Devil, and possibly a few cats of Bill's. Bill's big logging truck proved the best means to safely secure and transport Khizan,

Ranger, Prince, Katie, Fasaab, El Khilet, No Name, Grey Girl, Daisy, Tammy, Dixie, Goldie, Red, and Mouse. Bill, Ellie, Carl, Lynn, and George hauled various necessary belongings.

Amidst the delight of owning their own place, the Prince family quickly discovered that one feature, the Wyoming wind, would always be with them. It seemed to enjoy wreaking havoc on the first, and certainly not the last Sodergreen Ranch sign. One summer day, Bill took on the task of propping up a leaning sign. While he worked just inside the main gate to the property, Ellie busied herself exercising El Khilet. Nearing the end of the session, she rode the gelding to the spot where Bill was working, just to say hello. "I had been riding and riding and was tired. I wasn't on the ball. Bill was behind the sign, lifting heavy rocks into place to build up the rock wall that he hoped would cradle the sign in the strong winds that could blow from any direction. As El Khilet and I drew nearer, Bill stood straight up with a big rock. El Khilet had not seen Bill prior, so I guess he thought Bill was a monster. El Khilet was well-trained, but this time he reared, bucked me off, and raced away from the monster to the safety of the east barn. I was angry and fumed that this was not going to happen again." But that was as far as the anger went. It was only a quick flash. Anger never traveled to Ellie's animals. She thought it useless and incorrect. Instead, a lesson would take place. "Bill drove me up to the barn and, in spite of a bit of impatience on Bill's part, I had him, in front of El Khilet, stand up and down and up and down while holding big rocks. Then I ran Khilet up and down one of the steep hills nearby. But as needs to happen with horses, I, the rider, also learned a lesson: Don't go to sleep on a horse!"

When she was asked if she ever thought of giving up on the ranch in those early years, Ellie boomed, "Never!" It was just a matter of having more time there, figuring out how to do things, and doing them. "We knew the place was a terrible mess, but we took time to assess the blessings and value of the entire ranch. Goose Creek flowed through the property, from west to east, all the way to Harriman Road. We would have ninety acres of hay land for the horses and the cattle. We saw that we could divide the land into pastures and then rotate the pastures so that the horses didn't eat down to the roots or even pull out the roots. Some pasture near one of the barns would be available in winter, where the animals could find shelter from blizzards and cold wind. The north pasture would also be open to the horses in fall and winter. The south pasture, one great big field, had bigger acreage for summers."

Also, there was the benefit of a well on the property, and numerous springs, including a warm spring. The springs and pastures would be enough to accommodate at least thirty-five horses, and the horses could get water and still be kept from each other, during illness or breeding.

The final and most majestic of blessings was penned by Ellie for the first brochure that advertised the Sodergreen Horsemanship School at the new location. Pole Mountain in the Medicine Bow National Forest was a huge "recreational area providing hunting, fishing, camping, picnicking, hiking, riding, and Native American Study." Ellie extolled the scenic beauty of the nearby Happy Jack Hills and described the ranch's surrounding vista as mirroring nearby Vedauwoo, believed in Native American culture to be an ancient playground of the gods, "with its colorful, fantastic, wind-formed rock formations."

Near the ranch itself was land that the Prince family could not get enough of. Nestled between Saddleback and Twin Mountains, the terrain boasted Picnic Rock and the intricate formations of Vedauwoo-like creations in the distance. Along the creek and in swells stood massive, wide-branched cottonwoods. Ellie loved the trees, "and I loved to see the sky. At the ranch you could almost always see the sky. It was a beautiful landscape with a big, blue canopy over it. A gift from God."

As if all that wasn't asset enough, there was the history and lure of Remount Ranch, the property just to the northwest, against Saddleback Mountain—home from 1941 to 1946 to Mary O'Hara, author and ranch woman, and her second husband, Helge Sture-Vasa. There they bred horses and held a summer camp for prep school boys, a business venture they surmised as their best vocational option after the Depression.[46] The ranch, originally named Lone Tree Ranch, had been homesteaded in 1886 by Thomas Gunston, who was a social acquaintance of Tom Horn, "bounty hunter and range detective turned outlaw." According to some sources, the ranch had been Horn's hideout when he was being pursued by "Laramie County Sheriff Frank Roach and Federal agents seeking his arrest for killing a young boy named Willie Nichol."[47]

Stories circulate that O'Hara was inspired in 1941, by a nearby band of wild horses, to write a book called *My Friend Flicka*. *Thunderhead* followed in 1943, and *Green Grass of Wyoming* in 1946. From Sodergreen Ranch, Ellie and her students rode each summer to Remount Ranch to view, on display, O'Hara's long-hand draft of *My Friend Flicka*. A few of her students ventured to see the barn—just a shed, really—that had supposedly been used for the horse that the character Flicka was based on. What horse-crazy reader would not thrill at the similarity of Eleanor Prince's philosophy to the words spoken by O'Hara's fictional Remount Ranch owner, Rob McLaughlin, his last name drawn by O'Hara from that of an actual ranch family on Harriman Road?

> No bronco buster is going to break my horses. … It ruins a horse! … He loses something and never gets it back. … He's not a whole horse anymore. I hate the method, waiting until a horse is full grown, all his habits formed, and then a battle to the death, and the horse is marked with fear and distrust, his disposition damaged—he'll never have confidence in a man again.[48]

Work on Sodergreen ranch was never really work if Ellie was with her horses, but the days were often incredibly long and significantly busy, with challenge and critical creativity the norm. When evening's darkness settled over the ranch, Ellie and Bill welcomed time to relax. The two didn't watch too much TV. If they did, the program was usually something realistic, but for one exception. They loved the Western *Bonanza*. And, of course, they loved to read. Bill preferred nonfiction, and Ellie did as well, but she also favored adventure stories, mysteries, and tales of dogs and horses.

Although the house was drafty, Ellie remembered that it was cozy. There was the woodstove, and there was the big iron stove that had sat outside the abandoned schoolhouse at the top of the hill just south of Sodergreen until Ellie and Bill decided it had better use. With some dismantling and some innovative rolling, they got the massive stove into their living room and situated it by Bill's chair. At first, Ellie and Bill burned wood in the stove, but they switched to propane when creosote built up in it. "Before we took it," Ellie said, "it fell victim to drive-by shooters. It had a bullet hole in it, but that didn't bother us.

"Bill and I relaxed together," Ellie said, "and we worked together. I had my horse business, and he did all the haying, the mechanical work, and all the repairs. He cleaned out the barns. He had his cattle, and I had my horses. He had his cats, and I had my dogs. We complemented each other. That was a facet of our attraction to each other. We kind of thought the same, and we filled each other out. Even though he never thought of Wyoming as home, he had his beloved hay meadows and took such good care of them. But, oh, did he hate the wind."

Cattle, Cats, and Confrontations

Chapter 14

Wind gusts in southeast Wyoming, according to old-timers and modern meteorologists, have hit 100 mph. They also maintain, unofficially, that southeast Wyoming, with average wind gusts of 60 mph, is the windiest region of the windiest state in the nation. Bill Prince often told the story of the Wyoming rancher who drove a heavy metal spike into the ground and secured a length of heavy chain to the spike, announcing that the contraption was to be his wind vane. When the wind came up, the rancher watched the links snap off and blow away. Bill also remembered the time an awning salesman called the ranch. Bill never got any further in the story. He was laughing too hard.

The wind made ranching hard and the rancher irritable. It wasn't enough that Bill had to constantly deal with old machinery breaking down and the incessant toil of chopping out frozen water holes for the livestock. The wind made everything just that much more difficult. Ranch work takes place out-of-doors, for the most part, and out-of-doors is where Bill and the wind were in constant battle. A still day is an aberration in Wyoming. There has been more than one account of a resident of southeast Wyoming stepping outside, bracing for the ever-present wind, and falling face forward in its absence.

The wind was not the only overwhelming element of nature for the owners of Sodergreen Ranch. In the summer, Goose Creek provided constant, clear water for the horses and fishing for those who enjoyed fresh-fried trout, but after the frequent late-afternoon, late-summer thunderstorms, the creek turned into a torrent. By late summer, the first hay harvest usually had been mowed, raked, baled, and put up, but the flash flooding wreaked havoc on any hay still standing. The creek took loops, causing the swollen waterway to crash across the land and take downstream everything in its wider path. Hay and debris from the prairie and trash from upstream ranches got hung up on the wire fences. Ellie and Bill had to unwind and yank the debris from the wires while it was wet and pliable. If left to dry, the trash, mingling and knotting underneath the wire, might have broken the fence. The heavy, soggy hay could have broken the fence wires, too.

Cleaning up was a dirty job, but the more frighteningly urgent work involved bringing animals across the creek to safety before the flood advanced. "Sometimes," Ellie said, "we had to rescue the cats. As quickly as possible, we had to cross a bridge we'd fashioned with metal from a truck and railroad ties tied to each side. During the worst part of the flood, the water was higher than the makeshift bridge. Our neighbor Lisa once found one of the cats across the bridge after the bridge was submerged. Ingenuity kicked in, as it must for ranchers, and Lisa shoved the cat into a burlap sack and threw the sack across." Ellie added, "That was not a thing that any cat would like."

In constant battle with wind, water, and winter, Bill worried about the soundness of their newly purchased house's construction and foundation. He worried as well about the utilities. A Laramie County assessment of the property recorded that the house was built in 1950, but it had clearly experienced more than what might be a decade of neglect. Located at 7400 feet in elevation, the dwelling had been debilitated by wind and by freezing and thawing from the rough winters. Ironically, a good cement foundation existed on the property, but that concrete slab, the remnant of a full dairy operation that had existed prior to the 1950s, sat far to the north and east of the house.

It was the possibility of fire that upset Bill the most. When he was about six or seven, a fire had engulfed his parents' home in Windsor, Vermont. The memory was horrible and indelible for the young boy. He had raced from the blaze, with no time to put on his boots, to seek help from the neighbors. His effort was useless. As was the case on many New England farms, all the buildings were attached. All of them burned, as did all the livestock. Haunted by the death of the animals he had loved, Bill carried his fear of fire to the house off Harriman Road, and speculated that the old house, which was poorly built to begin with, might have unsound electrical wiring. He was, according to Ellie, fanatical that anything could cause a fire. An early task, for the safety of the horses, was to re-wire both the east and the west barns.

Whenever Bill and Ellie left the house together, which for ranchers was infrequent, all appliances had to be unplugged. Whenever they left a room, the lights and appliances had to be turned off. They watched with cautious eyes fires built in the living room's open fireplace, which Bill re-rocked with native moss rock. As soon as financially feasible, the appliances in the house were changed to gas.

It is appropriate to say that from the day they moved to the ranch, they were behind on their projects, but not out of laziness, neglect, or irresponsibility. Ranching in the best of conditions is more than a full-time job, evenings and weekends included. Bill's daughter Lynn, who worried at times that she might blow away in the wind, remembered that her dad was a hard worker, despite Wyoming's weather. "With the herd of Polled Herefords and the haying and the constant repairs to all the old equipment since they couldn't afford the new, Dad was always busy. If we did things as a family, I really don't remember those times because Dad and Ellie were always working. I learned quickly that on a ranch, there's little time for the fun stuff." She stressed, though, that "the ranch was a beautiful place. Dad and Ellie made it that way, and we didn't need much beyond Sodergreen."

The new Sodergreen Ranch, consisting of 972 acres, was located between the city of Laramie and the state capital, Cheyenne. Along Harriman Road, however, a bit of the Old West remained. The Princes soon discovered that civilized neighbors could turn cross when it came to newcomers and property lines.

The first year that Ellie and Bill were on the ranch, they had no cattle. To be neighborly, they shared a strip of their south pasture with a man who lived nearby in the summers and desired a path to run his cattle. He immediately took advantage of the Princes by doubling what was supposed to have been a small number of cows. Ellie and Bill saddled up their horses and moved the cattle back onto the man's property. A heated debate continued until a friend of the Princes, a practicing lawyer in Laramie and a well-known and ethical rancher, legally solved the issue in favor of the Princes.

When Warren Livestock sold some of their property, the family that purchased the acreage built a house and had all the fence lines of their new property surveyed. Unfortunately, they insisted that an edge of their property came thirty feet onto what the Princes knew to be their own Sodergreen property. The new family placed a new fence with disregard for the Princes' claim. Again, Ellie and Bill called in the Laramie lawyer, who cited to both parties the Wyoming law that states that if a property fence line is in one place for seven-and-one-half years, it stays. He went on to cite additional rules of ownership and fencing rights that clearly and legally put Ellie and Bill on the right side of the law. The family chose, however, to leave their fence where they had placed it, so Bill, within his rights, bulldozed that whole section of fence.

Ne'er-do-well drivers in Wyoming quite frequently practiced their target shooting on signs posted along highways and dirt roads, sometimes to the point of obliteration. Harriman Road was not without its population of these drive-by shooters. Ellie was upset by the senseless, destructive pastime. "We were plagued by this practice. We couldn't understand people who got a kick out of destroying property. In fact, in the middle of my first sign for the property, I had painted an outline of Khizan's head. The drive-by shooters delighted in shooting out the eyes of the horse. These people shot signs, and they shot antelope from the road. There weren't many of us on Harriman Road, so these intruders just did what they wanted. Poachers tried to fish out of our creek and shoot at just about anything on our land. We had people steal our calves that loved to lie along our fences by pulling them right under the fence. Horses got out because our gates were opened and left open."

Ellie described Sodergreen Zero, a foal out of Grey Girl, as a big, stout, friendly, sweet horse who was great as a school horse. One winter evening, the day before Christmas, a poacher came onto the land. Grazing by the tipi rings, Sodergreen Zero heard a noise and, as is customary for horses when they hear an unfamiliar sound, swung his head up. The poacher probably didn't even know what he was shooting at, but his bullet hit Sodergreen Zero right between the eyes.

"The police came," Ellie said, "but what could they do? It was then that we started worrying about the other horses and the cattle. Bill figured out that they came through one of the wire gates at the east-to-west fence. Bill drove large nails through a big board and placed it at the gate, nails sticking up. If they tried to come onto our land again, they would get nailed. Nothing came of it, but we figured the board might deter someone, sometime, and we felt a little better."

It wasn't just the animals who faced possible attack. Ellie once had her own confrontation, with a man who quite literally thought he owned the road. Ellie had driven only a short distance on Harriman Road, heading south in mid-day with her German Shepherds to visit new friends, the Hillens. Bill was back east with Carl, taking care of Bill's father. She spied a pickup truck parked across the road, so she slowed and then stopped. A man was standing in front of the grill of the truck. He held a rifle, which he pointed in the direction of Ellie's station wagon. Opening her car door, she partly slid from her vehicle and asked what the problem was. The man curtly told her that Harriman Road was his road and there would be no driving through for her. Ellie calmly replied that she lived just a ways up the road. The man kept his rifle on her and repeated that he would not be letting her through.

As the man steadied his rifle on Ellie, Ellie reached across the seat for hers, a .25-35 rifle her father had purchased on his trip west in the 1920s. Mr. Fracker had wasted no time sending his daughter the rifle when she had shared with him the story of the mountain lion prowling near the big house at the old Sodergreen. Ellie never traveled anywhere without the rifle as companion in her saddle scabbard or on the passenger seat of her station wagon.

"This is a county road," she said firmly and without emotion, "and I will go where I want to go, and you will get out of my way." Barry, Minx, and Minx's six pups, who always traveled with Ellie, began growling with purpose. After a moment, the man, who she would later learn didn't want any newcomers in the area and may have wanted to use the Princes' ranch for nefarious purposes, lowered his rifle. Fuming inwardly and admitting that the scene "was a bit scary," Ellie drove on down to the Hillens' place. She never saw the man again. "Lucky for him," she added.

"We had a lot of problems in the beginning," Ellie said. "It was fight, fight, fight, during all those early years, just like in the Old West, but we were not going to be pushed around." They eventually met nice and supportive neighbors, including the Resenbecks, who lived to the south, and the Willadsens, just north in the hollow where the soggy ground wouldn't hold a telephone pole. There was also Mr. Hillen, who lived twelve miles down Harriman Road and who had told Ellie and Bill about the ranch for sale. He loved a good conversation, and he was always willing, to Ellie's chagrin, to volunteer his wife Molly to handle any difficult chore that a neighbor might mention. One fine day, he set out to ride his horse along the Union Pacific railroad tracks that ran south of Ellie and Bill's ranch. Somehow, his horse's shoe got caught in one of the railroad ties. When the horse fell, Mr. Hillen fell under the horse. Luck shone on Mr. Hillen that morning in that no trains came through. However, in his haste to free himself and his beloved horse, he sustained quite a bit of bruising on his lower body. As news is always enjoyed by isolated ranchers, Mr. Hillen saw it his duty a couple days later to head post haste to Sodergreen Ranch to show Bill Prince his amazing bruises. Ellie wandered over to join the conversation just as Mr. Hillen, boasting of his escapade, dropped his trousers to display his well-earned injuries. He was wearing nothing underneath. Ellie pondered the moment and thought, "My goodness, why would someone want to do that?"

Despite all their hard work, skills, and diligence, Bill found the ranch, from the early days on, to be a source of constant worry. It was during their first year there that Bill suffered his first heart attack and Ellie discovered Bill's dark side—depression. World War II and the death of Bill's first wife surely took a toll as well.

Bill's son Carl knew from his dad's stories that Bill had served on the Rockbridge 228, commissioned November 18, 1944 as an amphibious attack troop transport. Bill saw action, which included kamikaze raids at Iwo Jima and Okinawa. Bill Wilkinson, a war veteran and good friend of Bill's, was able to capture in conversation some of Bill's war experiences. "Bill Prince told me of one battle. He said the fleet shelled the island for several hours before the beach landing, the loud shelling and rockets directly overhead as Bill's boat moved from ship to shore. On one run, the corner of the boat caught on a coral reef as they were getting ready to return to the ship. All hell was breaking loose, and Bill and his shipmates, in the water, rocked the boat until they freed it from the reef. They raced up the ramp, but Bill lost his footing and fell, driving his knee into one of the metal ribs of the ramp ironically placed there to provide traction for the troops. This injury would plague him the rest of his life. As the boat with exhausted troops motored back to sea, Bill laid back against the closed ramp instead of moving to his station. He felt a slap and saw light coming through a hole in the side of the landing craft that hadn't been there seconds before. An armor piercing round had come through the ramp just inches from his head."

Bill recovered from his heart attack and resumed his devotion to his cows and cats. His herd of Polled Herefords came from Rock River, about sixty miles northwest of the ranch. Although he raised the cattle for sale, Bill cared for his herd with the individual attention Ellie bestowed on her horses. Every sale was hard on Bill. He hated to part with the animals that he too often thought of as pets. In later years, Bill acquired and developed a fondness for the bull Ferdie and hung a photograph of the huge animal in his bedroom. When Ferdie died, Bill grieved.

It is an understatement to say that Bill also loved his cats. Most of his and Ellie's circle of friends remembered Bill in his chair, hugging a cat on his lap and cajoling it with totally uncharacteristic baby talk.

Bill had both outdoor and indoor cats. Of the outside cats, Ellie said, "They were catchable but not cute like the inside cats." Bill built a large outdoor cage with a runway access and a lock, to keep the coyotes and owls from the felines. The cats were always put in before dark and let out in the morning. When Bill was sick, herding cats was Ellie's job.

The inside cats, once numbering as many as seven, all got along and were never allowed outside. Bill made sure they were always clean, as were their litter boxes and feeding areas, and they were assured the best of nutrition. Ellie was partial to one large white cat that she insisted acted like a human. One of Bill's favorites was the all-black Mister. Bill tried to train Mister to a harness for outside walks, but all Mister did was roll on the ground to remove the awful object. Walking a cat proved to be an impossibility, even for a knowledgeable rancher.

Some of the cats earned fame. One lived to be twenty-eight years old. Another, Tippy, was once sitting and yowling on the stone wall behind the school's bunk house. Ellie went down to investigate and found Tippy and a young bobcat yowling and growling at each other. Knowing that the ferocious-hearted Tippy could not win in a battle with a bobcat, Ellie managed to whisk Tippy away as Bill charged after and chased away the bobcat. Usually, once a bobcat has been around, it will continue to come around. They never saw that bobcat again, thanks, they believed, to Tippy's courage.

Cats, cattle, kids, dogs, horses, and humans—many mouths to feed and a ranch begging for upkeep. In spite of the Princes' endeavors, and with their realistic reluctance to rely solely on the tuition from Sodergreen Horsemanship School, more money was needed. Driving a school bus didn't pay a great deal, but it did pay some.

Ellie took the bus route soon after moving to the new Sodergreen. Two years later, Bill took it. As soon as his class of '68 graduated from Laramie High School, Carl drove, recalling that even his visiting grandfather chose to ride along with Ellie. Only Lynn, just entering tenth grade at a Cheyenne high school, and George, soon in junior high, were exempt from the job.

Some might have considered driving a bus a mundane job. This was not the case in Wyoming. Drama was a part of the bus driver's life, especially in winter. Once, on the bus route near Remount Ranch, Ellie saw a wolf. That was exciting but not quite as dramatic as the day of prowling ground blizzards. Ellie's bus, at the time, was a GMC carry-all with four-wheel drive. On the day of the blizzards, Ellie started out on her morning route, which, simplified, went west, then east, then south before coming to the schoolhouse where I-80 exits to Harriman Road. The roads of the route, in Ellie's estimation, "were not kept well." She planned to go into Cheyenne after dropping off the kids at Willadsen School, to pick up a School District radio to use for safety while driving on the isolated country roads.

High hills rose up on either side of Remount Road. Ground blizzards swelled through this wind tunnel, and it was inevitable that Ellie would eventually get stuck in a huge drift, on her way to pick up her first passenger. She couldn't see the house. She tried to shovel, but the snow filled in as fast as she worked. Understanding safety as she kept the motor running, Ellie prioritized clearing the exhaust pipe and keeping a partially open driver door. She soon turned off the engine and, knowing better than to ever leave her vehicle in a snowstorm, settled in to wait. She sat for about five hours. "I knew that no one was expecting me back until much later, but it wasn't a problem. I had a lot of paperwork to do. I didn't get bored."

After the long wait, the wind died down, and a vehicle came up behind the back of the school bus. Ellie sent the driver, probably a father of one of the students, on to Cheyenne, twenty-six miles to the east, for help. Eventually, a snowplow arrived. Never one to leap into a situation without making an assessment as to all that could go wrong and should go right, Ellie instructed the plow driver to pull the bus slowly backward to avoid catching the partly open driver's door on something. Instead, the snowplow driver jerked the vehicle out, jerked the door, and the wind sprung the door. The bus's muffler was also damaged. Ellie remembered that "the incident was an all-day deal, but Bill and I fixed the muffler. It was a bolt problem, the bolt not being adequate enough to survive Wyoming's rough dirt roads." Needless to say, no children on that route were picked up that day. During the storm, Bill had no inkling of the situation, and instead assumed that Ellie had easily driven into Cheyenne. Ellie, however, was alone in the middle of life-threatening weather. "Gosh, though," she remembered, "I got a lot of paperwork done."

The ranch work and financial difficulties must have felt overwhelming at times. Ellie was immersed in making the ranch livable and in preparing for her first Sodergreen Horsemanship School session at the new ranch. She was breeding and training horses. She was drafting a book on horsemanship. And now, in her spare time, she was driving a school bus. "Yes," she said, "the financial situation was stressful. To hold onto the ranch, we had to hold onto ambition. We had to try. Worrying about failing was not a good mindset. We had to learn from our mistakes and then go on to the next thing. The main thing was to give it our all." Ellie clung to the fact that she was doing what she had wanted to do all her life. “I had that blessing; a lot of people don’t. I didn’t want to seem arrogant, though, in my short- and long-term goals. On the contrary, without the assistance of a Higher Presence and helpful, caring folks, I would not have had the life I enjoyed all those years.”

Ellie believed that she learned a lot about living from her mother. “Like her, I was always good at organizing and thinking ahead. I planned beforehand and didn’t wait for something to happen, whether financial or otherwise. Like my mother, I could switch things around till they got done. I went after things and made contacts. I couldn’t have the attitude that I couldn’t do it and so I wouldn’t even try. That’s a bad attitude. I didn’t wait to see if something was going to happen or not. I had to think ahead and move ahead. I looked for the positive in every situation, including when the gophers pulled up all the young trees that the university had given us to plant as snow and wind breaks along the lane from Harriman Road to the house.”

Ellie relied on her ability to meet a challenge. “Whether I won or not, at least I learned something. Sometimes I didn’t succeed, but I learned from my failures. Yes, sometimes doubt snuck in, but I learned from my mother that I shouldn’t focus on doubt. I should focus on my experiences, on what I had inside and around me to get the job done.”

Carl saw Ellie as a supportive contrast to his dad. Whereas Bill was the worrier and somewhat the skeptic, “Ellie was always happy, busy with art, dogs, horses, and her lessons. She had energy. She thought nothing of driving back in the summers to visit her folks. She was always positive and outgoing and didn’t let things get her down. And she was always having picnics.”

The gregarious Ellie, who, according to Deb Matthew, “never met a stranger,” knew that a great resource was the people she was getting to know. She was starting to make important and neighborly contacts, but her closest contact was her family. “Bill and I were learning how we could do so much if we worked together. He was a true helpmate. When I eventually went back east in the summer of 1975, after my parents died, Bill took care of the chickens, dogs, milk cow, horses, and Herefords. He took care of the stallions, who had to be kept in, fed, and watered. He took care of all these things even though he was doing the haying and all the background work that often doesn’t show. I couldn’t have done what I did without Bill.”

Carl, too, was a blessing. Besides driving the school bus, he helped with haying and other projects. During the worst of winters, when road graders were stranded for days, Carl helped his family bring in goods on sleds and then transfer them to the tractor.

Carl also developed a fondness for horses and discovered his skill, especially with a horse named Blue. The horse passed through several hands before she wound up with Ellie, but it was Carl who owned her. He trained Blue to jump into his old pickup truck. “She was always jumping in and out of the bed of the truck. I hauled her all over in that truck.”

Carl didn't need an excuse to ride, frequently riding Khizan down to Mr. Resenbeck's place, about seven miles south, to help when Bill was haying for the elderly and infirm neighbor. The rides were part of Carl's desire to help out in any way, including riding down over several days to feed Mr. Resenbeck's cows during a blizzard. "The roads were blown shut, and it took me half a day to get back, usually in the dark, but I was on a reliable horse."

Ellie and her new family thrived on reciprocity. As far as she was concerned, "it was all vice versa for us as far as helping each other." When Bill's father died, Bill and Carl drove back to Vermont. Ellie had never told Bill before that she could milk a cow, "maybe because I didn't want to do it. It had been a long time for me, but as they left, I assured them that I could milk the Holstein. Luckily, it was a nice cow with a good temperament. However, I had to use a three-legged milking stool, and I couldn't balance on it, so I found a five-gallon bucket, turned it upside down, and did just fine. It was funny that I could balance on a horse but sure as heck could not balance on a three-prong stool. Just as with my horses, I praised and petted that cow. She was really sweet, and everything came back to me. Like riding a bicycle, milking a cow always comes back to you."

With the reciprocity of chores, there were some rare times for fun. One of Lynn Prince's fondest memories was of the commemorative Pony Express ride that Ellie and Bill participated in, which probably occurred, according to Carl, around the summer of 1968. Never would Ellie have agreed to participate in any event had there been a hint of inhumanity to animals. The Pony Express was often depicted as horses being ridden hard, but in actuality, care and safety were of the utmost concern.

In the 1800s, the idea of the Pony Express derived from public concern that mail service across the expanding United States—be it by ship circumnavigating South America or by cross-country ox-wagon trains of military supplies and merchants' goods—was ever so slow. The first ride was on April 3, 1860, and its last was in October 1861, but it served its value to western expansion and was reenacted yearly, the hard-riding riders coming into southeast Wyoming from Nebraska, arcing up through the middle of the state and then crossing the mighty Green River before heading south and west into Utah.

Although there were deaths of the reliable and fleet-footed mounts, those who designed the Pony Express were fully aware that the venture depended not only on the courage and stamina of the riders but also on the excellent condition of the horses. Employees were required to sign a pledge written by Alexander Majors, one of the architects and backers of the plan: "While I am in the employ … I agree not to use profane language, not to get drunk, not to gamble, nor to treat the animals cruelly, and not to do anything incompatible with the conduct of a gentleman."[49] Violation resulted in discharge. "In writing that pledge and requiring his employees to sign and keep it, Majors was giving expression to his lifelong, stern, Calvinistic Presbyterian sentiments. He read his Bible regularly, attended church when he could, and sought to practice Christian principles …. Majors did not want men with a tendency for 'a generous application of the whip.'" He had worked his life with oxen and respected them. He was known to have a high regard for living creatures, which included the men he worked with, who grew to trust and respect him.[50]

"Five hundred of the best horses money could buy were required to start and keep the Pony Express in operation." Kentucky thoroughbreds and western mustangs were recruited. Mares were considered reliable. Their price ranged from $100 to $200 apiece. Their job was to run twelve-and-one-half miles per hour on the road with no stops between relay stations.[51] Stable and horse equipment included "brushes, currycombs, horseshoe nails, manure forks, bridles, horse liniment, rope, and farrier's tools," all for the care and comfort of the horses. Shelter, sheds, stalls, and corrals were maintained by station keepers and stock tenders at all stations. These jobs drew stalwart and steadfast men.[52]

The trans-continental Pony Express route stretched from the headquarters in St. Joseph, Missouri to Sacramento, California. The myths of horses galloping the full stretch were just that, myths. "About 119 way stations dotted the approximately 1,966-mile-long trail …. Every 75 to 100 miles was a 'Home Station' where a rider could rest for a short time before starting back. Each rider covered the route between two stations, changing horses on the average of six to eight times going in both directions."[53] The riders had to be young, agile, sensible, and knowledgeable horsemen, not to mention fearless and strong. "A man who did not know how to treat an expensive [and smart] horse on a ten- to fifteen-mile run was not wanted."[54] The rider's only equipment was the mail sack, called a mochila, a loaded cylinder Colt revolver, sheer courage, and total trust in and respect for the goodness of his horse.

Lynn Prince was delighted with the 1968 Pony Express reenactment and with the fact that her dad "seemed to really enjoy that ride. I stood on the same road, waiting for Dad to ride his section, with fake mail in his mail sack, and then pass the mail off to the next person." The reenactment in the area was sponsored by the Arabian Horse Club, so Ellie, carrying the mochila, rode Khizan, and Bill rode El Khilet. Carl remembered that "Ellie and Dad went out of Cheyenne and rode north out on I-25 toward Casper. They each rode about ten miles. Ellie brought back a pewter mug for me. I still have it."

Horses Were to Hug and to Love

Chapter 15

It was 1968, and Leslie Turner was only eleven years old when her mother saw an article in the *Dallas Morning News* about a four-week summer program that taught horsemanship and only horsemanship. The thought of summer camp had been intriguing, but Leslie, who at age ten already owned her own horse, didn't want to have to do all the other stuff, like dancing. She just wanted horses. "What my mother read about the school was right up my alley." Her mother made a call to the director, Eleanor Prince, at Sodergreen Ranch. The call changed Leslie's life.

"My mom, dad, and I arrived at the ranch, and we unpacked. My parents met Ellie and Bill, said their goodbyes, and drove off. I waved briefly and turned away from the departing car to the ranch. That was the first of ten summers with Ellie, from '68 to '77. During the last summer, I was one of Ellie's counselors, watching out for the girls, and when the classes got large, Ellie invited me to teach. I was invited back in the winters just to stay with Ellie and Bill. I was raised in Texas, but I found a second home in Buford, Wyoming."

Leslie clearly remembered that first day, when her family turned off Harriman Road and drove three-quarters of a mile, on a rutted two-track path, to the two-story house. "It was a beautiful day," Leslie said, "all sunshiny, with a clear sky, rolling hills, green grass, and horses all around. It was not a formal setting, but it was the one thing in my life that was love at first sight. It was comfortable, peaceful. I'm not shy, but I'm usually slow to open up. With Ellie and Bill, though, it wasn't difficult."

There were only five girls at the school that summer. The bunkhouse wasn't finished yet, so the girls lived upstairs in the Princes' house, in the bigger of the two rooms—an exciting arrangement in itself, as far as Leslie was concerned. Bill's three children slept on the main floor, and Ellie and Bill didn't seem to mind sleeping in the basement. Leslie immediately felt as if "the place was home. I wouldn't have been surprised that day if Ellie told me that six years later, she and I would be traveling to horse shows and sleeping in the horse trailer together. I just sensed that all this was a permanent part of my life."

Lynn Prince provided the explanation for the all-girls school. "I remember only one boy in any of Ellie's summer classes, and he joined the classes only because his mom was the school's cook and his dad helped with chores at the new ranch. The family stayed in their camper. Accommodation for co-ed classes wasn't possible. Ellie and Bill couldn't in any way afford financially to build another cabin for boys."

Robbie Wenske was nine years old in 1968 and doesn't remember when she wasn't infatuated with horses. Her dad bought Robbie her first horse when she was seven. She was nine when the horse died, and Maxine Wallace, an Arabian horse breeder from North Platte, Nebraska, recommended that the family contact a breeder and trainer named Eleanor Prince to find the best horse for Robbie. "This was the first time I met Ellie," Robbie said. "She studied the picture of the two-year-old black bay mare we were considering and helped us during the interview with the owner. The horse wasn't trained. It hadn't even been longed. Ellie recommended we buy the mare and then told me my homework would be to work with my new horse. I really wanted to learn, and I wanted to learn from the best."

In May of 1968, Sodergreen Horsemanship School, its postal address indicating its location as Buford, Wyoming, ran from June 20 through August 8. Four weeks of summer school, the minimum for Ellie's enrollees, could have been a long stretch for a nine-year-old girl. Robbie's parents worried that she would get homesick, but Robbie had her mind set. "Ellie made me an exception because the cut-off for enrollment was age 10. That would be no problem for me. I would turn ten on July 10th, and there wasn't a chance that I would get homesick because I had Ellie and I had my new horse, Fa-BGay, sired by Fasaab."

Early in July, Ellie took her students to Estes Park for the shows and competitions. This was the first time that Fa-BGay showed, and Robbie would never forget the experience. Her parents had come down to Estes Park, and before showtime, Robbie recalled that her dad walked her and her horse on the racetrack to calm them. "I was so nervous that I had trouble longeing my horse. Ellie was right there to guide me. My parents had come down in their trailer, but I didn't want to stay with them, even though I was glad to have them there, because I was feeling so independent, and I was almost ten, and I just wanted to be with Ellie and the horses."

Robbie showed Fa-BGay in breeding and showmanship, but the pair did not place. Even so, it was an amazing experience for the nine-year-old who, as noted, had only begun to learn to longe that summer. The scared little filly handled beautifully for Robbie and showed off the training of Eleanor Prince. Clearly, mutual trust and love was at work that day.

Robbie regarded Ellie as "so special, so loving. On the morning of my tenth birthday, I got up early, as was my habit, and Ellie made me breakfast. We visited, and that's when I had hot chocolate, Ellie's favorite, for the first time. It was just me and Ellie, and then Ellie gave me a gift. It was a picture of No Name, one of her nicest horses."

Robbie's parents came later in the day to take her home to Cheyenne for a birthday celebration. Robbie couldn't wait to get back to Ellie's. "I didn't want to waste my time away from her and the horses. I wanted to be back early the next day."

Robbie learned so much from Ellie "because of the way she taught. When she corrected, she did it gently. She always handed out compliments, and those were wonderful because Ellie was a perfectionist. I loved that Ellie mixed fun into her teaching. She took us on trail rides, and we camped out. Even if it rained, we loved it because we were with Ellie and the horses. It was Ellie who taught me that horses were to hug and to love."

In 1978, Kirsten Springer's dad, an orchard grower from New Hampshire, was helping Kirsten look for a place where she might work while enrolled as a student at the University of Wyoming. His search took him to Sodergreen Ranch, and that summer, Kirsten began teaching for Ellie. What she recalled most vividly from that summer was that "Ellie trusted me with her horses. She taught me her method of training them. That was the summer that she got the stallion, Kamars Sharif, and I was the first one allowed to ride him."

When she first started working for Ellie's school, Kirsten had her own way of working with horses. "But Ellie showed me her way, and I quickly knew that it was the best. Whether in class, clinics, or shows, she knew exactly what should be done and how. Her attention to knowledge and methods, whether feeding, cleaning horses, planning the curriculum, or matching students to horses, was all for the good of the horses and riders. All this came out in her first book, *Basic Horsemanship*. She even paid attention to electricity and water during the school terms. They were precious commodities, she told us, so we were allowed showers every three days and no hair dryers."

Kirsten insisted that it was Ellie who taught her how to teach. When Ellie later began teaching adults during the summer sessions, Kirsten was invited to help. "Ellie encouraged me to develop a curriculum for the adult students who were more advanced. She also let me and my first husband build a full-size dressage ring up in the pasture. We painted cement blocks with numbers and letters. We set up rails and jumps and a cross-country course with railroad ties. That's how Ellie showed her trust in me and my abilities. She let me take over on my own."

Kirsten admired how Ellie handled all situations, including those involving fearful or timid students. "If she saw fear in a young person or in an adult, Ellie's technique was to go step by step, from the ground up. Before the student got on the horse, Ellie had the student brush the horse, talk to the horse, move all around, touch the horse, and lead the horse. Ellie then worked on having the student mount and ride bareback to feel, understand, and gain trust in the horse and in herself. The rider next worked with the reins, noticing their feel and the horse's reaction. Ellie made all her students hold the bit in their hands to understand what it was like for the horse to feel it in his mouth."

Ellie pushed many students from their comfort zones, and Kirsten was one of them. "During my first summer, just nineteen with my first driver's license, we all went to Estes Park for the shows. Ellie drove the station wagon pulling the horse trailer. She decided I would pull the RV with the pickup, something I had never done. It was a rainy day, in danger of flooding, and I had to pull that trailer up narrow and winding mountain roads. I was scared to death, but because of Ellie I did it. She knew I could do it. And besides, Sharif was ready for the show ring. We couldn't let him down."

Kirsten grew close to Ellie and learned that life for her and Bill was a series of hardships. "They were always scraping money together, for the ranch and the school. It was scary at times when I went with Ellie to get groceries. We were sometimes over the budget's edge. But she was an innovative New England scrimper. She knew how to be frugal. In fact, one time she shared with me her invention of 'vapor barriers.' She said to just put bread bags over your socks and then put on your boots. They worked, in rain or snow, with no need to buy new boots."

Despite hardships, Kirsten saw Ellie as "a kind person, to all of us and to all of her animals. She cared so much about her horses. When a horse, a dog, or a cat died, it was so difficult for her. The cats were Bill's, but when Ellie's favorite cat Smudgie died, that was really hard. She was so full of love for any animal."

For two consecutive summers, Kirsten worked as an instructor for Ellie. A few years later, she became the school's cook and, during her free time, helped to train Sharif. During one of the latter summers, she became a co-counselor with Lana Brokaw.

Lana Brokaw grew up on her family's working cattle ranch, located just outside the wisp of a town northeast of Laramie called Arlington. It had been homesteaded in the late 1800s by earlier generations of her family. From at least the age of five, Lana had loved horses. She had endured the heartbreak of the death of her first foal. Her mother, Audrey, who had an affinity for Arabian horses, was a friend of Ellie Prince's, their connection made stronger through the breeding of Audrey's brood mares to Ellie's stallions. Audrey also loaned horses to Ellie for use in her school.

In the fall of 1982, fourteen years after Leslie Turner and Robbie Wenske discovered the joy of horsemanship instruction under Ellie Prince, Lana, then a first-year student at the University of Wyoming, realized that she had better take some coursework to boost her grade point average. She signed up for two classes that would guarantee A grades: singing and horsemanship. This was the first time she would meet her mother's friend as something other than "Audrey Brokaw's daughter."

Required reading in the horsemanship class was Eleanor Prince's first book, *Basic Horsemanship*. Lana was impressed. "I saw a great deal of common-sense information. I knew horses, but it was Ellie who gave me the vocabulary to accompany what my mom did with her horses. What Mom had taught me—basic seat, contact with legs and hands, handling on the ground—settled alongside what Ellie was teaching, but Ellie gave the words and the refinement to the techniques." It was in Ellie's classes that Lana learned a unique teaching technique. "Ellie taught us exercises. It wasn't easy, riding bareback on a moving horse, reins dropped, knees forward, and then knees back. I learned from all the different exercises to trust myself and to trust that I had the ability not to fall off while my hips were hating me. I stretched in places I didn't think I had stretch. It was overall strength training, and I discovered that it's best done on a horse's back.

"Ellie also taught us that the basics were the most important thing a rider could learn. You had to learn horse care and ground-up training, including the safe way to tie a horse and proper use and placement of tack. She taught us proper seat leg aids and contact with the horse's mouth. She made sure we were aware of our balance and kept our body and hands quiet. All this, so that our horse knew what we wanted."

It was the next year that Ellie invited Lana to work for her. Lana worked three summers, from 1982 through 1984. "As a ranch kid, I already knew how to work. Those were wonderful summers—cleaning out stalls, exercising the stallions, and helping with the breeding."

What Ellie expected and appreciated in her workers, who called themselves "the helpers," was what Lana had grown up with. Hard work, done thoroughly and properly, was a necessity. The animals were living creatures that needed their caregivers' best effort. To achieve this, Ellie set daily plans, presented her expectations and goals, and outlined everything from meals to break time. Ellie's helpers knew they had to be self-disciplined. If they didn't get something done, it was to be done the next day. Lana appreciated that "we focused our attention on the horses before the people. Mucking a stall was a daily thing. Trust was of the utmost to Ellie. When Ellie gained trust in me, she let me help train Kamars Sharif, her stallion from the Egyptian line. It was so important to me that she allowed me freedom with Sharif and that she believed in me."

Lana also quickly discovered that Ellie's mentoring extended into the world of business. She realized that Ellie was able to manage all the branches of her business because she had been raised by parents who had strong work ethics and were disciplined in their style of living. They instilled in Ellie how to turn a dream into reality by focusing patiently on the steps to achieve the goal. "Ellie made sure each day had a purpose. She understood the benefit of time management and took care of herself to make each day count. She began her day at 4:30 with exercises and slept well with satisfaction from what she had accomplished in a day. She also taught us that we were not alone. Like her, our lives would include others, and those relationships would matter a great deal."

Lana saw Ellie as a good boss. "She was quick to point out when something was done well. She didn't believe in shortcuts or not getting the job done thoroughly. If she thought a job wasn't finished for the day, she'd say, 'Well, let's just start again tomorrow.'"

Lana and Ellie didn't have theological conversations, but to Lana it was apparent that "Ellie knew she had blessings from God. She was always positive. When in the midst of depression, Bill saw his cup half-empty. Ellie just kept refilling hers. Ellie lived the saying, 'Not every day is good, but there is good in every day.' Joy just poured out of Ellie with every laugh, and nobody can laugh like Ellie Prince."

In the spring of 1991, Sandy Broyles discovered that her horsemanship abilities had not gone unnoticed by her instructor at the Sodergreen Horsemanship School. Upon high school graduation, Sandy was hired by Ellie. "Ellie liked how I worked with the horses. She hired me for three summers. During the week, I lived in the cabin with the students, as their chaperone. On the weekends, I went home." Home was also just outside Arlington, a little over sixty miles west of Sodergreen Ranch. Sandy's job was to teach the beginners at the school. "The summer school had such a positive atmosphere. The kids were enjoyable, and I don't remember ever having negative situations or problems."

Ellie asked for Sandy's help in other ways as well, including feeding, exercising, and assisting with the breeding of the horses. She called on Sandy to help with the grocery list. "Ellie hired cooks, and she often took me into Cheyenne so we could fill the RV with groceries. Ellie always mapped out the whole menu and day's schedule with set times for breakfast, lunch, dinner, riding instruction, and evening down time. There was never any chaos with all the kids and horses. Ellie was incredibly organized, and this rubbed off on her helpers."

What also rubbed off on Sandy was trust. "Ellie believed in me and her other helpers, and we then believed in ourselves. When Ellie had knee surgery in 1993, she entrusted me to drive the big station wagon into town for errands and groceries. I was just nineteen, but she said, 'You're going to have to do all this on your own,' and she made me believe I could. Bill and I went to the hospital

Bill begins the rock work on the house, supervised by his beloved cats.

Sodergreen

HORSEMANSHIP SCHOOL

BUFORD, WYOMING 82052

1-307-632-7954

Home of Quality Arabians

Presenting:

KAMARS SHARIF

112144

(Fabah x Roufina)

15.1 hands, black

Straight Egyptian Babson Stallion

Intensive Student Training Session

June

Black stallion Kamars Sharif on a 1970s school brochure. His photo was taken by professional photographer Ray Randall.

Wyoming ranch icons—buck fence and cottonwoods. The big picnic table sat under the trees' branches.

Eleanor Prince and Gay Collier,
partners in publishing.

Photo dated August 18, 1974, courtesy of the *Laramie Daily Boomerang*.

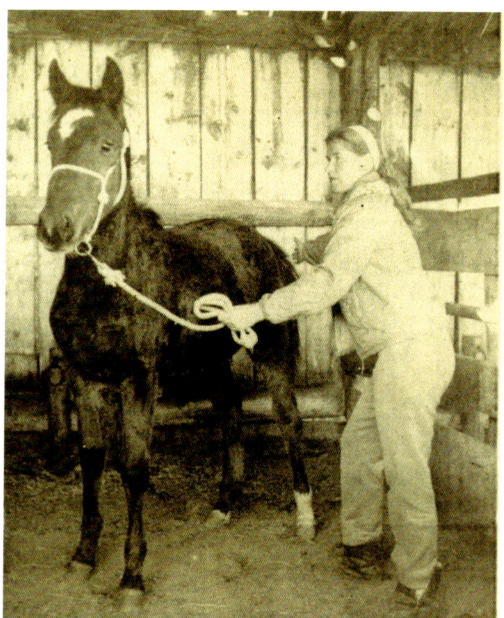

Ellie working with a young colt.

Photo dated Sunday Magazine, June 8, 1980, courtesy of the *Wyoming Tribune Eagle*.

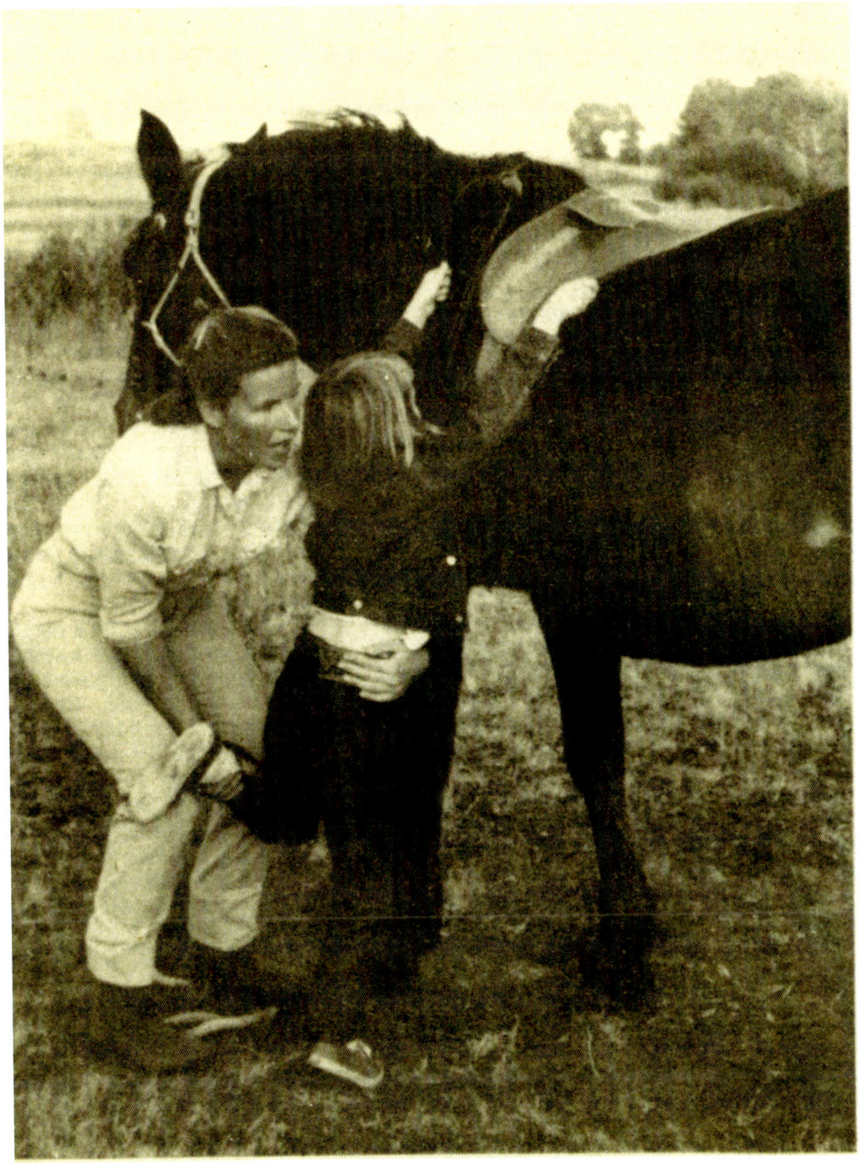

Ellie working with a youngster.

Photo dated Sunday Magazine, June 8, 1980, courtesy of the *Wyoming Tribune Eagle*.

Dr. Donna Marburger, retired as coordinator of the University of Wyoming Physical Education Undergraduate Program.

Photo courtesy of Donna Marburger.

Sharif, relaxed on his prairie.

Dorothy Feldman, partner to Ellie in the horse breeding business, with Mon Amie.

Kamar Sharif 112144
(Fabah x Roufina)
Stud Fee 1200/800

Khizan 7592
(Khebir x Fizana)
Reserve Champion-Estes Park 1960
Canadian Nationals TT Stallion 1961

Ellie Prince on Fasaab
(*Fadl X *Bint Bint Sabbah)

Sodergreen

Eleanor Prince • 307/632-7954 • Buford Wyoming
Dorothy Feldman • 307/632-4253 • Cheyenne, Wyoming

• 95 •

A page from the *1995-1996 Breeding Farms & Stallions Classic Black Arabian Directory.* Publisher unknown.

Christmas card design by Ellie.

Wood painting by Ellie. Carl cut and sanded cottonwood discs.

The holding pen, where the
horses patiently await their riders.

Photo taken by and courtesy
of Lisa MacGuire.

Cavalletti work, always
greeted with enthusiasm
in Saturday School.

Saturday School getting started
under the morning's big blue sky.

Ellie and Bill in front of
the moss-rocked house at
Sodergreen Ranch.

A cozy home in the midst of
the Wyoming wilderness.

in town nearly every day and I got my assignments, and then Bill bought us hamburgers at JB's before we headed back to the ranch."

Over the years, the helpers stayed in touch and checked in with Ellie. Most kept up their riding and, in some cases, their teaching. All maintained that they couldn't live without Ellie's love and believed that her mentoring helped them gain self-respect and self-confidence. They attributed to her their love, knowledge, and skill involving all things equine. A few of them knew that she was training them to carry on her teaching methods, especially in horsemanship. Kirsten Springer insisted that "the way Ellie taught horsemanship was the only way."

Sandy Broyles saw Ellie's teaching methods as a way toward "love, kindness, caring, and fun, for the horses and the students. Ellie was always patient and calm and encouraging. If a student had a problem, Ellie could solve it. She mixed fun days and contests, like riding while holding an egg on a spoon, with serious lectures and quizzes involving all aspects of responsible horse care." Sandy observed how Ellie easily modified her methods to teach young girls and, eventually, adults. "There was never chaos," said Sandy, "just enjoyment. And Ellie always wore that big smile. It lit up her whole face."

One of the highlights of the school featured big picnics at Picnic Rock. Invitations were extended to students, friends, and helpers. If pressed, Ellie might have gone so far as to say that picnics in the open air and under the blue sky of Wyoming were part of the basics of good horsemanship. Ellie and Bill provided the main dishes, but potluck was welcomed as well. A campfire was readied, and baked beans sizzled in their cans. If anyone were asked, they would probably say yes, they were part of this family. How could anyone not be, with the hospitality extended by the Princes? Loyal to Ellie, her schooling, and her philosophy, several of the helpers stayed on for the weeks after classes ended to help Bill get in the hay. Bill's tractor had a sweep, which gathered the loose hay into mounds. The hay was then stored in both barns for protection from snow and rain. The little prairie cottontails that Ellie called "cooney rabbits" annoyingly savored it for such protection as well.

Sandy appreciated that Bill patiently walked her through the steps of harvesting the hay and then trusted her to work with the machinery. "Ellie had instilled responsibility in me, and Bill knew it. Bill was really quiet, and I was a bit intimidated by him, but I respected his knowledge and his instructions. I worked hard, and he respected that I wanted to do everything right. Whether during school or during haying, Ellie fed us so well that at supper, we weren't too hungry. But sometimes Bill and I had supper in the kitchen at the house. I was honored that he taught me his favorite recipe: kidney beans in a bowl with salt and milk, heated up. I still like it. He also made and bottled his own root beer to share during haying. It was amazing. And after haying, he and I fished for trout in the little pools that branched off from Goose Creek."

It was clear to Sandy that Ellie and Bill didn't have much money, "but Ellie believed that even when things didn't work out the way she wanted, she had to press on. She had to be resourceful and clever. She was always saying, 'Do what you have to do with what you have on hand.'"

When Robbie Wenske was about fifteen or sixteen, Ellie asked her, even though she was not officially signed up for the school, to help with some of the lessons. "There were about fifteen students, and Ellie asked me to take the class through their warmups, exercises, and stretching. I only worked with each class for about fifteen or twenty minutes, but that was all that was needed. Ellie's style of teaching was now in me, and I was inspired that summer to choose teaching as my career. Years later, I did just that."

In Leslie Turner's second summer at Sodergreen Horsemanship School, the bunk house housed as many as twenty-five girls. The subsequent summer boasted twenty-eight. The girls, many of whom stayed for the full eight weeks, came with small trunks that included the requisite "layers" of clothing for chilly nights and brisk-breezy summer days. Blankets or sleeping bags were required as well. In the evenings, after lectures, demonstrations, and lessons, the girls congregated with Ellie and Bill and the helpers in the living and dining room of the Princes' house. Food was set out on the table, and the girls settled their hungry selves on the sofa, chairs, floor, and even the new stairs that made the second story accessible. Bill's chair by the woodstove-turned-propane stove was tacitly off limits to all but his beloved felines.

The New Englander Bill eschewed what he saw as silliness in the behavior of some of the ranch workers, so Leslie was pleased that he "tolerated" her. He didn't engage in many conversations, preferring instead to study people, but she loved the stories that he told. When classes ended for Leslie's second summer, she stayed on to help Bill with haying and with gathering the moss rock that Bill planned to use to "rock up" the exterior of the Princes' two-story house. She helped move Bill's cattle and shared his interest in shooting black powder rifles. In the evenings, they fished.

"During the school, there was little free time," Leslie recalled, "although we didn't care because our busy time was with Ellie and the horses. That constant busyness was what made the school unique. It was Ellie's plan to totally immerse her students in horsemanship."

A typical school day began with early rising and breakfast at the house. Afterwards, the students were required to clean up the cabin, which Ellie then inspected for tidiness. Lectures, tests, and assigned reports followed. After that, the girls donned their riding boots and headed to the arena for the routine: English riding in the morning, lunch, rest, and Western riding in the afternoon. Rest, dinner, and study time came after lessons with the horses. During study time, Ellie invited the girls to use the books in her library in one of the upstairs rooms to prepare for oral reports.

Meals were simple and frugal but, under Ellie's watchful eye, hearty and healthy. At some of the summer sessions, the cooks were helpers who just couldn't stay away, including Kirsten Springer and Margaret Smith. Breakfast consisted of cereals and juices, and sandwiches were the mainstay of lunches. Dinners were easy casseroles, comfort foods, and desserts. On occasion, Ellie made her favorite meals, which were popular with the girls: clam chowder, corn chowder, and ranch pudding. On Sundays, after donuts and other such sweets, Ellie took the girls into Cheyenne, where they did their laundry, attended church, or indulged in junk food.

In the first two weeks of the school, Ellie assigned two girls each to the care of a foal or an older horse, which they then used to practice halter showmanship and prepare for showing "at halter" and "under saddle" at the Estes Park All Arabian Horse Show, during the July 4th weekend. As Ellie led her students from shows to demonstrations to sales to facilities where the horses were cared for, both helpers and students, some of whom had never before been around horses, were fascinated with Ellie's narratives. She taught them what was going on, what to look for, what to do or what not to do, and gave background on the popular breeds of horses. The helpers all agreed that Ellie seemed to know everything. She was always teaching, and she gave her students every opportunity to learn.

The uniqueness of Sodergreen Horsemanship School was easily traced to its scope of activities and styles. The school dealt with every angle and range of horses and horsemanship, with no other main activities. Ellie covered every topic imaginable: horse farms, breeding situations, livestock auctions, different lines of horses, stable care, ethics in the show ring and in breeding, and even the Colorado State University vet lab. The girls attended Cheyenne Frontier Days, rodeos in Laramie, and the Pony Express reenactment.

Ellie focused her lessons on dressage, show training, and jumping. She taught gaming and gymkhana races, such as keyhole racing, barrel racing, and pole bending. When the school started, Ellie helped her students avoid a dependence on saddles for balance and seat by having them first ride bareback. Only after they had grown used to their horses were the girls given saddle pads that Ellie had purchased from England. Placed over saddle blankets, the pads were equipped with detachable safety stirrups. Ellie was adamant that bareback and the pads were the only way her riders could get to know the movements of their horses. According to Ellie, feeling the horse was everything.

Sodergreen Horsemanship School displayed organization and accountability, yet the atmosphere was relaxed and never formal. Safety was paramount for Ellie, and it influenced her approaches and practices to riding and horse care. Leslie knew that Ellie, as an instructor, "was always on the alert and understandably so. She was dealing with horses and people and had to be ready to react to any danger. She made sure that she got the critical notion of safety across to everyone under her care."

Ellie's attention to the connection of horse and rider was unique in the pedagogy of horsemanship. Early on, Leslie Turner was intrigued that Ellie believed, in most situations involving a choice, that the animals were correct, not the riders. It was up to the rider to figure out what she was doing wrong and not blame the horse. "Ellie explained that animals can't think things through like humans do. A horse's brain makes the animal only react in self-preservation. They may not notice a rider, since the rider is much smaller than the horse. The handler is often trying to do too much and just confuses the horse." Always cognizant of the individuality and differences in horses and riders, Ellie's major goal was communication between the two.

Ellie's philosophy and pedagogy were working. Enrollment grew, with one summer session serving thirty-five girls. Ellie's loyal helpers instructed or cooked meals in Ellie's old RV, parked just outside the house's front door. The helpers acknowledged that "everybody helped with everything." The students came from every state in the union but Arkansas. They came from South America, Canada, and Mexico. Eventually, Ellie opened the school gates to families, who often came in campers for the newly established ten-day sessions. New chapters were unfolding in Ellie Prince's life, including those that were captured in a book that would contribute significantly to the scholarship of basic horsemanship.

New Chapters

★

Chapter 16

What Eleanor Prince's helpers so aptly described as a type of pedagogy involving communication and understanding between horse and rider was a methodology unique to its time and location. That uniqueness had to be captured for a wider audience. Gay Collier had long ago realized the value of the published word. After Ellie announced that she was writing a series of five articles on basic horsemanship for *Arabian Horse News*, Gay knew it was time to present Ellie's methodology and her wisdom in more than articles. It was time for Ellie to write a book.

Once Gay shared her idea with Ellie, the horsemanship instructor envisioned a textbook as an invaluable primary source for those who placed anywhere on the "horse lover" spectrum. It would provide material for Ellie's students who would go on to teach, as Kirsten Springer had said, in "Ellie's own way." It would unfold and preserve Ellie's psychology and philosophy: If immersion was the scaffolding of her instruction, and the impetus was love, understanding, and care, then the beautiful art of dressage, which Ellie taught as a part of both English and Western riding, was the spirit which would be captured in writing.

When asked the meaning of "dressage," Ellie introduced it simply as the French word for training. "It's common sense in training," she further explained. "A type of response from the horse is required for each precise movement from the rider." In her elementary classes, Ellie introduced elementary dressage. First and foremost, the rider had to see the horse as unique. The horse's individuality had to be recognized by the rider, through thorough grooming and conversation before the horse was saddled and bridled. Listening and understanding were key, as was a mixture of gentleness, firmness, respect, and trust. Ellie's horse training involved step-by-step ground work for suppleness, balance, cadence, obedience, and trust. Longeing taught and perfected correct gaits, including the halt.

Ellie trained her riders, often using metaphors and analogies, to be consistent and clear in communication and to reinforce what Ellie's horses had been taught by applying the same sensitive and subtle aids: voice cues, reining techniques, leg aids, and body weight. Cavalry movements, similar to those in advanced dressage, found their way into the lessons. Ellie shared that "when the horse and rider connect, it is a beautiful thing. It is nearly like dancing. The two anticipate directions, steady gaits, maneuvers, and moods as if they are one." For Ellie, the big advantage of dressage, whether in Western or English riding, was that it trained a horse to be responsive and sensitive. "It is so important," she believed, "to be your horse's friend and partner."

Dressage, for Ellie, was more than a semester of lessons. It was a culmination of months, perhaps years, of training. The rider spent long periods training the horse to be supple and sensitive; every muscle, including the eyes, became part of a flowing and gently controlled organism. Ground work with the horse was essential, the movements repeated patiently and with enough variety that rote was replaced by cues given as lightly as a whisper and received with an attitude of grace. Finally, a boot found the stirrup, the gentle human settled into the saddle, and horse and rider became a blend of majesty and benign power. The result was equine portraiture. With what seemed like merely a thought on the part of the rider, the enormous horse began to move about the ring, executing gaits, turns, reverses, a turn-on-the forehand, a flying change of lead, a halt—with the rider's attention to every detail, from heels down to peripheral awareness; with the horse's head held high and every muscle synchronous. With light, hardly perceptive fingering, the rider persuaded the massive animal with nary a battle, only trust and love. This was not merely horseback riding. It was elegant cooperation. It was artistry. It was *danse*.

This aesthetic of horsemanship was important in Ellie's book. She was blessed at the start to have a partner in Gay Collier. Gay was a poet and an artist. Her senses were keen. Gay also had experience and success in writing and in publishing. In her memoir, *Just Beyond Harmony*, Gay called writing a joy and revealed that she depended on the words of the 139th Psalm when she felt "daunted and unsure of my ability to cope"[55]: *If I take the wings of the morning, and dwell in the uttermost part of the sea; Even there shall thy hand lead me, and thy right hand shall hold me.*[56]

Gay wrote poetry, short stories, and essays, including her later tribute to Ellie's stallion Fasaab in "Monarch of the Mountains."[57] She still used the typewriter that had been a gift for her sixth-grade graduation. When she first met Ellie in the 1960s, Ellie had accumulated reams of mimeographed material for her various classes and expressed the desire to "find a textbook that contained all the information she wanted her students to study." When it finally occurred to Ellie that she herself was the best person to create a textbook on basic horsemanship, Gay reminded Ellie that with her background in art study from Boston's Museum of Fine Arts, she could provide her own diagrams and instructional illustrations as well. Gay signed on as photographer, researcher, and editor, typing drafts on newsprint to save money.[58] As Ellie pointed out, "we had no technology back then, but we did just fine."

The seed for the book, in addition to Ellie's handouts and lecture notes, was the five-article series published in 1964 in *Arabian Horse News*, titled "Is It—Magic?" From the beginning, Ellie made sure that the draft of the book stressed the basics. "You couldn't start anywhere but from the basics, and from there, the sequencing and steps of training had to be cohesive. Too many horse books jumped all around. The European books tended to focus on the last stages of training. That was not what I wanted."

Through the years of writing and editing, Ellie steered the book to focus on her philosophy and basics, which became the substance for the book. Long hours of drafting and revising took place in Gay's small cabin or the big house at the old Sodergreen, usually in the evenings when ranch and school chores ceased. When Ellie and her husband Bill moved to the new Sodergreen and Gay took a position at the circulation desk at the University of Wyoming's Coe Library, Ellie and Gay rendezvoused curbside at Laramie's old Safeway parking lot on Grand Avenue or met in the old Laramie public library on the corner of Grand and 4th Street. During collaboration on their second and third books on horsemanship, published in 1979 and 1986, Gay moved northeast to Sundance, Wyoming to become the head librarian at the town's public library. The two writers arranged to meet at Ft. Robinson, in northwest Nebraska, where they worked outside or in Ellie's RV and took breaks to explore the fort. Ellie reminisced that "we took walks and even stagecoach rides there. The stables for the officers' horses were in wonderful shape, fitted with glass and mahogany wood. There was even a veterinarian and a farrier at the fort. I know we'd say we had to get back to working on the book, but the fort was a wonderful and educational setting for two horsewomen writing on horsemanship." There was no fancy, permanent office for these writers. They worked anywhere, preferring where there were horses.

Gay was not surprised that seeking publication for the first book led the two women on a long and rocky road. The manuscript was considered by then-Doubleday senior editor Ellin K. Roberts, who, according to Gay, rejected it "in the nicest possible way" and recommended they submit it to William Steinkraus, editor at then-Van Nostrand and captain of the United States Equestrian Olympic Team. Steinkraus, too, rejected the manuscript, but he also provided a detailed and valuable critique, accompanied by the note to "try me again."[59] Van Nostrand eventually accepted the manuscript, but the company changed hands, and the search for publication was forced to continue. Ten years after Ellie and Gay put together a rough outline for the book they envisioned, the manuscript was subjected to a mountain of revisions and was then published, on March 5, 1974, by Doubleday.[60] Fasaab, who once had delighted being in the limelight, carrying his Bedouin-costumed rider in competition, was immortalized in portraiture with Ellie on the book's back cover. Ellie regarded the portrait, taken by the famous horse photographer Johnny Johnston, as "the best picture of the horse and myself, correct in everything, even the double bridle." Fittingly, a photograph of a grinning Gay Collier on one of Ellie's horses was also included.

In the Introduction to *Basic Horsemanship English and Western: A Complete Guide for Riders and Instructors*, by Eleanor F. Prince and Gaydell M. Collier, published by Doubleday & Company in 1974, Ellie and Gay set out immediately to inform the rider that horsemanship is a partnership. "Understanding," the Introduction read, "is the essence of harmonious horsemanship. Anyone may climb on a horse and with a little practice manage to stay there; but without understanding, harmonious horsemanship is almost impossible. Understanding is a distillation of knowledge and experience. It is the comprehension of how and why a horse behaves or reacts, and what you should do to motivate the behavior or counteract the reaction. With understanding as a basis, you will work consistently with kindness, confidence, and ability."[61]

The purpose of the book, the authors wrote, "is to establish … a basis for continuing on to a full and intelligent understanding of horses …[,] to offer the reader a solid foundation for continuing on to advanced or specialized equitation … [and] to present the whole of the American riding scene as it is today." Unique to the book is the erasure of "contempt" for any particular riding style. "We emphasize the similarity of English and Western Horsemanship, [noting that] there is something to gain from each style."[62]

In eleven chapters, with over 300 pages, the book covers just about everything, including the reminder that "good horsemanship entails understanding, patience, and love. … [Your horse] will, in effect, teach you to ride."[63] Online customer reviews as late as 2023 would still give the book five stars.

The book and the many responsibilities of running a ranch and a summer school—let alone those that accompanied her contribution in founding the Colorado Arabian Horse Club, her tenure as president of both the Wyoming Arabian Horse Club and the Laramie Kennel Club, and membership in myriad local and national equine-related associations, as well as her participation in Laramie Jubilee Days and Cheyenne Frontier Rodeo parades—could have caused Ellie Prince to say, "Enough." But she fully accepted her responsibility to the expanding community of young riders who couldn't get enough of horses, and she also understood that she had to build her profile, her community, and her reputation. What better way to do it than to reveal to a greater population a thorough demonstration of her teaching techniques? So, as her husband Bill began the arduous task of fortifying the exterior of their house with large, flat, colorful moss rock found on their property, Ellie began preparations for events that would attract the eager, the inquisitive, and even the skeptical to Sodergreen Ranch.

The Sodergreen Ranch Open House occurred in the late 1970s, in the month of April. Bill's son Carl had graduated from high school in 1968, worked for a time in the oil fields and at the nearby quarry, joined the Navy Reserve, and eventually met and married Kim, a Wyomingite from Casper, Wyoming. Lynn, after graduation in 1971, had returned to Vermont to care for her grandparents. George left junior high school and set out for work and a place to live south of Jackson, Wyoming. A number of Ellie's helpers, however, were available and ready to contribute their time and training to help Ellie and Bill make their first Open House a success.

Crowds from Cheyenne attended the Open House, and many admirers quickly earned status as new friends. Ellie recalled that there were "so many people, so many cars. They were parked almost to the gate at the end of the property. Somehow, there was enough food—crackers, cheese, drinks for everyone. I think we had nearly the population of Cheyenne." From one building to the next, from one grassy area to another, demonstrations by Ellie's helpers offered information on many and varied topics unique to Ellie's horsemanship instruction, including breeding, training, and general equine care.

Despite being scheduled on the heels of a late snowstorm, snowdrifts still abounding, the event was well advertised and well attended. Most of the attendees were used to snowdrifts in April, and most wore footwear for sloshing through spring mud in prairie ruts. Ellie's plan was two-fold: to advertise and showcase her breeding stallions, and to publicize and promote her training methods for horses and riders. Ellie's helpers assisted with demonstrations, and her new dog Mostly, purchased after Devil's death and named such because he was mostly German Shepherd, was there to greet as many guests as he could. The Polled Herefords took it all in stride, and Bill's new kitten, Panther, was safely tucked inside the house.

At one station, Lana Brokaw was responsible for showing the effects of ground work on Kaliph, a three-month-old foal. At the west barn, throughout the day, Lana explained that imprinting—taking every opportunity, every day, to touch every part of the foal's body, including teeth, tongue, ears, stomach, legs, and hooves—was critical to future ease and gentleness in caring for and working with a horse. She first demonstrated how Kaliph accepted his halter and lead rope. She then explained that horses' hooves must be cleaned out as part of the horse's health regimen and in preparation for riding. Time after time, Lana bent down and, thanks to imprinting, gently slid her inside hand down Kaliph's leg, the signal for Kaliph to calmly lift his leg as if to welcome a hoof cleaning. Toward the end of the day, Lana had only to point, and the foal would raise a hoof. Lana explained to her audience that "behaviors are set in horses' brains. They learn by rote. Ground work, constancy, and gentleness are what we do and who we are, as Ellie's instructors, helpers, and students." Surely Lana's last sentence rang out at every demonstration that day.

Horsemanship clinics, as teaching tools, were also frequent events at Sodergreen Ranch. Despite her experience and research, Ellie was humble enough to believe in the benefits of learning from other instructors. She wanted her students to be exposed to new perspectives and methods. From the 1970s until 2001, Ellie ran seasonal clinics, composed of individual instructional classes, sometimes as frequently as three or four times a year. On occasion, a summer clinic coincided with the school. Session costs were low, and Ellie rented out her horses if participants were in need. Ellie made sure that any person who wanted to attend was welcome.

Learning, according to Ellie, was necessary and never-ending, and Ellie wanted her participants to learn from incredible practitioners and teachers of dressage. She wanted them to meet innovators in the field of horsemanship. She brought in Mary Rose and Dominique Barbier, both of whom held impressive resumés in dressage teaching and training, publication, awards, and international tours. She brought in Ida Richards, an eighteen-year-old award winner from Farmington, Maine. And in the 1990s, she organized a clinic on Equine Massage and hosted Monty Roberts and his program on the Arabian Horse. Even her highly experienced former students offered clinics.

Leslie Turner, who over a ten-year period had worked with Ellie as a student, instructor, and horse trainer, was Ellie's co-coordinator and clinic presenter in 1977. In 1973, Leslie qualified for the American Horse Show Association Junior National Dressage Finals. The finals were divided into three locations, and Leslie entered the Midwestern Division, in Bloomfield Hills, Michigan. "It was a 300-point dressage test, and the judges gave me a final score of 226. I took fourth overall nationally." Leslie knew without a doubt that Ellie's instruction and encouragement were instrumental in Leslie's earning that award. In turn, she was honored to instruct in the clinics.

Kirsten Springer, also a student and instructor, found that teaching in the clinics helped her to improve as an instructor. "At one clinic, I was trying to look and act older, and at one point, when I was having the riders move the horses in small circles, I corrected a woman who was an experienced rider. When I told her that she needed to try again, she dismounted, and snapped, 'I'm not riding with you! You're a drill sergeant.' That wouldn't have happened with Ellie. Ellie's teaching voice was always calm. She didn't show stress or any negative emotions. Always positive, she corrected in a respectful and helpful way. That was a great lesson for me to learn."

The clinic sessions revolved around English pleasure, Western pleasure, and trail riding, and their common link was dressage training. Classes ran from one hour to ninety minutes, with one morning class and one afternoon class. A lecture and a Sodergreen-hosted lunch were offered midday. Judges often provided their critiques at the end of the class, but most never hesitated to assist the riders during the demonstrations.

Ellie appreciated that she learned much from the clinics, including learning from her own experienced "helpers." Ellie knew that her former students considered her an expert, and she knew that they had grown immensely in horsemanship. "I never stopped learning from books, magazines, and my own students and instructors. In fact, one of my helpers, from Montana, taught me that if you're having trouble loading a horse, use a broom. Touch the horse under the tail. It's amazing to see that horse jump right in. But of course," she added, with her own touch of expertise, "that might not work on every horse. We must accept that they are all individuals."

During clinics, Ellie made sure that she did not interfere in any outside instructor's presentation. She was always available to assist people in getting ready and finishing afterwards. "But I didn't interfere during a class. That was not professionalism."

It was not long before reciprocity kicked in. When instructors or organizations needed programs for clinics and shows, Ellie enthusiastically accepted the invitations to present, whether in Wyoming or neighboring states. She easily related to any mix of audience. She was a born communicator, a professional speaker, and a talented artist. She provided engaging presentations, what some called accessible college-level lectures. She expertly wove artwork and slide presentations into her talks. She could speak impromptu on just about anything relating to horsemanship, from English to Western, from trail riding to dressage. She never walked away without totally engaging her audience.

However, there was a clinic, many years later, during which a four-horse trailer upstaged her. In mid-August, 2016, Ellie received a call from the office manager at the University of Wyoming Engineering Department. The office manager explained that the Engineering Department was hosting thirteen English-as-a-second-language students from Japan for two weeks. The department wanted to welcome and entertain them by giving them a glimpse of the West. Would Mrs. Prince be willing to provide a clinic for thirteen students and two instructors on the 15th or 16th of August? Of course she would, and Ellie agreed to the 15th, from 2:00 to 5:30 p.m. She excitedly thought of all that she could not only teach but also learn from these international students. Her scribbled phone-conversation notes indicated—so typically Ellie—that she would host as well, for the students and instructors, a picnic party at the tipi rings.

Ellie's finalized schedule and her handout masters assured a thorough, appropriate, and entertaining series of lessons on ranching and horsemanship in Wyoming. Her stepson, Carl, visiting the ranch at the time, was listed as her co-teacher. The handouts included: The Western Saddle and Western Tack, Bits and Accessories; a pictorial of ranch clothing suitable for ranching and a tractor and scythe (probably reminiscent of Ellie's Grandfather Fracker's scythe); and finally, Mammals of Wyoming. Topics and related tours included: the use of and care for the land, seasonal weather and necessary equipment and practices, methods to preserve the land and such archaeological finds as tipi rings, financial issues in ranching, Sodergreen Horsemanship School, her background in horsemanship and ranching, the uses and versatility of horses, all the roles that a single rancher needs to assume, and finally, all the equipment used on a ranch including four-horse trailers.

According to Ellie's notes, the cost of the clinic was $10 per person. As was always the case with Eleanor Prince, everyone got their money's worth. If the "tests" turned in—by students Keiko, Hikam Takayashiki, Genta Sawasato, Yutaro Tanaka, Ryosuke Sasahara, Jun Tamada, Mac, Manami Hoshi, Kana Konno, Chihiro Watanabe, Amiko Miyake, and Shuhei Kodama—were an indicator, the students learned a great deal. An amused Ellie, however, had to admit that the highlight of the day was the Japanese students' reaction to the four-horse trailer. "They kept going in and out, exploring it all over." Ellie's ego was hardly crushed by the young students' rapt attention to the trailer. In fact, she delighted in it, intrigued by the students' interest and desire to learn more about these modes of transportation. It would be safe to say that questions flew in both directions while the students explored every corner of that old trailer.

Even though she considered herself a life-long learner, Ellie was aware that she was gifted with the knowledge, experiences, and resources she had accumulated over her many years as a horsewoman. She knew that just as the audiences flocked to her open house and her clinics, she had much to offer to and share with any community where there were horses and horse lovers. In the 1970s and 1980s, reciprocity continued as she offered her expertise as an events judge to state shows and competitions.

In Wyoming and the expanded west, it wasn't often easy to just get on the road and get where you wanted to go. Sometimes you had to be innovative. Sometimes you had to wait for a small plane to be going in your direction. One of Ellie's earliest judging gigs involved getting quickly to a horse show that was in Lander, Wyoming, in the middle of the state. A generous friend, Carolyn Rowe—who, as a horsewoman and breeder, had learned the equivalent in diamonds from Ellie—heard of Ellie's situation and said, "My husband can fly you." In record time, Carolyn's husband Don, a licensed pilot, was flying Ellie over the vast countryside. It was also a practice, at least in Wyoming, that if an obstacle appeared, you merely went around it or over it. Carolyn's husband determined that the only place to land was on one side, the wrong side, of a substantial fence. In Wyoming fashion, Don landed the plane, and pilot, pilot's wife, and judge simply scurried over the fence to the judging complex.

Nostalgic images of county fairs often portray judges standing under large shade tents, their feet comfortable on cool and lush grass, tables of iced tea at the ready. That was not the case for Ellie when she drove one very hot summer to a competition in Riverton, Wyoming. "I spent most of my time standing on the sand that felt like it was boiling. My feet actually did burn. Every evening, and it was a several-days event, I forever ran cold water over my feet. I had no lasting effects, like blisters, but, oh, my feet hurt. I soon learned and accepted that, at least in Wyoming, many of the show rings are mostly hot sand."

Ellie accepted these judging jobs for money, but she prepared for and studied the events with her usual fascination, curiosity, and thoroughness. "I always learned while I was judging and made sure I did research before events. All types of animals are at these events—pigs, dogs, horses, and more. All types of events occur. You have to learn everything." Ellie even judged, in July 1990, the all-women Cheyenne Foxy Trotters, a cavalry team that based its maneuvers, according to its Drill Team Competition brochure, "on the U.S. cavalry manual used by the original mounted military units. The Trotters ... used the ... maneuvers as training exercises to prepare horses and riders for drill team participation."

Ellie believed that judging would be much easier if a judge didn't have compassion for the participants and their animals. Ellie's strong sense of compassion caused her to examine the motivations and feelings of not only the event participants but also the judge. "Judging is a personal thing," she discovered. "Of course everyone thinks they should be awarded a ribbon, and everyone wants to know why they weren't awarded. A judge has to look at the animals objectively. Even though the judge has an opinion, what he or she decides cannot be personal." Seeing judging as an interesting process, she revealed that owners would go so far as to "learn the history of the judges. They learned what certain judges preferred and entered where they believed their animal might compete well. Many owners went from show to show, following the judge who just might award that ribbon."

For Ellie, shows and competitions were integral to the business of breeding and showing horses. "You wanted your horse to get awards. You had to get your horses noticed, especially your stallions, and the reason was that it was all about the money." Money was a factor for Ellie, but there was the human side as well. She enjoyed judging but didn't like to disappoint owners or riders. She preferred meeting afterwards with competitors to explain her decisions. Sometimes a horse may have had a blemish, and it was just a matter of the judge seeing or not seeing the horse at the angle that showed the blemish. A judge, she insisted, had to be entirely "in that moment" with the horse. "I hated to disappoint people, but that was a part of being a judge. It was all about what happened and what was in that particular moment. Just like life." Ellie herself was living every moment and all that happened in each moment. "How did I handle all these things?" she wondered. "I guess I was just satisfied with the present and looking to the future. There was that much more in the future to handle, and I knew I could handle it."

Higher Ed Horsemanship

Chapter 17

Despite all that she and Bill did to keep the school and the ranch going, and despite her acuity in all things financial, Ellie Prince could not change the basic dynamic of the life she had chosen. Ranching in Wyoming put a rancher at odds with the weather, a bad hay crop, sick animals, and never-ending repairs. It sucked up every penny, and the general way of the rancher—one of sharing, bartering, and generosity—didn't solve matters. Ellie was frugal and clever, but she was generous. She did not let people take advantage, but she gave when giving was appropriate. It was not her nature to hoard or to accumulate, be it money or materials. She had no desire to build wealth. She and Bill had accepted the hardship that came with the vast and beautiful blue skies and the freedom feeling of the prairie. Had they sold the ranch, they might have afforded a lovely condo in the suburbs. Ellie's response to the notion of leaving her beloved Sodergreen was an emphatic "Never!"

Through the fall of 1971, Bill finished the construction of the indoor arena and a corral system for the Polled Herefords. Panther was the newest kitten, and the haying season had been good. Bill and Ellie stole time, afforded by helpers filling in at the ranch, for a deer and turkey hunting trip near Newcastle, Wyoming, with Robbie Wenske's parents. Bill drove to the hunting area, humming all the way. Later, helpers again helping, the Princes made a two-week trip back east to see "the folks." All might have seemed placid, but the money that came from Sodergreen Horsemanship School and Ellie's services as a trainer and breeder just wasn't enough, and her membership and leadership in the Wyoming and Colorado Arabian Horse Associations, the Rocky Mountain Dressage Association, the International Arabian Horse Registry of North America, Al Khamsa, and the Pyramid Club yielded no remuneration. Ellie set out to find an additional source of income—one, of course, that did not take her far from the ranch. That same autumn, Ellie, who had once doubted her choice of classes at Boston University, signed a contract to teach a course on basic horsemanship through the University of Wyoming's Physical Education Department. The course included English and Western equitation and was, according to Ellie's course description handout, for "anyone who is interested in riding and learning about horses. No experience is necessary."

This was not the first time that basic horsemanship had been a part of the curriculum at the university. The story began with Ruth Eleanor Campbell. According to information provided by Dr. Donna Marburger, Ruth Campbell, born in 1899, served as Head of the University of Wyoming's Women's Physical Education Department from 1924 until her retirement in 1965. In addition to her administrative duties, she taught physical and health education and coached the women's varsity ski team. In the 1930s, she established horse-riding classes in the wide pasture to the east of the few buildings that made up the UW campus. According to a circa-1984 article in the *Laramie Boomerang* town newspaper, by the columnist Erne Linford, Miss Campbell also organized polo teams, open only to women students, faculty, and townspeople. The three teams competed at the old fairgrounds, which were then located near what is now 21st and Grand Avenue. Linford maintained in his article that in the late 1930s, Laramie "had no paved streets, no traffic lights and no sanitary pickup service." But there were horses and those who loved to ride them.

The source of Ruth Campbell's horses for her riding classes is not clear. The horses may have come directly from the Wyoming Army National Guard stables in Newcastle, 246 miles north of Laramie. They may also have been dispersed remounts or retirees from Fort David A. Russell (now F. E. Warren Air Force Base), in Cheyenne, which maintained a cavalry until 1927.[64] Wyoming in and of itself had been, since WWI, "prevalent in breeding war-horse stock."[65]

Eleanor Prince and Ruth Eleanor Campbell were both disciplined and passionate horsewomen. Other similarities existed. Ellie's drive to give young women opportunities to learn confidence, resilience, tenacity, generosity, and self-worth could be mirrored in Ruth's accomplishments. Accolades to Ruth Campbell were recorded by Erne Linford in his 1984 tribute to Campbell after her death, which he titled, "Laramie Loses a Gracious Lady."

"Girls," Linford wrote, "were tolerated in university sports, but they were second class in the schedule for playing and in equipment." According to Linford, Miss Campbell revised the men's and women's curricula and graduation requirements, securing equality for all physical education majors, regardless of gender. Linford described her as "one of Laramie's outstanding leaders in civic and health affairs" and the organizer of "the first Girl Scout troop in the community." Miss Campbell served as a city council member, acting mayor, and a member of the Mental Health Board for Albany County. According to Linford, though, Ruth Campbell believed her greatest contribution to the university and to Wyoming was "the creation of health education in the university's curriculum." During WWII, she took a leave of absence "to serve as a health education consultant in the Wyoming State Department of Education" and later served as chairperson of the Red Cross.

In 1955, some would say, Ruth Campbell engaged in her most significant work for humanity. In a missive dated October 11th of that year and sent to her friend and former student Donna Marburger, she provided a poignant account of the work of many professionals and volunteers, including mountain climbers and skiers from Denver University, Colorado University, and UW, to retrieve the remains of the sixty-six crew members and passengers of United Airlines Flight 409 after its crash into the Snowy Range Medicine Bow Peak on October 6, 1955. Ruth Campbell was head of the large Red Cross crew at Base Camp No. 1 that provided the massive operation's personnel—from FBI to ambulance drivers to horse wranglers—with "coffee, hot chocolate, tea, milk, sandwiches, stew, candy, cigars, cigarettes, and even chewing tobacco from 8:30 to 6:00" throughout the operation.

Ruth Campbell retired from the department in 1965, six years before Eleanor Prince was hired to teach basic horsemanship. Barbara Breeding was hired and served as coordinator of women's physical education until 1972. Breeding delighted in re-connecting with her old classmate and friend Donna Marburger, who joined the department in 1967 as an associate professor of physical education, responsible for teaching undergraduate classes to PE majors and advising and acting as thesis director for graduate students. Donna Marburger received her Bachelor of Science degree from UW in 1954 and went on to earn her Master's degree at the University of Colorado and her Doctorate at the University of Northern Colorado, citing, "I may have been the first female faculty member in the department to have a doctorate." The two women, who had been undergraduates together, reminisced about their love of horses and riding, including pack trips, runaway horses, and bad storms in terrain that did not afford the best of shelters. They also remembered earlier days as counselors at a girls' summer camp in Maine, where Barbara had taught English riding and Donna had been head counselor. In her short term as coordinator, Breeding was pivotal in reinstating the UW horsemanship class as part of the Physical Education Activity Program.

Eleanor Prince, Breeding's vibrant and well-educated hire for the fall 1971 and spring 1972 semesters, was pivotal in expanding the horsemanship program. That academic year, there were no appropriate facilities on the campus, and the riding arena at the Sodergreen Ranch was only partially completed, so the university arranged for Ellie's "classroom" to be north of town, adjacent to the Diamond Horseshoe restaurant and bar. A corral would be her arena, and she would lecture in the vacant bar. Healthy Quarter horses were at her disposal, and Ellie appreciated the condition of the stalls and tack. However, these horses presented a problem for Ellie's students. She explained that "the horses were too well trained. If an inexperienced student exaggerated a command, even slightly, the horse might magnify what the rider, often mistakenly, requested. For example, pull the rein just a bit too much and the horse might do a roll back. I appreciated the owners and caretakers, but lessons were a challenge for my inexperienced students."

In direct contrast, the owner who leased horses to the university the subsequent semester was, in Ellie's words, "an awful person." Ellie was horrified to see that "the tack was just left on the ground, the saddle and bridle leather was dried out and old, motheaten blankets replaced saddle pads, and the bits and bridles were in terrible, filthy condition. The horses were wild and skinny, and when they were brought in for the class, they were treated roughly, with ropes just thrown over them. I was worried for the horses and for my students."

Ellie also worried about the university's reputation, with students coming from all over the country to the state's only four-year school. She told the owner of her dissatisfaction and her intent to do something about the neglectful and unsafe situation if her concerns were not addressed. She was ignored. Not long after, Ellie finished a lecture in the empty bar and dismissed her students to get their horses. As she was preparing to leave the area, the furious wife of the owner of the horses attacked Ellie. "She went right for my throat. I may have been smaller, but I was stronger. I shoved her to the ground, finished my class, and contacted the police." The State Brand Inspector and a veterinarian arrived in an unmarked car. After their investigation, the woman ran after their departing vehicle, threatening them with a broom.

Ellie was not intimidated by the incident at the Diamond Horseshoe. To the contrary, she grew more determined than ever to make excellence in instruction her unwavering goal and would settle for nothing less than to teach at her own ranch with her own horses. At the semester's end, the PE Department agreed to move the horsemanship class to Sodergreen Ranch.

In 1972, when Dr. Marburger became the coordinator of the Physical Education Undergraduate Program, Ellie's class, PEACT 344D, remained part of the Physical Education Activity Program. Thus, it was available for ½ academic credit for PE majors as well as for non-PE majors, who were required to have two years of PE in order to fulfill UW graduation requirements. The class met on Thursday afternoons in the fall and spring semesters. As Ellie's supervisor, Dr. Marburger pledged to support Ellie in what she had already established. "It was fun and easy to continue Barbara's work through Ellie. Ellie had answers to my questions, and we sorted out the details such as the need for students to have transportation to Sodergreen Ranch, the weather's potential effect on attendance, and the issue of the additional required student fee of $125."

Like Ruth Campbell, Donna Marburger was intelligent, well-educated, and dedicated to cultivating gender equality for students throughout the department and in encouraging young women to achieve their goals. It is no wonder that Donna Marburger and Eleanor Prince became lifetime friends as well as amicable colleagues.

Dr. Marburger was quick to see Ellie's potential as a college instructor. "Ellie carried into the riding ring her enthusiasm for both riding and teaching young riders to practice safety and to have fun. She was confident but never overbearing. She instilled in her students a great respect and love for horses and helped the timid ones overcome their fear of these big creatures. She never lost her temper and was always gentle with the horses and her students. And, of course, she had that delightful New England accent and that big smile." Dr. Marburger was from a family of horseback riders and knew that she could leave Ellie on her own. She enjoyed observing the horsemanship classes and meeting the horses, and a few times she even participated.

As coordinator of the Physical Education Undergraduate Program, Dr. Marburger fully endorsed the Basic Horsemanship class. She saw it as something unique to Wyoming and an exceptional opportunity for students to learn about horses and how riding could be such a joy. She accepted that there were private stables where students could study riding, "but they wouldn't get the extent of knowledge as in Ellie's class, or the same breadth, since Ellie taught both English and Western equitation."

Besides, Donna was a horse-loving person herself. "I like horses," she said exuberantly, "even if they are bigger than I am. A person can have a really nice relationship with a horse. When I rode, I loved to talk and sing to my horse. There's something appealing about a horse, maybe because they're so big and strong yet are sensitive to our voices, our legs, and our handling of the reins. And just imagine all the places you can go and the scenery you can take in." Connect all that with the joy of an instructor like Ellie, and it was no wonder, Dr. Marburger professed, "that Ellie's students' course evaluations were always excellent, and there was always a waiting list for the class, in spite of the additional fee required."

Those who wrote positive evaluations and never forgot their experiences in the class included Wyoming native Lana Brokaw, daughter of horse breeder Audrey Brokaw and one of Ellie's first students and helpers. After completing the class, Lana was hired by Ellie as an assistant instructor and ranch helper in 1982 and 1984. Lana appreciated Ellie's teaching that every horse is different and that every rider must sense that individuality. "Just as Ellie knew fully her horses and her students, she made sure that her riders understood their horses and engaged in two-way communication." Lana also stressed that Ellie's teaching went beyond the riding arena. "Probably recalling advice from her mother, Ellie taught self-confidence. She reminded her riders that just as they would make concessions in life, they were never to forget or devalue their own individuality."

Linda Goodnight (now Haynes) was another student who praised Ellie in her evaluation of the course. Linda had loved riding bareback on her father's farm in Pennsylvania. "I grew up thinking I knew a lot, and I even took riding lessons when I was older. Those riding lessons were just that, though—riding. We were put on our horses, we rode around the ring, and the instructor's only words were 'up, two, three, down, two, three.' I assumed that was all there was." As a grown woman, Linda moved to Wyoming "to be on a ranch and be around horses." Thanks to a new friend, Lois Beckett, she soon learned that riding horses was more than "up, two, three, down, two, three." Lois, also horse-crazy, convinced Linda in the mid-1970s that they should take a fall semester UW horsemanship class, where the lessons were taught on a ranch.

Linda's plan for the class was to ride, ride, ride. At the first class meeting, then, she was hugely disappointed to learn that the first hour of every two-hour class would be devoted to lectures and lessons about horses and horsemanship. Her disappointment wore off quickly as Ellie talked of how the health of a horse was dependent on thorough grooming, hoof care, mouth inspection, and a comprehensive care regimen both before and after riding. "I didn't expect," Linda said, "to learn so much in those classroom hours, all the intricacies and critical minutiae important to the horse. I realized I hadn't been prepared for that kind of care. Ellie made the material so engaging, but she also indicated that we had no choice but to learn, and we did learn. It was terrific."

The class remained a fond memory for Linda. "Ellie's classes were comprehensive. She was also a kick, so at ease and at one with the environment. There was no artificiality, and she made us feel at home. She loved having us there and sharing what she knew, and everyone picked up on that. She made us feel as important as the horses. Being with horses was just, well, Ellie."

Lois Beckett also loved the class. "With the lessons, the horses, and the ranch, it couldn't get any better." She recalled that during the lectures in Ellie's inviting living room, before the arena was finished, Ellie shared with the students the "personalities of the horses we would ride so that they were not abstract animals or merely tools for the class. Ellie taught that the pre- and post-riding grooming was for us to get to know the horse, but it was also for the horse's health and comfort and our responsibility as riders. Everything was all about care, from beginning to end."

Ellie encouraged a proper seat and the benefits of balance in the saddle "so that we were engaging with our horses," Lois said. "We learned exercises, posting, arena riding, right and left trot diagonals—all done through control of the body and shifting our weight." Calling Ellie an "apt" teacher whose enthusiasm and confidence were contagious, Lois insisted that even Ellie's exams were good training. "They caused me to be serious about these new skills and the knowledge of horse care. This may have been just a PE class, but it really was a true college course with useful instruction if ever we were going to do things with animals that were in our care. I learned everything Ellie taught us because, without a doubt, I never wanted to disappoint this special teacher."

Ellie made Lois believe that she could do whatever Ellie told her to do "because she believed in me, and I knew I could trust in her." From the start, Lois was confident that Ellie was "invested in all of us. Without breaking the student-teacher relationship, she invited us into her world as if to say, 'You are my friends.' What was most important to her was sharing her love of horses and the ranch life. She lived Western hospitality, and she was an active part of that connected community."

Lois still carried in her old Basic Horsemanship textbook an index card with the names, distinct markings, and personality points of Ellie's school horses. There they were, still famous after so many years: Dixie, Badjur, Grey Girl, Brandy, White Cloud, Suzy, El Khilet, Faazan, Kataffa, Red I, Mouse, Gail, Queen, Serra, Blue, Barney Blue, Jinx, Babbette, Pickle, and Red II.

Part of the key to Ellie's success in teaching Basic Horsemanship as a departmental elective credit class for thirty-five years was her ability to anticipate and address the needs of all manner of students. The other part was her passion for connecting people to horses. There was no greater joy in her school and in her college classes than to see a horse and rider fully commit to each other. She fashioned her UW course after the Sodergreen Horsemanship School curriculum's philosophy, purpose, and methods. In spite of the brevity of the course, the basics of horsemanship were thoroughly covered. Riding methods showcased the need for understanding, communicating with, and caring for the horse. Lessons involved step-by-step instruction, with demonstration and repetition as needed, with sensitivity toward both the confident and the timid rider. Ellie taught in increments, slowly and cohesively, with repetition mixed with patience and encouragement. Ellie did not believe in student attrition on her watch.

Her method in working with the timid rider involved first taking time to fit the student with a horse that was older and quiet and in no way intimidating. Her experience was that "if a horse just coughs or moves his head, it can scare the heck out of an unsure rider." The first lesson for the wary rider, then, was to take the time necessary to halter the horse and then lead and talk to the animal. Grooming, during which Ellie instructed and quizzed the students about the anatomy of the horse, was imperative for the timid and braver students alike. Grooming included having the students soothingly run their hands all over their horses. Ellie then had the students work with a reining board, which was simply a sawhorse covered by a blanket. The board, mounted on a wall with reins attached, simulated both feeling the horse and using the reins while sitting on a wide plank that acted as the saddle. In this saddle, the students were encouraged to practice looking and reining in whatever desired direction. Finally, the students were ready to mount a real horse, with the help of the instructor or by using a mounting block. Ellie made sure that every step up to this point was demonstrated as often as each student needed, in a quiet, calm, and encouraging way.

For the first several sessions, Ellie's students paired up, with one riding bareback and holding the reins while the other led the horse, calmly walking around the arena at the horse's side. Eventually the lead rope was removed. The riders were led through halting, turning, and moving forward. They engaged in stretching and balance exercises that encouraged relaxation, self-confidence, and awareness of the horse's movement. Bareback riding was essential to feel and get to know the horse and gain confidence without reliance on a saddle. The students soon discovered how a proper seat, balance, and subtle but clear aids communicated to the horse what the rider desired. By this time, the timid students had forgotten they were timid.

This method was the reason Ellie preferred group lessons to private ones. "The students learned from each other," she explained. "Even the person on the ground learned. Because everyone was riding and helping, the riders didn't get upset, and they felt safe. Everyone was courteous, and the rider always felt like there was someone near as an anchor." Ellie saw additional benefits to the calm, gradual group work. "It built in my riders a motivation to perhaps teach horsemanship someday. It helped them realize that they could help others learn to ride. It also gave them confidence to eventually try, next time, a more challenging horse, with safety always being a primary component." Every lesson was held in the new arena, the seasonally chilly air warmed by the presence of the calm, working horses and Ellie's nurturing voice. "Otherwise," Ellie said, grateful for her lovely arena, "I'd have had horses going everywhere." That is difficult to imagine, as Ellie always seemed to have at least six sets of eyes and total, harmonious control of her classroom.

With their confidence building, the students graduated, as they chose, to Western saddles or to English pads with safety-release stirrups. An adventurer herself, Ellie encouraged the students to try something new, be it Western or English equitation. She cited the benefits, challenges, and similarities of both. In Wyoming's old days, as she put it, most training was in the Western style. It was considered "sissy" to ride English. However, Ellie shared with her students that English riding no longer carried a stigma out west. In fact, dressage, jumping, and polo exhibited the same challenges and skills necessary for ranch work done in the saddle. Whenever she could, Ellie offered the students new adventures and challenges. As the students grew in confidence and skills, Ellie unfolded, piece by piece, so much more, as indicated in her course description handout.

The course's purpose was "to give the student the necessary information to enable him as handler/rider to ask a horse to do what he desires: when he wants it done and the way he wished it performed; in short, the student should learn how to communicate with horses and produce the desired effect. This course should help a student to realize the pleasure that riding and working with horses can be." The required textbook was *Basic Horsemanship: English and Western*, by Eleanor F. Prince and Gaydell Collier.

Ellie's "Specific Course Objectives" handout included learning how to catch, halter, tie, groom, and tack up a horse; stable management; equine conformation and health problems; personal safety; learning to ride in the correct position at a walk, trot (jog), and canter (lope); learning exercises on horseback to promote muscular development and coordination; learning equestrian games and patterns; and learning how to handle horses while trail riding. Preparation for the class was time-consuming, and Ellie, as was her way, was always quick to thank those who helped with any task, including university-level paperwork. Her work was made easier because of the support of the PE department, including that of Jennifer Martin, office assistant, who assisted Ellie in preparing the course's teaching materials. The invaluable and resourceful Department secretary, Carolyn Hough, who worked in that position from 1975 until her retirement in 1992, was also a great asset to Ellie. Ellie was fortunate as well to have the respect and support of her first Department of Physical Education head, John Woods, and later Ward Gates, as well as the entire Physical Education faculty.

Close to the time she began teaching for the University of Wyoming, Ellie was instrumental in assisting in the development of an evening Equine Program at Laramie County Community College, in Cheyenne. She provided valuable input for an arena built for the program. The class met once or twice a week and, in the wintry months, did not require the participants to bring their own horses. Ellie, however, transported El Khilet to use in demonstrations, often driving on I-80 in the dark and in snowy conditions. When the students' horses were invited, Ellie quickly saw varying levels of training in both horses and riders. Ellie called this "a potential for pandemonium" and after one semester gracefully resigned. In 1975, Ellie taught what she called a "dry course" on horsemanship for the Cheyenne Parks and Recreation Department. Actual riding was not involved; the class focused on equine issues, such as health, conformation, and tack. How, Ellie wondered, could one teach a horsemanship class without horses?

In the fall of 1978, Laramie County Community College (LCCC) hired Ellie to teach, at the college's facility, Basic Horsemanship and Basic Riding, both credit courses in the college's Agriculture Department. Problems arose immediately. The male instructors, well established in the Agricultural program, were the dominating types and did not want women in the program. Before her teaching responsibilities began, one of the men, who saw himself as the head of the Ag Department, called her to a meeting, during which time he and his male colleagues made it clear that they didn't believe she could ever live up to their standards. As the semester began, the men resorted to petty acts. More than once, they locked Ellie out of her classroom, forcing her to find a key before the students arrived. In the arena, they resorted on several occasions to turning the aluminum bleachers the wrong way.

Ellie Prince was not going to take all this. She realized that if she was going to be given peace and expected to do a good job, she would need the support of those in power. She went straight to the college's governing board and made it clear to them that she wanted to do a good job and would, if they backed her. Promptly, the board called in Ellie and the troublemakers. In Ellie's account, the board "lambasted those guys," insisting that "under no uncertain circumstances was this action to continue." No one bothered Ellie Prince again.

After a year of teaching at LCCC, simultaneously serving as a part-time adviser on the construction of the new facility for equestrienne study and shows, Ellie learned that the college had decided that all equine classes would be scheduled during the day in Cheyenne. Ellie could not be gone from her horses and the ranch during the day, nor did she even want to, so in 1981, she resigned. She reaped benefits from the LCCC experience, however. First, she learned a great deal about design and acoustics for event purposes. Second, several graduates from the evening class came to her, wanting to learn how to teach horsemanship. When she invited them to her UW classes, they eagerly attended. It worked for Ellie just to teach; from her class performance, they would learn. She taught some of these students for several years, and Ellie maintained that it was a valuable experience for her, as she believed that one's education never ended. Surely it was a valuable experience for the young women. They had the best of teachers teaching them to become the best of teachers.

Throughout her life, Ellie gave so much and insisted that she gained so much. However, in the mid 70's, as she was embarking on her experience as a college teacher, and only a few years before she was hired to teach at the community college, she lost so much. In February of 1975, Ellie's father had decided that it was time again to visit his daughter. Ellie's mother, Maxine Fracker, in her seventy-fourth year, had chosen to stay at home in Freedom, New Hampshire. She died soon after Mr. Fracker arrived in Wyoming. With her father, Ellie mourned her beloved mother's death, both of them inconsolable that Maxine Fracker had died with neither her husband nor her oldest daughter by her side. On the grayest of days, the prairie unsettled by snowdrifts and swaths of icy patches, Mr. Fracker, seventy-four years old, began experiencing chest discomfort. Ellie piled him into her "reliable on ice" yellow Chrysler and raced him to the hospital in Laramie, where he had two heart attacks and died. A grieving Ellie sent her father's body back to Freedom by train. In mid-summer, Ellie drove to Freedom with her old dog Devil as her traveling companion. There, she attended the memorial services for her beloved parents.

The Sires of Sodergreen

Chapter 18

It is considered by many only a legend, and thus, like the sands of the Arabian Peninsula desert region, the details have shifted since the time of the Prophet Muhammed, approximately 5th century CE. The legend is still told. It may have been after an arduous trek over the dunes. It may have been just before a battle, of which there were many among the nomadic Bedouin tribes. Either way, Arabian horses, muscular and elegant, had been denied water for some time. They were a reliable means of transportation, and they were, as well, war horses; the legend depicted them as swift and enduring, responsive and trustworthy for centuries. They surpassed camels in their maneuverability, and their conformation was well adapted to the desert environment. Their high tails cooled their bodies, their strong hooves held purchase on the rocks and sand, and their dense bones and short backs provided them the endurance they would need in battle. They easily traveled great distances with little food or water.[66]

The Arabian horses had physical prowess, but equally great was their loyalty to the Bedouin warriors and leaders, who considered their Arabians part of the family and thought nothing of inviting these animals into their tents at night, thus nurturing the bond between human and horse—what today is known as imprinting. "The foals were raised with the children, the mares protected in the tents."[67] The strong bond formed with the humans instilled in the horses the desire to seek affection and to please.

As the legend would have it, a particular tribe came near an oasis. The horses—all mares, as mares made the better equine warriors—were released to drink. At this point, the legend takes two avenues. Warriors might have released the horses, or the Prophet may have. Nevertheless, the parched horses turned toward the water and began to drink. In moments, an enemy appeared, or it might have been that the Prophet decided to test loyalty. A call was sounded—perhaps the warriors shouted or perhaps Muhammed blew on his horn—for the horses to return to the riders. Only five mares complied: Kehilan, Seqlawi, Muniqi, Dahman, and Hadban.[68] The five—in Arabic, *Al Khamsa*—chose obedience over a cool, sweet, and rejuvenating drink. As the centuries unfolded, the blood of these Al Khamsa mares would indicate the true Arabian horse, the living example of the warrior horses of the Bedouin tribes.

According to Eleanor Prince, the Arabian horse was recorded as having been brought to Mexico in 1518 by the explorer Hernando Cortez. By the 1730s—when the Arabian horse was introduced to America, England, France, and Holland—the descendants of the primitive horses of Arabia were renowned as the forebears of many of today's European breeds. About half of the Al Khamsa population is now also known as "straight Egyptian," with both bloodlines sought after by reputable breeders.

Al Khamsa "strains," supposedly originating from the five mares, were first regarded as categories of different outstanding physical characteristics. They now also represent traits of temperament and are keenly regarded by breeders. For example, the Kuhaylan strain indicates a compact, masculine horse, and the Seqlawi represents a refined, feminine horse. Traits of temperament, which might also be considered as traits of family lines, might include courage, nobility, agility, endurance, intelligence, and even a photogenic way.[69] Interestingly, the family strain is passed from generation to generation only through the dam, or female, line.

Breeders themselves are highly influential in the world of breeding. Reputable breeders purchase and breed to maintain provenance and strains. They purchase and breed to preserve the bloodline traits of temperament. The best of the breeders are expensive. However, to someone who treasured beauty and brains in a horse, as did Ellie Prince, the expense would be well worth it. Her hope was to someday have the money and means to do business with the Arabian breeders at Babson Farm.

Al Khamsa Straight Egyptian is the most numerous breeding group within Al Khamsa, and traces back to ancient Egypt in the days of the pharaohs, who absorbed the Arabian horse into their stock through capture and purchase.[70] In 1932, Henry Babson imported to Babson Farm, in Springfield, Illinois, five Al Khamsa and Straight Egyptian mares and two stallions from Egypt. Since that day, when Henry Babson established Babson Farm and began his breeding program, Babson-influenced horses, according to Ellie, have proved not only their athleticism and endurance but also their intelligence and aptitude for training; they have excelled in the show ring. Babson's stallions were, as was critical, the best examples of their breeds.

According to an *Al Khaima* article titled "Babson Influence Group," the farm's Arabian horses were "calm, kind, trusting horses … with an amiable sense of joy of life [and] proud but not overbearing."[71] It is no wonder that Henry Babson was highly respected in the world of Arabian horses and served as President of the Arabian Horse Registry from 1949 to 1957. Ellie respected him as well, describing Babson Arabian horses as "true gentlemen of classic pedigree with a disposition to be well-behaved while breeding their mares." She admired the Babson-bred horses as "well-conformed, sweet-tempered, smart, and people-loving."

Majestic in body, a true Arabian horse, according to Ellie, is only as valuable as his temperament—in breeding, showing, training, and horsemanship. One summer, Ellie gave a presentation at the 10th Overland Trail Open House, sponsored by Overland Trail Arabians—the ranch and breeding business owned by Audrey Brokaw of Arlington, Wyoming. As indicated in her extensive presentation notes, Ellie extolled the virtues of the Al Khamsa Straight Egyptian Arabian horse on a working western ranch. She began her presentation by asserting that in all-around ranch work, the Arabian horse showed endurance, steadiness, and cow sense, even over rough and scary terrain. She described the Arabian horse as "beautiful in mind and body, a breed that likes to please and learns quickly, is gentle yet spirited, and is curious and alert." Speaking for the horse, she maintained that his attitude was one of "just show me; don't make me."

Lynn Hornby Hiatt, most assuredly in attendance at Ellie's presentation, gained in her youth an appreciation for what Ellie referred to as the Arabian horse breed's tractable nature. Lynn learned that "Arabian horses have the looks and the flash, but they are easy to work with. They're not hard-headed and they're not resentful. They're smart, and you can work with them around a problem."

To prove the strong and enduring physicality of the Arabian horse, Ellie, truly a scholar and an expert, listed in her presentation the following features: "intelligent face and large eyes, nostrils that close at rest to keep out the dust, a wide jawbone which allows for a large windpipe, a high head carriage to allow oxygen intake, a long mane and forelock to shelter the head and neck from direct sun and to protect the eyes from glare and dust, a short back which can carry more weight and makes for an easy keeper, well-sprung ribs, legs of dense and flat bones, and sensitive skin which responds to cues."

During the riding demonstrations that followed the presentation, Ellie's notes indicated what she wanted her audience to see in the Arabian horse under saddle. Her chosen words were like that of a proud mother: "animated, smooth, collected, willing to obey, brisk, smart, cadenced, balanced, able to lengthen stride and cover ground, obedient, responsive, well-mannered, relaxed, surefooted and careful, steady-paced, tolerant of noisy objects, calm with children, and powerful."

Ellie praised this amazing breed of horse, whether in show, cutting cows, or driving. The Arabian horse might well have praised Ellie. Her knowledge of these horses—their conformation, history, bloodlines, psychology, abilities, needs, tendencies, and temperaments—was astounding. Her professional library of books, magazines, and research notes was immense. Her accumulated wisdom was precise and inerrant.

In 1972, Eleanor Fracker Prince and Dorothy Feldman started a partnership to preserve Al Khamsa horses through the breeding of Egyptian/Babson/Blue List/Al Khamsa bloodlines. Dorothy grew up in Cheyenne, Wyoming, and was described by Nancy Palmer in her Summer 1999 article for *Khamsat* as "a warm, soft-spoken woman, whose very demeanor suggests Western hospitality." A shrewd and organized businesswoman with artistic talent, who professed to have been horse-crazy for as long as she could remember, Dorothy quickly learned everything she could about breeding and bloodlines. She meticulously and accurately printed all the business's pedigree records. She provided financial backing. She even traveled with her husband to France in an attempt to prove that Ellie's stallion Khizan was a pure-bred Egyptian Arabian, despite the lack of papers confirming that fact.[72]

While Ellie worked with the horses, Dorothy, whose parents had never allowed her to have a horse, used her artistic ability to design the stallions' breeding advertisements and also took on the delightful task of grooming and desensitizing the magnificent animals. Her gregarious and generous personality came in handy. The two women were two parts of a whole, and their close friendship made it a pleasure to spend days attending sales, clinics, and shows. Mutual trust was an element of their relationship. Carolyn Rowe, who purchased and lovingly trained at least one foal from one of Ellie's mares, saw a vibrant energy in the two women's relationship. She described their breeding business as "a fierce dream shared by two unstoppable women."

What became a fifty-year partnership involved Dorothy's expertise in researching, advertising, and maintaining records for Feldman-Prince, and Ellie's ownership of two fine horses named Khizan and Fasaab, both, according to Dorothy, with wonderful temperaments. Knowing Ellie's expertise in training, Dorothy wasn't surprised by and often told the story of walking with Ellie in a barn to see one of Ellie's young fillies. Dorothy suddenly lost her footing and fell directly under the filly. Some horses would have jumped. The young horse never moved. Thereafter, there was no doubt in Dorothy's mind that Ellie's number one priority—to breed for sensible temperament and a sweet, gentle disposition—was an excellent one.

Ellie and Dorothy often vied to tell the story of a young mare who had the freedom to roam her grassy paddock during the day but for safety was locked in her stall at night with the gate fastened with a chain and hook. One evening, Ellie went up to check on the filly, in her stall, and discovered that the curious mare had worked the chain, mouthed it, and caused the hook to run through her lip. Ellie moved slowly toward the calmly standing horse, unhooked the hook, pulled it free, and, as soon as possible, applied an antibiotic. There was no reaction from the young horse, who was obviously frightened and in pain. Ellie knew that if the horse had reared back, she would have badly torn her mouth. With both relief and admiration, Ellie and Dorothy asked of anyone to whom they told the story, "How many horses, other than Arabian horses, have the common sense and trust to stand still like that?"

The temperaments of the Feldman-Prince Arabian horses were long ago bred in. However, only proper training could bring those traits to the forefront. From the minute one of her horses was born—or for that matter, any horse that came to Sodergreen—Ellie, perhaps unwittingly, was training the animal to be like her: gentle but spirited, proud but sensible, curious but smart, trusting and loving. Ellie perhaps saw those traits in her new business partner, sharing that "we never had any disagreement or anger. We always talked and worked things out. We accepted each other for who we were, and we were optimists." Ellie remembered that Dorothy was always helping out, including at the Sodergreen Ranch events. At the huge Open House, Ellie shared that "Dorothy was wherever she was needed. She was the one who provided the endless supply of cheese and crackers and help for the event. She was reliable and generous."

The sensible and serious Dorothy had a playful, spirited side, as did her business partner. Often the two women set out in Ellie's motorhome and in no time had an adventure. "We never seemed to get home in time," said Ellie, "or when our husbands thought we should. We knew Bill and Dorothy's Joe were calling each other, wondering where we were, but we didn't pay attention. We did not want to be reined in." Nor did they mind bringing traffic to a standstill if it paid off for the horses.

Dorothy found a red, wooden building in Cheyenne and immediately knew that Ellie needed it for the horses. She bought it, and she and Ellie hired Tommy McLaughlin, the neighbor down Harriman Road, to bring the building to the ranch on his flatbed truck. First, the building had to be freed of its cement moorings, which needless to say was a time-consuming job for Tommy. Tommy made it out of Cheyenne and onto I-80, which was then still Route 30, but he didn't get far before the police stopped him. It was Labor Day weekend, and his huge, lumbering truck transporting the wide and wobbly building was holding up traffic. The police said that the building had to sit on Tommy's truck on the side of the road till the weekend holiday traffic ceased. When Tommy got moving again, all manner of friends decided it would be great fun to pitch in to help situate the structure on the Princes' property. Ellie realized that once everyone was at the ranch, she would have to feed them. Dorothy, self-selected organizer of the project, came through, with buckets of Kentucky Fried Chicken. Ellie remembered that Joe and Bill were not happy about the huge project. "They were annoyed, and the whole process was a stressful thing, because we kept wondering how the building, without a floor, didn't fall apart." A corral was built around the structure, and it proved its use as home to stallions who were being trained.

Khizan, a Babson black bay ninety-eight percent Al Khamsa Arabian, was Ellie's first stallion. The young horse, ignored and ill-fed by his owner, was in poor condition when Ellie purchased him in the mid-1960s, but according to Carolyn Row, "Ellie could see potential in horses when others could not. She could see beyond the infirmities to the real value of the animal." The stallion, born in 1951, quickly responded to Ellie's constant exercise and nutrition regimen. Ellie showed him at the 1960 Estes Park show and the Top Ten Arabian Stallion Competition in Canada in 1961, and, acknowledging his progeny (Khebir x Fizana), began breeding him. To her delight, many of his get, or offspring, were black. Equally valuable was that Khizan showed himself to be a willing "do-it-all" horse with the very temperament, disposition, and level of endurance that Ellie had previously only dreamed of someday acquiring in a horse. In 1961, Khizan sired El Khilet, who as a gray gelding would become one of Ellie's favorite "do-it-all" mounts.

Fasaab was another dream come true. Ellie purchased the foundered, weak horse from Dr. James H. Quinn of Salt Lake City, Utah, and soon, with her care, he was in top shape. Photos of his beautiful head adorned Ellie's brochures and breeding advertisements. A Babson black Straight Egyptian Al Khamsa stallion (Fadl x Bint Bint Sabbah), Fasaab excelled in the show ring, loving the lights and attention and returning the appreciation with an outpouring of willingness and delight. Ellie and Fasaab went on to win ribbons in Park (Ellie defined this category as "showing off but with good manners and form"), English Pleasure, and Arabian Costume classes. Fasaab, born at Babson Farm in 1948, sired over thirty-seven beautiful foals, many of them black, until his death in 1974. While Ellie longed Fassab during his early days of training, Gay Collier rode him, recalling "sitting on his glossy black back and feeling his muscles rippling under my thighs. It was like riding a thunder cloud—smooth and soft but seething inside with power and spirit and the fire of his breeding."[73]

In 1978, Ellie, in full partnership with Dorothy, purchased from Babson Farm the stallion Kamars Sharif (Fabah x Roufina). Sharif, born April 30, 1974, was a true black Babson straight Egyptian, the son of a full brother to Fasaab. Like the other two stallions of Sodergreen Ranch, the beautiful, stunning Sharif, noble and dignified, had an amenable personality and a gentle disposition. Like Khizan and Fasaab, he was intelligent, level-headed, and willing. Used in Ellie's classes, he was powerful and proud, yet affectionate and obedient. In fact, Sharif exhibited this nature, as did Khizan, during one of the clinics at Sodergreen Ranch. At clinics, Ellie's intent was always to display her two popular stallions individually, separate from each other. This was because two stallions in close proximity, even stallions with breeding and training for tractability, could decide to prove who was superior. When it was time to show the stallions to the crowd, one of Ellie's helpers assumed that it was time to lead Khizan down from the east barn just as another helper assumed that it was time to lead Sharif down from the west barn. As the two stallions drew closer to each other, the young women, realizing the potentially explosive situation, calmly cued each horse to halt. The stallions complied but swung up their majestic heads and from low in their throats emitted snorts of dominance. On their own, they then quieted, ready for a cue from their trusted handlers, who calmly led the stallions away from each other.

As breeders, Ellie and Dorothy were always in attendance at local, state, or national Arabian Horse Association meetings, once traveling as far as California. Former Sodergreen Horsemanship School instructors and helpers who wanted to attend were invited along. The conventions' shows exhibited all aspects and histories of the Arabian horse breeds as well as provided access to breeding registers. The huge area was filled with vendor booths, videos, silent auctions, and the latest information on equine equipment. At a four-day event in Denver, Ellie was a featured presenter of critical information for Arabian horse owners.

Dorothy and Ellie—sometimes with Audrey Brokaw and her daughters, Lana and Lois—never turned down a chance to visit the beautifully maintained Babson Farm. The women from Wyoming and the Babson family of Illinois shared a common philosophy, which Ellie described as raising horses to please. She explained that horses "want to be a part of you. The secret is to spend time with them when they are young, when they can learn that people are friends. You need to touch their heads, feel them all over, pull their tails, pick up their feet, and mess with them with brushes and combs."

In the late '50s and through the '60s, television channels were packed nightly with "cowboy" Westerns. *Rawhide*, *Maverick*, *Gunsmoke*, *Bonanza*, *Wagon Train*, *The Virginian*, *The Rifleman*, and *Black Saddle* brought the Wild West into many a family living room. Rapt viewers learned that the only way to dismount was to leap off, reins in hand, while the horse was still galloping, and then jerk the horse to a full stop. If a stallion was part of the herd, the rider first rode the buck out of him and then raced the animal in circles or over the prairie until his spirit subsided. Breeding was not displayed, but any stallion at any time reared, bucked, fish-tailed, and pulled away from the handler, nostrils flaring, eyes wide. Stallions were recalcitrant handfuls. At Sodergreen Ranch, nothing could have been farther from the truth. Ellie assumed the responsibility, without question or hesitation, of swirling her stallions in a sea of calm voices and gentle handling. Her stallions grew accustomed to loving human attention. Like the ancient Bedouins, Ellie worked with her stallions to make them people-lovers. Combined with the assurance of bloodlines that produced proud but placid animals, Ellie's stallions were sensible, intelligent gentlemen.

To illustrate, Kamars Sharif, under Ellie's training, became a Class A winner at Halter, Driving, and Dressage. In November of 1984, at the Regional Convention of the North American Trail Ride Conference (NATRC), Carolyn Rowe, a young student of Ellie's and an impressive clinic instructor, rode Kamars Sharif through long and intricate patterns to demonstrate training techniques for competitive trail riding. What was amazing about the routine, titled "Variations on a Theme," was that Carolyn rode with neither saddle nor bridle. In a profile of Kamars Sharif for eventual publication, Ellie wrote that Sharif "shows how very sensitive, obedient, and responsive he can be to unobtrusive aids—in fact, he will perform dressage and arena movements with only a rope around his neck (and this is mostly for the rider)."

It was no surprise that Kamars Sharif was also quite the willingly photogenic young fellow. Soon after his purchase, he became the poster horse for the Sodergreen Horsemanship School brochures. 1979 saw the release of the movie *The Black Stallion*, starring Kelly Reno as Alec Ramsey, Mickey Rooney as the retired jockey Henry Dailey, and Cass Ole as Alec's black stallion. Based on the 1941 classic children's novel by Walter Farley, the movie was a smash hit. Eleanor Prince, a fan of the book and the movie, placed an ad for Sodergreen Horsemanship School in the Cheyenne newspaper. The newspaper clipping displayed a gorgeous picture of Kamars Sharif. Beneath Sharif's picture was an invitation to visit Sodergreen Ranch. Above, and in a larger font, were these words: "The BLACK STALLION of Sodergreen Ranch recommends the adventure movie THE BLACK STALLION. The photography and color are superb."

The remarkable Kamars Sharif sired SG Sharifs Flag, the last stallion to be born at Sodergreen Ranch. Flag was never bred, although some profiles for advertising described him as the stallion who carried the potential to continue the Sodergreen Ranch legacy. Born on Flag Day, June 14, 1997, Flag did not carry on the breeding legacy. Instead, he became Ellie's gentle and affectionate pet, tasked only with offering his cherished owner the unique love and pleasure that only a horse could give.

Ellie knew that "a stallion must be the best example of its breed and must be advertised as such." Ellie's goal, early on, was to be able to advertise "Proven Stallions." These were stallions that had proved their "prepotency," or ability to sire foals that are out of the ordinary. What "out of the ordinary" meant for Eleanor Prince was disposition. "It's ninety percent of the whole horse," she said, explaining that ancestry and pedigree were important if the stallion had not yet been used for breeding, but disposition was always critical. Granted, Arabian horses were bred to be tractable, but according to Ellie, they had to be constantly surrounded by loving, gentle, and trustworthy people who taught them to trust. Training interactions had to be calm, with cues obvious. The stallions needed to be exercised daily, fed well, and kept from each other but not from people. As potential show horses, they had to be introduced to travel, new settings, noise, and the unexpected. Prone to stress during breeding season, they required good food and loving hands. "It was the touching all over," Ellie said, "that was so important to my stallions."

The Sodergreen stallions may have provided the flash, but Ellie saw her mares as equally important to her breeding business. Mares, she was quick to share, carry the progeny, and thus "the stallion and the mare must be complementary. What a mare doesn't have, a stallion must have, and vice versa." She insisted that breeders "must offer well-cared-for, sensible, tractable mares as well as stallions. Nothing less."

Ellie's stallions were gentlemen. What mare wouldn't look their way? Her brood mares—Grey Girl, Tammilass, and Kataffa (Katie)—and Audrey Brokaw's brood mares were ladies. What stallion would refuse to contribute to the progeny of such class? The descendants' decorum carried to shows, competitions, and presentations.

Back home, at Sodergreen Ranch, a love story came to pass each spring. According to Leslie Turner, the lovely mare Grey Girl threw beautiful foals with Khizan, the handsome stallion. There was more to the relationship than just the act of breeding. The two horses were in love with each other. "Before the breeding," Leslie said, "I could lead Grey Girl right up to Khizan's corral, face to face, and they would serenely touch cheeks. After breeding, they calmly stood side by side. You have to be alert in breeding because things happen in a hurry, and powerful stallions can cause injury. But Grey Girl and Khizan? They just melded."

Liabilities, Lightning, and Losses

Chapter 19

THE ROMANTIC VIEW OF RANCHING SPEAKS MUCH OF EXCITING CATTLE drives, evening horseback rides on the prairie, and large reunions of family and friends. Little is said of the many financial fears, disasters, legalities, and unexpected circumstances that can plague ranch owners. A ranch's profile is neither placid nor static.

As if to reveal the tenuous nature of ranching, one might consider a landmark that those people who lived near it or knew it said would stand forever. Known by the Johnsons, the Smiths, the Princes, and the Colliers as "the big house," the building that shared its reputation with the beautiful old barn, both solidly built by a strong, skilled Swedish homesteader, burned to the ground, cause unknown, on December 13, 1979. Gay Collier memorialized the majesty and demise of the old house in an unpublished 1980 poem titled, "When the Sodergreen House Burned Down." The house of "hewn heartwood" disappeared in ash, even though it was "made to last forever." Gay, like many others who knew the structure's personality, lamented that no more would dwellers "hear the footsteps of the old times running through the halls / feel the warmth and feel the lifeblood beating in its walls."

Bill and Eleanor Prince, despite their constant and often exhausting projects and repairs, were not immune to liabilities and losses. They knew that their ranch off Harriman Road and the dreams and goals that came with it were not made to last forever. A disrupting and potentially catastrophic event occurred in the early 2000s, late in their ranching lives. At that time, Ellie depended on her UW classes, which she described as full to overflowing, and relied on their going smoothly. One of the students in the class had borrowed her boyfriend's truck to drive to Sodergreen Ranch. She parked above the arena, facing the wide, high, sliding metal doors that made up most of the north side of the building. Just inside the doors was a substantial and well-organized area full of well-maintained and—as far as the Princes' finances were involved— irreplaceable tack. To create the tack area, Bill had securely fastened a long board to the thick, stout wooden framing of the metal arena and, at intervals, had fastened round wooden pegs, on which Ellie painted the name of each of the Sodergreen school horses. Each horse's bridle and halter hung neatly on his or her peg. Below and about two and one-half feet off the ground were sturdy racks for the saddles and blankets.

The young woman who had driven the flatbed truck neglected to take into consideration that she had parked on an incline above the arena and failed to set the emergency brake before she left the vehicle. When the truck finally stopped, after having gained enough momentum to slam through the whole north front of the arena and through the tack room, only its bed and rear wheels were still on the outside. All the saddles and tack were embedded into the thick sawdust floor of the tack room, which itself was badly damaged. Luckily, the porta potty was not knocked over, and the horses were nowhere near. Also, the crash, which Ellie described as a violent scene, occurred just before Ellie and the students headed to the tack room.

The violent scene soon turned into one of high disorder. It was the beginning of the semester, and Ellie did not want to proceed in a state of chaos or declare it impossible to hold her remaining classes in the damaged arena. In the next week, before class, Ellie and Bill, with some of Ellie's beloved helpers, moved all the tack and every saddle far to the south end of the arena. Using cross pieces and racks of poles, they fashioned a bridle rack along one inside corner. Saddles and tack were carefully cleaned, repaired, and restored as well as possible and then moved to the makeshift tack room. The work was time-consuming. Classes would be held in a condensed area of the arena; Ellie would have to make do.

Years earlier, when they sought financing for the construction of the arena, Ellie and Bill established themselves with the Farmers Insurance Agency. A familiar agent and friend assigned himself to the damaged arena case. That was a good thing, because it was quickly determined that the truck did not belong to the student, and the settlement became a drawn-out affair. The young woman said that the vehicle belonged to her boyfriend, who, when finally located, was not forthcoming. After some time, the agent tracked down the actual owner, who turned out to be the boy's rather uncooperative grandfather. The agent finally negotiated a settlement for repairs that was advantageous for Bill and Ellie. However, all that they might have lost in income from classes and loss of equipment haunted the Princes. Their professional lives and financial well-being depended on their ability to hold onto the ranch, the equipment, the school, and the cattle and horses. At times, that hold was fragile.

Ellie's entire livelihood depended on animals, and animals, of course, grow old and die. Some even die well before old age. Ellie was in accord with this fact of life, stating, "Because we had so many animals, we lost so many—horses, dogs, Bill's cattle, and even the cats. We had to accept that they were not going to live forever, but when some die young, their deaths are still so painful. I always had to remind myself of all that I did for these animals to make their lives happy. The fact that I made them happy dulled the grief. With a long sickness, though, it was a little different. I was sad but relieved when these horses were finally out of pain and in Heaven somewhere."

Regardless of the cause or time of death, it was emotionally draining for Ellie to lose a horse, but it was financially upsetting as well. "They were necessary to my programs. I had to have enough horses for classes and enough that could be used for so many different students. I couldn't afford to lose them. We did everything we could for an injured horse if we thought we could save him and often had to look the other way at the mounting costs."

When a filly by Sharif and out of an Egyptian mare broke her left foreleg, Doc Allen, a veterinarian in Laramie, and Dr. Green, a family practice physician, engaged in long discussions over how to treat valuable Ru-Anna's compound fracture. A solution for setting the fractured leg was devised, but extreme skepticism regarding recovery care was shared by the two doctors. It had to be excellent. Ellie couldn't afford less.

Ellie decided to hire a young girl to come to the ranch, her sole job being to watch over the injured horse for as long as necessary. Ellie didn't care about the cost for the filly's care. All went well until the filly started chewing on the cast. Ellie researched a way to stop the chewing, and Tabasco sauce was the answer. She bought out all the Tabasco sauce in all the stores in Laramie and Cheyenne. The horse eventually grew to like Tabasco sauce, and in spite of a small limp, the registered filly recovered and was placed with a caring family. And Doc Allen's fee? Doc Allen knew ranchers, knew their lives. "Nothing," he said.

The deaths of the ranch's horses by lightning strikes were the most traumatic, in that they were sudden, unexpected, and violent. There was nothing to be done to prevent them. On the western prairie, thunderstorms travel fast, appear suddenly, and are often vicious in the frequency and severity of the accompanying lightning. Ellie remembered a day when all was peaceful, the horses were out on the south pasture, and the clouds were easily five miles away. Bill and his son Carl were out in a field, hunting another liability—the gophers that dug networks of holes into which a horse could plunge and break a leg. A thundercloud soon appeared, and it didn't look threatening. Bill, though, knew the weather. He instructed Carl to place his rifle on the ground next to Bill's and get away quickly. The two men ran twenty or thirty feet away from the metal of the guns and crouched in a hollow while the lightning's tendrils cracked all around them. As soon as it was safe, they grabbed their guns and hot-footed it back to the house.

Ellie, at the house, had just received a phone call that one of her horses had been struck by lightning. No one had seen the strike, but neighbors going along

Harriman Road had seen the dead horse. "You know it's lightning," Ellie said, "when at the lower part of the horse's leg and foot, they show signs of burn. There's little else to go by." When they got to the horse, a gray mare out of Grey Girl named Sugarfoot, they found that she had been singed from her front legs to her withers, nose, and forehead. She lay a very short distance from where Bill and Carl had taken shelter. Another horse killed by lightning was Silver, a beautiful and favored school horse. "The horses don't understand," said Ellie. "Silver was in the north pasture, standing in water from all the rain we'd had."

Ellie never had her dead horses carted off. There always was the option of the landfill, but Ellie said no. "It's better on your own place. You can always think of them as still being nearby." The animals were family and were treated with dignity, but disposal was a practical thing for the Princes. An arroyo was right above the house and just over a couple of hills. The horse's hind legs were chained together, and the animal was dragged to the top of the arroyo. A deep hole was dug, and the tractor was then used to maneuver the body in and cover it with dirt.

"Sometimes," Ellie said, "we had a little ceremony. Carolyn Rowe danced or said words from Native American wisdom. Our friend Bob Dougherty, whose beloved Reveille was buried on our property, sent up balloons." Happy memories were shared, such as No Name's tendency to tear home at a full-blown run, and Babbette's executing of a command before Ellie finished saying it. Sad memories surfaced as well: Prince's death from complications of a broken leg, Fasaab's early death in 1973, El Khilet's and Khizan's in the 1980s, and Sharif's in 2000. An oft-resurrected memory that surely brought a smile to Ellie's face was how her beloved Khizan—and weren't all of them beloved?—helped to herd Bill's cattle by running up behind a cow and biting it on the rump when it wasn't doing what it was supposed to be doing.

If lightning was frightening and loss of animals inevitable, unrealized liabilities lurked as well for Ellie and Bill. One in particular was labeled by legal experts as "attractive nuisance." Ellie's highly intelligent dog, Devil, provided a canine introduction to the term. When the Princes first arrived on the property that would become the new Sodergreen, Devil was keen on exploration. Old, discarded farm equipment was strewn about the ranch in the neglected fields, and the curious Devil soon chanced upon a disk harrow, partly buried and mostly hidden in the tall grass. Ellie and Bill would eventually find the huge comb of metal disks, repair it, and use it in the outdoor riding ring to turn and level the soil. However, on that day, it was a curio for Devil.

At one point in his playful examination of the contraption, Devil leaped, and one of the disks cut so deeply into his chest that Ellie, running to the rescue, could see Devil's heart beating. The good news was that Devil's injury took Ellie once again to the veterinarian Doc Allen, in Laramie, "who knew everything and quickly became my long-lasting friend." The bad news was that, had Devil been a human youngster, his human parents could have sued for damage caused by something accessible, attractive, and life-threatening.

Cornell Law School Legal Information Institute defines an "attractive nuisance" legally as "a dangerous condition on a landowner's property that may particularly attract children onto the land and pose a risk to their safety. … The … doctrine imposes a duty on property owners to treat trespassing children the same as an invitee, and as a result, must exercise reasonable care to eliminate potential dangers or provide adequate warning."[74]

Ellie and Bill came terrifyingly close to an actual attractive nuisance lawsuit when a friend with two little boys came to visit. The little boys were like Devil in their curiosity, and in the blink of an eye, one of the youngsters managed to climb to the seat of the ranch's tractor, which always had to be parked on an incline so that it could be started by coasting. The boy called out for attention just as the tractor started moving. The terrified child lunged and was able to jump free of the moving machine. Had he stayed on the tractor, which was heading toward the creek and the potential for overturning, he might have been killed. "We were thankful the boy was safe," said Ellie, her voice displaying a hint of horror still, "but even at that, Bill and I were so upset. If the mother had sued, we might have lost everything in a minute, after we had worked so hard to get the ranch. I knew I would never forget this. It was one of those times when your heart is in your mouth." The friend was a good friend and chose not to sue the Princes for her child's tractor ride.

The fear of lawsuits may have played a part in Ellie's decision, in 1993, to revise for re-release her first book, *Basic Horsemanship: English and Western*. She and Gay Collier met in Ellie's old RV at Fort Robinson in Nebraska to go through the book with an even keener eye for safety for both horses and riders. Numerous requirements were added, such as wearing heeled boots so the rider's foot didn't get hung up in the stirrup. Likewise, the authors stressed the necessity and even in some cases the requirement for all riders, regardless of experience or skill, to wear riding helmets. Even as she wrote about and employed these new safety precautions, Ellie estimated that the high cost of insurance removed any possibility of her making much money on her UW classes. "I didn't want to go up in fees just to cover insurance. I had to consider the UW students' finances and the cost to get out to the ranch." As she often remarked, she didn't want anything, especially money, to stand in the way of anyone's learning to love a horse.

Despite Ellie's riveted attention to safety procedures, her classes and school sessions were not immune to accidents. On a ranch, she said, "accidents do and will happen. It's just the nature of people." Once a student parked her car in the wrong place at the ranch, where the horses had access. One curious horse came over to her car and started chewing on the red paint—which, according to Ellie, horses seem to enjoy—and may have even damaged a mirror or a light.

Another time a rider got a bit cocky and decided to ride her horse at a trot away from the barn. Her horse broke into a canter stride, a canter that included a high buck or two. The woman fell, broke a bone, and spent time in the hospital. Luckily, in neither case was Ellie sued for damages. Both women had signed the requisite release form.

All of Ellie's University of Wyoming students and parents or guardians were required to sign this release form, titled "Warning, Agreement to Obey Instruction, Release Assumption of Risk, and Agreement to Hold Harmless." According to Ellie, the signers of this form accepted that equine-related dangers and risks existed and that they were signing to accept the importance of obeying instructions. The signers assumed all risks associated with participation and agreed not to hold the University responsible for any and all liability. The signers agreed as well to purchase accident insurance coverage.

Likewise, Ellie was required, as are all Wyomingites whose businesses involve horses in close proximity to humans, to post noticeably on the premises a sign titled the Wyoming Equine Liability Act. The sign acted as a "release" for the owner. The words stood out on the old sign nailed to a thick post just inside Ellie's arena, where horses were tied, tack was gathered, and Ellie lectured. No one missed it, and if they did, Ellie pointed it out:

> Any person who takes part in any sport or recreational opportunity assumes the inherent risks in that sport or recreational opportunity, whether those risks are known or unknown, and is legally responsible for any and all damage, injury or death to himself or other persons or property that results from the inherent risks in that sport or recreational opportunity. A provider of any sport or recreational opportunity is not required to eliminate, alter or control the inherent risks within the particular sport or recreational opportunity.

According to Ellie, the rider had to accept partial responsibility. "However," she explained, "there was an unpredictable variable to this—the horse. If you wanted lessons, you acknowledged that you knew and accepted this variable." Ellie understood the serious need for legal definitions, forms, and signatures, and even though she was "going into the hole" because of the cost of insurance, she looked at the bright side in her optimistic way. "I was grateful that at least there were still the university horsemanship lessons for all the students who wanted that free feeling of being with a horse."

Owning the ranch, in and of itself, posed burdensome challenges. Leslie Turner saw early on that "Ellie and Bill, as committed as they were, constantly felt tied down to the ranch. They were scared to death to leave it for five minutes. They were worried to the point of borderline paranoia about it being cared for if they both had to be gone at the same time." Leslie rued that Ellie and Bill missed "having fun by getting out. Sometimes I think that going away might have made them happier together." She could see that Ellie wanted to reach out to friends and family and help them more by being near them. "She honestly didn't think she did enough to help people because she was so tied to the ranch."

Bill Wilkinson recalled, in an account of the temperamental and aggravating Sodergreen Ranch equipment to which the Princes were also tied, that what the Princes owned was potentially ancient, without any hint of vintage value. "Bill Prince had an old one-and-a half-ton Dodge dump truck that had no muffler or brakes. He had International H and M tractors that he had to park on a hill to start. He only had one tractor that would start on its own using a battery. He had an old swather that was always out of adjustment. He had a hay tedder that was probably made in the 30s or 40s, and a 1932 crank-start Caterpillar Dozer that he luckily knew how to take apart and rebuild from top to bottom."

All the old equipment was daunting, but Bill Wilkinson maintained that Bill Prince "was clever and creative in fixing it all." If equipment couldn't be repaired, Bill Prince, as ingenious as his wife, figured out a way to use it elsewhere. He owned an old Harley Davidson 250cc Enduro, but it couldn't be driven on the road because the kick starter was broken. He explained to Bill Wilkinson that he used the motorcycle to herd his cattle, and Bill Wilkinson had to admit that it was perfectly suited to the task.

The adjective "old" was also ascribed to the Prince's well, their source of water for the house and barns. The well was hand-dug and therefore shallow, and thus could easily become contaminated. When they were first considering the land for purchase, Ellie and Bill had seen the well as an asset. This asset, however, became a constant source of trouble and irritation. When they first moved to the property, Ellie and Bill discovered that a dead animal had been in the well for some time. The pressure tank and pump were in a covered pit below grade, the plumbing and wiring were jury-rigged, and working in the well pit was dangerous and damp. A full well was dependent on ground water, from Goose Creek's springs. As the drought moved into the area, the creek water level dropped, and the well threatened to go dry. Often, the pump quit. To fix or replace the well or dig the existing well deeper would cost money that the Princes knew they would never have.

Like the horses standing out in the open fields, even the farm equipment and the house itself were susceptible to the constantly overwhelming forces of Wyoming weather. Bill Wilkinson recalled a story Bill Prince told him about being on his tractor when a lightning bolt hit a fence post twenty or thirty feet away. "Bill watched a trail of white light travel across the grass to the tractor. The next thing he remembered was lying in a field, opening his eyes, and realizing that he had been thrown off the tractor, which had kept running and had driven through a fence. He had to get up and chase that tractor to turn it off."

On another occasion, before lightning rods were secured to the house, Leslie Turner was visiting with the Princes in their kitchen, leaning against the porcelain sink as was her habit. Just as they heard a big bang of thunder, lightning hit the high, metal windmill by the school bunkhouse and raced up the water lines. Fire blew through the kitchen faucet, and Leslie leaped a mile. Calm eventually ensued and Leslie, out of habit, again leaned against the sink. Lightning again followed the same route. Lightning rods were soon purchased, and Leslie Turner, from then on, found a new place to settle while visiting her dear friends.

Ever vigilant of possible accidents, Ellie focused on the safety of her students, her horses, and herself, but even she was vulnerable to injury. In 1987, at the age of sixty-one, she was running her programs with the agility and health of a thirty-year-old. One wrong move, however, slowed her down. That year, she was hosting a "Good Morning" program for newcomers to Cheyenne. For the group's weekly sessions, she usually saddled all her horses before the riders arrived. She never forgot that one of her horses, Gail, did not like to be cinched while she was tied and often reared up if that happened. On one occasion, while Ellie was tying the horses for saddling, Bill hurried down to the arena to tell Ellie that a foal was in trouble. Since horse care was Ellie's responsibility, she finished her tying and took off to take care of the foal.

When Ellie returned to the group's horses, she felt a bit hurried and forgot to untie Gail before cinching up the saddle. Gail reared and came down on Ellie's left knee. Her knee was, in Ellie's words, a bloody mess, but she knew that no one had seen the accident, "so I went ahead and got the horses and riders ready and rode with my injury." She later cleaned her knee but didn't go to the doctor. In a tone of gentle self-reprimand, she said, "That's what happens when you hurry, when you're not careful, when you don't follow the rules. But I had work to do for others and couldn't stop for the pain, and, yes, I took everybody on a good ride that day."

Years later, Ellie agreed to knee replacement surgery. With Bill's help and that of Sandy Broyles, who happily traveled with Bill to the hospital in Laramie to receive work assignments related to the school, no students, staff, or horses missed a beat, and Ellie was very soon up on her feet and in the saddle.

In 1991, Ellie Prince began saving copies of her long, descriptive, and illustrated Christmas letters. A pattern of events emerged from the handwritten pages adorned with sketches of sleds, bells, snowflakes, frolicking horses, dogs, and cats. The family grew closer with frequent summer visits. Bill's son Carl and his family visited often from Oregon, daughter Lynn and her family traveled from Virginia Beach, Virginia, and George visited from Alpine, Wyoming.

The ranch finally began to don a cloak of "old." In March of 1991, Mostly the dog died after nearly eighteen years by Ellie's side. In the same month, because of a severe heart attack, Bill, mourning the loss of his beloved cat Panther, was scheduled for triple bypass surgery and faced the fact that he would have to give

The stove with the bullet hole.

Bill looking proudly over his hay fields.

Former helpers and students at Bill's memorial service.

More former helpers and students.

Awssie, the last dog of
Sodergreen Ranch, living the life.

Flag, the last horse of
Sodergreen Ranch, as a foal.

Flag taking instruction from Ellie.

Flag's paddock at the west barn.

Ellie's helicopter ride, second to the last item on her bucket list.

Lynn and George, Bill's daughter and younger son.

Michelle Huff, at the reining board, attentive to Ellie.

Photo taken by and courtesy of Lisa MacGuire.

Spring snowdrift blocking the west barn door.

Ellie at 91, ever young.

Carl and Ellie.

Photo taken by and courtesy of Lisa MacGuire.

Ellie heading to the west barn in her late 90s. Ellie never missed a feeding.

up the more physically demanding parts of ranching, including raising cattle. According to Ellie, finances were a huge worry, and the yield of hay later in the summer was almost ruined due to the flooding of Goose Creek.

From 1994 on, Ellie made mention of relentless, torrential summertime floods that brought in debris and nearly wiped out the hay meadows. She wrote in the Christmas letters of the milder and unpredictable winters that hinted of impending drought. She wrote of the spring blizzards characterized by extreme winds that caused heavy, horizontal snows that formed into packed, icy drifts sometimes as high as Ellie's shoulders, necessitating that she lug buckets of water to her horses. She described her herd of horses each year as "getting mighty old," but the Sodergreen Horsemanship classes were "full and going strong."

In 1995, Badjur, a favorite horse among the students, died at the very old age of thirty-three, and Wobbly the cat turned twenty-four. Bill, in 1996, applied more paint to the old house siding and constantly repaired fences. Ellie finally dared to take two trips away from the ranch—one to the Olympics, attending the Individual Dressage and Show Jumping competitions and seeing the sights in Atlanta, Georgia; and one to the Al Khamsa convention in Springfield, Illinois, where she also visited the Babson Farm. Wobbly the cat turned twenty-five.

In 1997 and 1998, Ellie lost Fabir, Candy, and Zag. In 1998, "another hard year for our old horses and heartaches for us," the ranch saw the deaths of Turol, Kevish, and Fataff. A five-year-old Egyptian colt died of a possible aneurism. Bill's heart condition worsened. Wobbly the cat turned twenty-six and died, leaving one Sodergreen cat, Stubby, age unknown. Three more "mighty old" school horses—Blue, Princess, and Chico—died in 1999. Monty, Ellie's loyal German Shepherd since 1992, died in 2000, as did three horses, including Ellie's "beautiful beloved black super stallion Sharif, our wonderful Gail, who in her prime was our best lesson horse, and Sunshine, a lovely old riding horse." However, that same year, Lisa Pontoriero, the neighbor on the hill to the south, and a loyal and excellent helper to Ellie since 1992, brought new life to Sodergreen by starting a partnership with Ellie. She began to pasture her horses on Sodergreen Ranch meadows. Ellie supplied the arena, and Lisa loaned her horses and her time as an instructor for UW lessons. Lisa also helped Ellie with the development of Saturday School, a new idea and opportunity, as Ellie said, "for those who just couldn't get enough of horses."

The constant wind was described as "getting mighty old" at the house on the Wyoming prairie, but pushing it were the breezes of new life and ventures. Ellie did not have the temperament to let things get her down. As Carolyn Rowe put it, "In any difficult time, Ellie found support and peace in the very life she lived."

For Those Who Can't Get Enough

Chapter 20

When Eleanor Prince shared that she accomplished more in the 1970s than in any other decade of her life, she wasn't kidding, although numerous accomplishments spilled over into the 1980s. Sodergreen Horsemanship School and the University of Wyoming Basic Horsemanship class continued to boast record attendance. Ellie's second book, written with Gay Collier, titled *Basic Training for Horses: English and Western*, came out in 1979, published by Doubleday. A review of her book in the magazine *Horse Play* focused on the uniqueness of both the authors and the book's content: Both Ellie and Gay grew up in the East and settled in the West, and the book was written for both English and Western riders. The reviewers remarked on the ability of the writers to "cite differences and similarities in both 'camps' and to compress the confluence of thought and method." That compression was revisited by the authors in the book's final paragraph, which the reviewers repeated in its entirety: "If [those committed to working effectively with horses] are to be successful trainers, our knowledge of horses must be thorough and sensitive. We must transmit our desires to the horse in a way he can understand, and in a way that causes him to desire to obey and please us. It's a tall order, but the rewards are worth our effort, patience, time, understanding, and love."[75]

The book was still filling the shelves when Ellie and Gay's third and final book, *Basic Horse Care,* was published in 1986, also by Doubleday. A January 1987 review in *Arabian Horse Country* focused on the abundance of information provided by the authors. "[The book is] an authoritative reference designed to meet the needs of both the novice and the most experienced horse enthusiast. ... [The] profusely illustrated volume contains the most up-to-date information, advice, and counsel currently available on the maintenance, training, and stabling of horses. ... *Basic Horse Care* gives you all the information you'll need to enjoy the companionship, beauty, and performance of a healthy, happy, intelligent animal."[76]

Ellie was innovatively providing more opportunities for riders to enjoy healthy, happy, and intelligent animals. The Sodergreen Horsemanship School, which began in 1961, was originally in session for eight weeks. At the new Sodergreen school, Ellie shortened the program to six and then 4 weeks. In 1974, after learning that adults and families were interested in the school but could not attend because of work schedules, she and Bill cleared a parking area for RVs and horse trailers, and Ellie adjusted her curriculum to create a "ten-day intensive school" to accommodate the spectrum of ages. Despite the range in ages, Ellie adamantly adhered to her philosophy and goal of teaching thorough horse care and horsemanship basics, as evidenced in a 1994 letter to a Mrs. Kiser who, with her husband, intended to become horse owners and were considering taking the ten-day intensive course. Ellie wrote, "We do not expect to 'finish' our students in just ten days' time. However, we do tailor our program to the needs and desires of our students. Since you and your husband wish to own, care for, and ride your horses, you need lectures and 'hands on' information about feeding, basic stable facilities, ground training, health, and especially safety for you and your horses. You should also become knowledgeable in how to select a horse suitable to your temperament, size, and experience. We have an almost complete equine library, and we give lectures and demonstrations in all the basics. I feel our program will be very beneficial to you." She diplomatically ended the letter thus: "I do hope you can adjust your vacation time to join us."

Graduates of Ellie's early private lessons, Sodergreen Horsemanship School, LCCC classes, and the UW courses were all hinting that they needed more, and Ellie was not about to ignore the plea. Circa the mid-70s, she started Saturday School, specifically for her advanced and committed students, and even more specifically, for those who couldn't get enough of horses. The devoted riders soon started showing up, men and women, middle-aged and older. Audrey Brokaw and her daughters were some of the first students. Lana Brokaw remembered that getting to the ranch and back was not for the faint of heart. "We left our ranch in Arlington early enough to make the two-hour drive to Ellie's ranch, and of course we had to add on the time it took to tack and load the horses in the trailer. The Saturday class started about 9:30 or 10:00, but despite the time and distance, the wind and weather, and having to drive over the Sherman Hill summit, there were few cancellations."

A Saturday School session was about three hours long and began with lecture, demonstration, and Q&A time. Lana remembered that there was more than talk about horses. "There was dog and cat conversation, and friends just talking and laughing."

Training and discipline were the core of Saturday School. Along with fostering the jovial camaraderie, Ellie made sure that learning took place. She quickly realized that every session had to be different, that each Saturday she had to come up with some new focus. These students, she said, "knew how to do things. They had the skills and the basics. It was up to me to provide what was beyond their equine education."

The curriculum fanned out to cover just about any unique topic Ellie thought of. Having used cavalry maneuvers in her SHS class, she decided that advanced cavalry methods, garnered from her manual from Fort Riley, Kansas, would be advantageous to her advanced students. She began lessons with the tried-and-true cavalry exercises that relaxed both horse and rider and made them one. Favorite exercises included the rider stretching an arm across the horse's withers to touch the opposite foot. Another involved lying back on the horse's rump and peering up at the blue sky and white clouds while maintaining awareness and control of the gentle animal as he walked.

Ellie enjoyed taking her students through the cavalry maneuvers, which she called "a fluidity thing in the midst of precise execution of commands." An initial practice involved the riders positioning their horses in a single line and then by twos, then threes and finally fours. The horses were then brought down the center of the arena, where they were turned to the left or the right, depending on Ellie's command. Ellie formed her riders into drill teams that weaved in and out, the riders focused on delivering frequent but slight aids to their horses. "No one got bored," Ellie said, and despite a few traffic jams, the class had a great deal of fun and, to Ellie's pleasure, learned from each other how to maneuver safely among other horses and riders while Ellie gave crisp commands from the center or side of the ring.

Ellie also challenged her riders and horses by asking the students to circle the indoor riding arena or outdoor ring over sets of cavalletti. Up to four cavalletti (log poles) were placed parallel, and from two-and-a-half to three feet apart. Each specially built cavalletto (with wooden X's fastened to the ends) could be rotated to lie as poles on the ground or jumps of six inches. In addition to other benefits, cavalletti served as training for a horse to prepare for jumping, or as precision practice to improve rhythm, cadence, and balance during the walk and the trot. Training in jumping would soon follow for Ellie's eager students.

If students indicated interest in a topic she hadn't covered, Ellie didn't hesitate to bring it into her Saturday School curriculum. She even pulled out her two side saddles when the students asked her what it was like to ride side-saddle. She shared her memory of attending a horse show with her sister Carolyn when they were both little girls. Watching the women riding side-saddle, the young Ellie was baffled as to how the women in their costumes stayed on their horses. "Those women were brave, because it was obvious that if the horse went down, the rider, who would not be able to free herself from the saddle, went down as well. She had to sit square during any gait, with her left leg pinned under her right, holding a whip in her right hand and wearing a long, full skirt, since women in the

1800s weren't supposed to show their ankles." So, intrigued by what she saw, Ellie searched for and bought two side saddles when she came to Wyoming. One had the tree for the rider's legs on the left, and the other had been made with the tree on the right, possibly, Ellie figured, to allow for conversation when a duo was out riding. Considering it a good way to have her students balance their weight while looking straight ahead, Ellie encouraged them to try the side saddle, but only at a walk or trot, of course. They all did, and laughter mounted as each student, tossing gracefulness aside, attempted to stay in the saddle.

Ellie researched and prepared an interesting history lesson to go with the side-saddle experience. This included her observation that "most of the horses in the last century that were trained for 'ladies' mounts' were gentle. Any horse that offered to buck was not considered as a mount. Men eventually tried the side saddles and got a sense of the ladies' courage. The side saddle brought the male riders down a peg."

In Saturday School, some of the students had favorite mounts, but Ellie always had the last word in matching horse and rider. The match might have been to challenge or encourage a student or to help a student master or revisit a skill. Of course, the match was for the horse's benefit as well. "On occasion," said Ellie, "I had to work with ego. Once, a rider with an ego wasn't as gentle as he should have been with his horse. I had to match him later with a horse that could work with that ego." Ellie also had to consider particular riders' needs. "With older students, as were a number of my students, the needs didn't show, and I had to find them. There were also physical limits that I had to work with, including knee replacements." Always meeting the needs were Ellie's trusted and loyal lineup of school horses, which included Red #1, Mouse, Badjur, Grey Girl, Gail, Suzy, Blue, Pickle, Jinx, Babbett, Red #2, White Cloud, Serra, and Dixie.

One of the regular attendees, now Lana Brokaw Clark, referred to those who had been riding for fifteen to twenty years as Ellie's perpetual students. Their ages ranged from the twenties to the seventies. Some came from Cheyenne, and some came from Laramie and Arlington. Some found the more advanced work difficult, but none of the group, numbering on average from four to fifteen riders, gave up. All of them insisted that the class was good for horses and riders alike. They, like Ellie, knew there was always something to learn, even during trail rides out to the tipi rings, Ellie accompanying them, side-saddle on her 6-wheeler.

Deb Matthew, returning to Sodergreen Ranch as a retired Air Force Reserve Officer, was grateful that Ellie didn't make the riders take tests anymore, but she spoke for the regulars when she shared that "while we rode, we didn't worry about anything except riding. It was like tai chi, yoga, and pilates on horseback. Ellie was inspiring and charismatic, and we all laughed a lot. She provided an opening joke, and an excellent lesson, and at times initiated or encouraged conversation about major concerns in the world." Deb was impressed that Ellie, as a horsemanship instructor, had carved a unique niche for herself. "Ellie taught English and Western, the basics and beyond, and trail riding and book learning. The eternal common denominator was love of horses."

Cheryl Mair, a flight nurse in the Wyoming Air National Guard, learned about Saturday School from her good friend Julie Wilkinson, also a Wyoming Air National Guard flight nurse. Taking the Saturday School lessons in 2018 and 2019, when Ellie was in her early nineties, Cheryl delightedly saw the group itself as mostly "eccentric older women, all in love with horses. I wish I had started Saturday School ten years earlier. Ellie challenged me, and I felt I was the luckiest horse lover on earth. The lessons were a treasure, and Ellie became uniquely special to me."

Julie Wilkinson also attended the school. In 1987, she had seen a long article about Eleanor Prince and the Sodergreen Horsemanship school in the Cheyenne newspaper. It was the first she'd ever heard of Ellie Prince, but as a recently married woman, she knew that she wanted to get back into riding horses. She picked up the phone book, looked for "Prince," and dialed the number. She offered to help the friendly woman on the line with the University of Wyoming students, and Ellie accepted her offer. While Bill Prince and Bill Wilkinson worked together on projects on the ranch, Julie had the opportunity to ride and to build a friendship with Ellie. "I felt an instant connection with Ellie. When you meet her, you love her instantly."

When Bill Wilkinson was transferred to Oklahoma to work with the Department of Transportation, Julie vowed that she and Cheryl, who she had met during a military tour, would visit Ellie often. They braved blizzards, often "winging it" on the snow-drifted prairie to get to Ellie's house. A coffee cake or birthday cake was usually part of their luggage.

Julie was awed by Ellie's courage in living on the Wyoming prairie. "She lived a completely unintimidated lifestyle. She never put on airs about being some kind of pioneer woman. She didn't mind eventually living alone and being isolated from neighbors." Julie claimed that a person had to live in Wyoming in order to understand the state's demographic of isolation. When Julie was traveling the state as a night shift Home Health nurse, she always had to pack everything she might need, including sleeping bag, food, and survival items. In snowstorms, Julie took the frontage roads to avoid the semi-trucks flying past on the highway. "I drove at 20 miles per hour and had to open the car door periodically to make sure I was on the road and not on the grass. I couldn't see beyond the hood of the car. I could have wound up in a ditch and no one would have known for a long time." What existed between the tiny towns, small cities, and ranch houses of Wyoming, she quickly learned, was total remoteness.

Julie remembered that Ellie was okay living in a remote area. She was okay with the wind blowing out the water heater pilot light and with the occasional lurking mountain lion. Over the years, the Princes had constructed ways to protect their animals, and Ellie and Bill were fine if the animals were fine. In fact, Julie pictured the Princes' home as an inviting oasis of coziness in the midst of Wyoming's wildness: the little stone house on a hill, surrounded by huge cottonwoods, and within, the living room walls and shelves decorated with Ellie's carvings and pen and ink drawings of her horses, horse show snapshots and ribbons won in shows, and books and magazines, lots of them.

After retiring as a science teacher at Carey Jr. High School in Cheyenne, and after a right hip replacement, Robbie Wenski Wilson signed up for Saturday School. She rode bareback the gentle horse April and benefitted physically and mentally from Ellie's patience and encouragement. Robbie was a regular attendee at Ellie's tack parties, when all the saddles and bridles were cleaned with saddle-soap and then rubbed to suppleness with Lexol. In spite of the late August chill hovering in the large, metal arena, Robbie remembered that "we spent our working time reminiscing about horses and Ellie's classes. We talked about horse problems and concerns, and Ellie provided answers. Afterwards, she invited us up to the house for chili or a casserole, and some of us provided the rest of the meal. It was always like family in her living room."

"Family" didn't stop with the tack parties. Often, Ellie invited her Saturday School students down to the Willadsen School for the Harvest and Craft show and always planned a cookout at the end of the fall session of the school. For Robbie, the class was a community where concerns and troubles were left behind and nurturing took place. Robbie remembered that even though Ellie had never trained in hippo-therapy, she did so much to help Robbie when she broke her ankle, and to work with Nola Shafer, not only when Nola was pregnant with her second son but when she shattered her ankle in a ski accident. "In Ellie's class," Robbie said, "we regained confidence, self-esteem, and pride. It was as if Ellie was telling us that, in a safe environment, we could do more than we thought we ever could."

After completing her MFA degree in Creative Writing and settling into an office staff position at the University of Wyoming, Beth Buskirk decided to fulfill her faculty gratis UW credit courses by taking the Basic Horsemanship class. Ellie then encouraged her to sign up for Saturday School. Beth had misgivings: "that it would be expensive and dangerous and that I would be the oldest one in the class." She signed up regardless. On the first day, "they were all talking social security, and I knew that this was my tribe."

The Saturday School stretched Beth as a rider, but she saw in the school something else. "Ellie's legacy was one touching so many people's lives through riding. She provided a way of allowing older horse-lovers such as myself to keep their fingers in riding, and she nurtured friendships, which were constantly being created." Beth described the classes as "endearing times" and remembered the trail rides and "Ellie's corny jokes from *Reader's Digest*." Tipi ring picnics and potluck lunches were festive times for riders, friends, and families. The arena lessons, though, were disciplined and organized, always focusing on a daily theme and valuable instruction. "Ellie had an incredible eye as a teacher," Beth noted. "She could tell right away what a rider had to do to improve seat, hands, and legs. Her gentle suggestions were right on the mark, and we paid attention to them."

Beth was impressed that Ellie stressed safety as part of her general education. In her calm and direct way, Ellie made sure that her students were prepared beforehand for any potential problem. "It was all preventative," said Beth. "We were taught what to do ahead of a risky situation. For example, if in a real situation a horse started to get ahead of the rider, we had already learned to take that horse in a circle, round and round."

Beth stayed with the class for ten years before she and her husband retired to the Southwest. "Ellie's students never got enough," she remembered. "We were always coming back. We were friends, and we were completely in awe of Ellie. She was a joy to be around."

Esther McGann, a retired financial planner and investment manager, was introduced to Saturday School by Beth Buskirk. It had been sixty-five years since Esther had ridden a horse, and she was "missing the fragrance only a horse will have." She signed up for the school. "Ellie was a mix of knowledge, discipline, and infinite kindness. She was intuitive and sensitive to a horse's feelings and could see things in both the horse and the rider that others could not. She respected both the horse and the rider and offered care and tenderness to each. She didn't mind that I sweet-talked every horse I rode."

According to Esther, everything was done gently and subtly around the horses, so that the rider gained trust from the horse. She remembered that Ellie spoke emphatically of dressage training for the horses. "Ellie told us that dressage horses often remain in the Olympics for twenty years or more because they have been treated biomechanically correctly through dressage techniques. Their muscles remained strong, and their joints were taken care of. The horses were never forced to do anything that didn't come naturally."

Ellie, Esther noted, was a gracious instructor. "There was never any bravado or braggadocio, and when Ellie had to correct a student, there was no belittling. She simply explained what was to be done instead and asked the student to then notice the difference in the horse. She wanted the class to be enjoyable as well as safe and informative."

What Nola Shafer appreciated most about Saturday School, besides being on a horse and with Ellie, were the exercises. "I would have loved a class just doing exercises on one of Ellie's horses. It was wonderful to know and feel the animal. You weren't on a La-Z-Boy, though. Ellie gently prodded and pushed you to know the horse. She made us focus on what we were doing and on what was coming ahead, but it was a warm focus." Old class notes revealed that Ellie's warm-up exercises numbered at least twenty-three.

Feeling safe and confident around Ellie's horses, Nola believed that their distinct personalities resulted from the love and care they received at Sodergreen Ranch. Fataaf, an Arabian horse, was Nola's go-to horse. "He was so well trained that my three kids also rode him, one with a pacifier, and I rode him up into my second trimester of pregnancy." Rudy was another of Nola's favorites. "Rudy always made me look good and was so well trained that once, after helping Ellie set up cavalletti in the ring, I casually said to Rudy, without giving any command, that I was finished. He came right to me."

Nola saw Ellie's essence as artistic, in that she brought her sense of visual art into her training and teaching—including her artistic, detailed, and thorough handouts on many topics, from the history of horsemanship to the polite and proper way to take a horse through a gate. Although Ellie frequently reminded her students that even she had so much more to learn, Nola believed Ellie to be "encyclopedic" about horses. "One day, she told us that even the movement of our eyes could affect our horse. She told us we needed to have soft eyes. In other words, we needed to see peripherally as well, so that we'd be prepared for what was happening and what might happen. She told us that horses use peripheral sight as well because their left and right eyes focus separately."

During each class, Nola and the others were assigned individual tasks with the horses. Some tasks were hard, but the riders would always cheer each other on. When Nola was having trouble getting her horse to take the correct lead during a canter, she announced that she wanted to give up. "But someone called out, 'You can't retire. You still have work to do!'" In Saturday School, Ellie made sure that the students benefitted from and were happy in their accomplishments. In one class, Ellie called out, "Show off!" after Nola executed a difficult task. "That," said Nola, "was the greatest compliment ever."

England is known for its dressage history and expertise, yet in the late 1990s, Valerie Scott, of Norfolk, United Kingdom, had nothing but accolades for her Wyoming instructor. Introduced to Ellie by Robbie Wenske Wilson, Val signed up for the fall and spring Saturday School classes "mainly for the pleasure of seeing Ellie." Although a competitor in dressage and jumping/cross country classes, Val "enjoyed the walk and trot lessons with Ellie as they kept me grounded, and Ellie kept me honest with regards to my riding position and riding habits. I had actually read Ellie's book on horsemanship, but I admit it took a while for the penny to drop with me that she was THE Eleanor Prince."

Referring to Ellie's lessons as "solid and pertinent and always a mix of work and fun," Val was "thrilled to find an English riding instructor in Wyoming whose methods gelled so much with what I had learned and believed to be good horsemanship." Ellie's teaching style, in Val's opinion, did not "overface either horse or rider. It was non-judgmental and quick with praise and slow with criticism." Val observed that on occasion, Ellie's students included "some very nervous amateurs who had purchased horses that were not suitable for them.

Ellie was always able to find some insight for the rider in dealing with the horse, to the benefit of both of them."

Looking back over her memories of Ellie's lessons, Val confirmed that "they were always fun and fruitful," even when Val rode her own draft horses. Val remembered Ellie "sitting in the sun, smiling broadly, and watching the lesson participants trot over poles in front of her. She clearly loved every minute of it." Ellie became a role model for Val, as to "how to live my life and age gracefully. At the tender age of sixty-four, I continue to ride horses in England and try to be like Ellie in all that I do. I have become involved in volunteering in my village, and I hope Ellie would be proud of me."

The men who attended Saturday School, if they felt like outsiders, were not outsiders for long. They instantly sensed and were drawn into the camaraderie and warm sense of family. Shawn Reese's uncle, an attorney, convinced his nephew that he needed to enroll in Ellie Prince's Saturday School. Mike Reese had been an avid participant in Ellie's school for ten or twelve years. Shawn agreed, if only to have "windshield time" with his uncle, who was the family historian and an interesting storyteller. Shawn, the executive director of Wyoming Humanities since 2020, found himself the youngest member of the group in the spring of 2018, but after meeting Ellie Prince, that didn't matter. He continued for two more semesters.

Class gathered, Shawn recalled, with the students seated on benches around a small wooden desk that Ellie had set up in the arena. "After the customary joke, she shared copies of articles she had pulled from magazines. The articles, always interesting, were about such topics as saddlery, riding positions and posture, ways of communicating with horses, and riding techniques."

Early on, Shawn pondered why the class was called Horsemanship rather than Horseback Riding. He soon learned why. "What Ellie taught was more about the relationship between humans and horses than about the act of riding. Whether a student rode English or Western, Ellie emphasized communication with the horse. She taught how the rider made eye contact and how horses see things. She taught us how they are built and how they think and respond. She made us aware of the power structure and authority between horse and rider and how this dynamic is created."

After lecture and lessons, Shawn remembered, the students went from the arena up to the holding area to halter their assigned horses. By that time, most of the horses were from Lisa Pontoriero's herd. Ellie rode side-saddle on her four-wheeler to make sure the gates were all closed as the students led their horses to the arena for grooming, saddling, and bridling. Ellie settled herself on a five-gallon bucket in the center of the ring, moving frequently during the lesson for closer observation or to shovel away newly dropped manure. Shawn observed that Ellie's stern but encouraging critiques were about "the most subtle of movements, seeing or sensing all the tiny things that were happening between horse and rider as they moved around the arena. I realized that only someone who had been doing this all her life could do what she did to instruct the class."

Ellie began ringwork by addressing a particular skill or movement and then moving into what Shawn described as more athletic material: trotting and then slowing the trot to move in tight circles or change directions. Cantering occurred when earlier skills had been mastered. The after-class procedures focused almost entirely on the care, comfort, and safety of the horses. When the students returned their horses to the corral, Ellie again followed, enjoying, Shawn said, "the extra task of swatting the resident donkey out of the way."

When Ellie talked of the horses she had owned, "it was clear," Shawn said, "that she had been a very influential woman in the world of horsemanship." He saw her as "quite a character, someone who had lived a very rich and unique personal life. That accent of hers was new to my ears, her opening jokes were quaint, and the time she spent finding articles to share with us showed that she cared about giving us gifts of diverse knowledge. One minute Ellie would be discussing horse safety and the next, she told of the Native American medicine wheel and the skull found near Jelm Mountain."

Shawn easily detected that "the ranch itself had a strong sense of place." He remembered the "quintessential ranch house, with its antique stove in the middle of the big room, as cozy and cluttered with horse paraphernalia. It was a little Ellie museum."

Everyone felt welcomed at the ranch, Shawn said, "and Ellie was attentive and complimentary to me as the newbie." In fact, Shawn saw everyone in the class as equally supportive. Noting that they had been together so long, he saw them less as students and more as close friends. The group bond was certainly evident when, at the start of each lesson, "Ellie asked everyone what was going on in their personal lives and was truly interested in their responses." Perhaps this explains why the original rate of $20 per lesson never increased over the years.

Shawn realized early on that Ellie was "grounded in life-long learning of equine behavior and interaction as well as cause and effect. She had a deep understanding of horse and human relationships because her life was dedicated to learning lessons about behavior and interaction. It was more than textbook understanding. She sensed it all, especially with her eyes, and saw it as a pleasure and a duty to teach others. She was a good educator. I may no longer remember how to tie the knots the right way, but I remember Ellie."

Shawn didn't remember the bad weather that occasionally cancelled class, or the muddy road up to the arena, or the puddle-dodging that the riders had to deal with. "It was chilly at times, but we were in the warmth and scent of our horses." Seeing how the hardy and independent Ellie met the hardships of weather and ranching, Shawn bestowed on her a title: "The most quintessential of Wyoming people I've ever met."

Connected Community

Chapter 21

In the summer of 2001, Eleanor Prince held her last session of Sodergreen Horsemanship School. Several reasons factored into Ellie's difficult decision to close the school. Despite the interest and enthusiasm still felt by loyal helpers, including those who showed up for the last session—Lisa Pontoriero, a helper since 1990, Patsy Nelson, Mary Weinstein, Susan Abraham, Danelle Peck, and Kirsten Crawford—the schedule required of them was not doable. Early and late feedings as well as class times, coupled with Ellie's inability to pay the helpers during down times at the school, resulted in their having to secure additional jobs in Laramie or Cheyenne and then drive back and forth to the ranch. Even if the helpers wanted to stay at the ranch, the already-once-rebuilt cabin roof was showing its age, and Ellie and Bill soon deemed the building unsafe for overnight residents. Even if the chance was taken to allow helpers to stay in the cabin, the regional drought had its say. Springs on the ranch provided water for horses, but there was certainly no extra water for baths. The helpers sadly sought paying jobs elsewhere.

Bill's poor health, the drought's contribution to dwindling hay yields, and the aging of the ranch equipment were additional factors for closing the school, as was the diminishment of Ellie's equine herd. When Lisa Pontoriero purchased land south of the Princes' to add to her own ranch acreage, she and Ellie combined resources and formed a partnership, which allowed for at least Saturday School and the UW classes to continue.

Some forty years earlier, in the late 1960s, Bill Prince had begun a battle with health problems. A heart attack led to his eventually having to receive a pacemaker. Over the years, his fight with heart disease and bladder cancer took away his strength and stamina, and in 2009, he was rushed to the hospital, placed on oxygen for the remainder of his life, and faced time in VA care, nursing home care, and hospice care. Illness and infirmity were difficult for any rancher to accept, and Bill Prince was no exception. Bill had spent his adult life building, repairing, and shepherding his ranch—livestock and equipment—through the challenging and often vicious seasons. He took his responsibilities seriously and never rested until the work was done. Like most ranchers, he was a genius of ingenuity, using what was on hand to do what was needed. He was a master of ranch ownership jury-rigging. Worry and hard work took its toll.

As Bill's health declined, the inability to do his own work or to accept that kind friends had to do it for him must have diminished his pride. It must have hurt when he made the decision to sell his Polled Herefords and his tractor to a neighbor. He died on Saturday, April 21, 2012, at the age of 86. His youngest child, George, who had returned after many years to Sodergreen Ranch to help out in any way he could, had died one week earlier from cancer.

A memorial service for Bill Prince was held at the Cheyenne VA Medical Center the following summer. Bill received a twenty-one-gun salute, and Ellie was given the military funeral flag. When the ceremony was over, a group of veterans drove through the parking area on their motorcycles. An intrigued Ellie noticed that one was a three-wheeled motorcycle, from Canada. All the motorcycles were, to Ellie, "quite fancy with silver all over." When she realized that most of the riders were wearing spurs, her thought, stemming from practicality, was incredulous. "What were they wearing spurs for? I could only think that those spurs could get caught in the motorcycle gears." After the ceremony, Ellie's thoughts turned to those still alive and still in her care. "I have to get home to feed," she characteristically announced.

A number of Ellie's helpers, long-term students, and those who had helped Bill with haying over the many years attended the service and were invited afterwards to return with Ellie to the ranch. Even Val Scott, with family visiting from England, was scooped up into the basket of the many friends who made it their purpose to always be available to Ellie in whatever ways she needed. Ellie reminisced, "We gave Bill the best tribute we could. We scattered his ashes in his beloved west hay meadow."

Kirsten Springer, who had often stayed with the Princes in their house during summer school sessions, stayed again with Ellie while Bill was dying in Cheyenne. "Ellie was like family. She gave me love, warmth, and a special sense of connection. She never said goodbye on the phone without telling me she loved me." After Bill's death, Kirsten, whose family had set up a Sodergreen Horsemanship School scholarship in her dad's memory, helped with planning Bill's service and came later to help Ellie go through Bill's possessions. "It was an intimate time, but Ellie and I have always been intimate. At times we talked about faith, which was strong in Ellie even though she didn't attend church because she couldn't leave the ranch. Occasionally, we talked about hardships, especially when Bill was ill. Sometimes, we didn't even have to talk."

One year later, Ellie's world was jolted again. As the instructor for the University of Wyoming Basic Horsemanship class since 1971, Ellie had depended on that income, especially after the Sodergreen Horsemanship

School ended. In the summer of 2013, she received written word that the university was dropping the class as a credit course. For several weeks, she was fretful. Not only did she fear the loss of the income, but she also feared losing connection with the university and, most importantly, losing the chance to teach a class she loved. Relief washed over Ellie when she was informed that the class would continue, but not as part of the Physical Education Department's basic instruction program. Instead, it would be housed under the UW Outdoor Program for students and staff, and would meet on Sundays from 1:00 to 4:00, with those enrolled providing their own transportation. The transition was rocky, with erroneous or vague information mixed into the facts. Also, unlike the PE department, the Outdoor Program did not provide the hard-copy visual advertising that Ellie saw as essential. Everything related to the class, including advertising, was posted on the computer. Ellie remembered that when the class started in the '70s, "we signed up the students in person. I had to get used to all these changes, but luckily, I didn't have to do anything on the computer because I didn't have a computer."

Ellie, however, had Lisa Pontoriero. When Ellie was teaching horsemanship classes at Laramie County Community College, Lisa enrolled for a semester. Ellie was impressed with Lisa's horsemanship skills and invited Lisa, in 1992, to sign on as a Sodergreen Horsemanship School counselor. Lisa accepted the invitation and signed on every summer thereafter. "Lisa did such a good job with the students," Ellie said, "even the very young ones." When Ellie's class was shifted to the UW Outdoor Program, Lisa shifted as well. A future partnership had been developing for some time, and when Lisa and her husband purchased acreage from Ellie and Bill, the partnership became a reality. Ellie supplied the instruction, tack, arena, pasture, and hay meadows. Lisa supplied the horses and assistance in instruction, harvested the Princes' hay, and named her firstborn daughter Eleanor. "It was good," Ellie said, "to have a partner and to have the pastures again full of horses."

When Lisa divorced her husband, she decided that she alone would fully manage and maintain her ranch as well as continue her lucrative farrier service. "Working hard and working all the time" was how Ellie described Lisa, and she appreciated that Lisa also assumed "some responsibility for my health, checking on me, helping me, coming over and doing some of the things that needed doing." Ellie would not become dependent, though, and she completed tasks with the attitude that what had to be done, she could still do. With her typical practicality and ingenuity, she cared for her ranch and her animals every single day.

When Bill was hospitalized, Ellie recognized the need for a ranch dog and canine companion. In 2011, she adopted from an animal rescue center in Cheyenne an unregistered German Shepherd and Husky mix pup, who she named Awssie, a derivative of "awesome," she explained. Until Ellie could get a bit of training into the exuberant and loving pup, she referred to her as "my wild girl." At the end of each day, Awssie trotted alongside Ellie as they walked in the chill of the advancing evening to the west barn where Flag, Ellie's only remaining stallion, waited for his late-day meal and Ellie's affection. Flag's needs met, the stallion nickered his satisfaction, and Ellie and Awssie returned on the rutted, sloping lane to the house. Stubby, the last cat on the ranch, mewed a greeting from his perch. The three animals, Ellie fondly recalled, "gave me exercise and pleasure through those later years." As night settled, Ellie, Stubby, and the massive and furry Awssie cozied up for the night in the small stone house surrounded by leafy cottonwood trees and blanketed by the star-filled Wyoming night sky.

Ellie and her animals were never alone for too long. As Julie Wilkinson put it, "Ellie's attitude was always one of welcome. She was always saying, 'Just call and come.'" Her old friends in Cheyenne and Laramie called, and they came, often toting lunch or sweet treats to share. They came ready to help with chores or carry her mail to and from the post office. They brought news, and of course they came with their horse questions. Those who moved afar kept in touch. Constant calls, cards, and visits gave credence to one former student's observation that when someone met Ellie, they weren't a stranger for long. Ellie had opened her heart and her home to many, and they were simply paying back the love.

Old friends cherished moments with Ellie and were touched that Ellie was so grateful for the smallest of things. Ellie's close friends knew that there had to be dark moments in her life, but she didn't share them. Ellie politely accepted both the praise and the help she received but was always humbled on both accounts. She could not stop her friends from describing her as fearless, feisty, and strong; they offered stories that validated the descriptions. Indeed, she did hoist feed bags, and she did shovel drifts. When pumps froze, she carried heavy, awkward buckets of water to Flag. She never complained about glass ceilings and barriers and just figured out how to accomplish what she needed. She could not afford to be weak. She dealt with the weather and myriad hardships and, according to Deb Matthew, "even made it fun sometimes." Lana Brokaw Clark, recalling the Fruits of the Holy Spirit from the Bible, Galatians 5:22-23, said that her whole life, Ellie possessed and shared those fruits: love, joy, peace, patience, kindness, generosity, faithfulness, gentleness, and self-control.

As far as Ellie was concerned, the many friends she collected over the years were her greatest gifts and blessings, and she was amazed that there were so many. Perhaps her constant time with horses instilled in her this attitude of welcome and sociability. Just as her horses were gregarious, sensing the benefits of herd mentality, so was Ellie. "I knew so many people. My mother's favorite saying was, 'It's the friends you have who shape you.' My friends did shape me, they made my life, and some even helped me to see where I thought I wanted to go. They helped to send me in different directions. They're my breadth and depth. I learned so much from them, and now so many want to help me." She carried a mental list of those who had helped her, in ways small and large. She remembered Robbie Wenske's dad, Bob, who had rebuilt the Prince's brick chimney and put a new fireplace in their living room as barter for the horse that Ellie gave to Robbie. She remembered Tom Rinehart, who had taken on all of Ellie's work one summer so that she could go to the 1996 Summer Olympics. She remembered Bonnie Rinehart, who had made all the arrangements for Ellie and her to attend that year's Olympics. Ellie had flown to Washington, D.C., where Bonnie worked as a lawyer, and the two then drove to Atlanta, Georgia, where they stayed in Bonnie's in-laws' house. Together, they attended venues for equine cross country, dressage, and jumping. Ellie repaid Bonnie by caring for her Airedale dogs so that Bonnie could go to other venues.

As the profile of Harriman Road shifted from old folks to new, Ellie was not about to ignore the presence of the new property owners; a significant number of them were retirees. Ellie, viewing this crowd of new friends as blessings, donned the hat of community organizer. She would not be, according to Deb Matthew, "the aging lady living all alone on the windblown plains of Wyoming." Community dinners were held for socializing, but Ellie's purpose for the gatherings had a second and new focus: respectful and informed activism. She was definitely Mrs. Walter Fracker Sr.'s granddaughter.

In her new role as activist, Ellie was adamant that the quality of life be maintained for everyone in the large neighborhood off Harriman Road; she organized the neighborhood to hold true to that objective. "Someone was always trying one destructive thing or another," Ellie said, "but we were ready to fight. At first it was the idea to use the end of our ranch's road for a landfill. Then, someone came up with the idea to create a spur between the rail lines that ran north and south of our area." In the early 2000s, plans came forth to build a large rock quarry northwest of Sodergreen Ranch. The quarry operation would reduce the ground water level, the quality and safety of roads, and, in blasting, result in a decrease in air quality and increase noise harmful to wild and domestic habitats. It could also shatter the glass windows in homes. Ellie again gathered the neighborhood to confront the quarry company and possibly block its progress. She never let the fight get her down. As Cheryl Mair recalled, laughter was the cornerstone of Ellie's life. "Ellie always said, 'How bad can things be if you can still laugh?'"

As the battles were being fought, Ellie's community of old and new friends held to their vow of forming a support system around their cherished neighbor, who was now in her nineties. One of the aims of these many friends was to give Ellie something she couldn't imagine for many years—a night out. She no longer needed to worry, as she had for years, that she "had to get home to feed." Ellie's animals would be cared for by a dear and loyal friend to Ellie, named Ann.

For several years, Robbie Wenske Wilson arranged to take Ellie to the Frontier Days Cowgirls of the West Style Show. Robbie was thrilled that Ellie dressed up for it. "She wore a pretty, slightly dressy white blouse with a Western-style skirt that was decorated with little silver conchos. Her earrings were small silver posts, and her moccasins were Western style." And, of course, Ellie wore a touch of the red lipstick that had been a trademark in her younger years. A friend named Vickie Engbretson had cut Ellie's hair short, and the once-long ponytail had given way to white curls.

Bonnie Walno, who lived five miles south on Harriman Road, had met Ellie when they served together as volunteers with the Laramie County District #10 Fire Department Auxiliary. Ellie was a member of the Board of Directors, serving as notary. The two women became instant friends while coordinating money-raising events and organizing the annual Christmas dinner. Bonnie took Ellie into town for groceries, and the trips soon included lunches, often two hours long. "I could listen to Ellie for hours," said Bonnie. "A woman of her age, yet she was still so interesting and so mentally quick. We had the same love of horses, and I was impressed with her as a trainer. And what an artist she was. She actually captured the personality of any animal she painted."

Lunch talk, however, often turned to the potential quarry. Bonnie saw that Ellie was worried, "but Ellie wasn't one to avoid an opportunity or challenge. When Ellie spoke, whether to commissioners or company representatives, people listened. She was a force in herself about many a debate." Always eager for a new challenge, whether for work or play, Ellie was one of the first to volunteer to take her first-ever ride in a helicopter at one of the Auxiliary Fire Department's get-togethers. According to Bonnie, "After the helicopter landed, a grinning Ellie announced to the waiting group that riding a zip line above a jungle was next on her bucket list."

Esther McGann, a fellow activist, saw the refreshingly feisty side of Ellie. On a trip to the Wyoming Legislature, to attend an early hearing on the access for the granite quarry, Ellie and friends wore Granite Canyon t-shirts, representing opposition to the development affecting not only housing areas but also the ranches on Harriman Road. Although the old injury to Ellie's left knee caused a limp, she never considered her injury a handicap. On this day, however, when the Legislative session caused a dearth of parking spots, Ellie insisted they park in a handicap-only space so that they wouldn't miss a single moment of the hearing. Grabbing a ski pole that she wielded sometimes when walking the ranch, Ellie announced, "I'll just get my cane. They won't ticket an old lady walking with a cane." When Esther gently commented on the "naughty streak" in Ellie, Ellie responded with her trademark robust laughter.

Esther knew that Ellie, when she needed something done, could be highly innovative. During a season that marked a shortage of hay, Esther's husband was able to purchase a load packed in huge square bales and have it loaded onto his truck. But how to get it off? Ellie was 95, and Esther's husband was 80. Ellie disappeared but soon charged back on her "summer use" four-wheeler to the truck with a long rope tied to her vehicle. She promptly tied the other end to a single bale. Ellie gunned her vehicle into reverse, and after a loud and large jerk, a bale flew off the truck. The procedure was repeated till the ground was scattered with the bales. Lisa, Ellie said with assurance and satisfaction, would take it from there.

On another occasion, deep in winter, Esther McGann and Beth Buskirk, Saturday School students, invited Ellie to attend with them a large horse show in Denver. On their return, as a snowstorm raged, the friends dropped Ellie at the turnoff where Ellie's lane met Harriman Road. Ellie would have to drive overland in snowdrifts to get to her house. The worried younger women cautiously watched as Ellie gunned the motor, but, Beth said, "Ellie knew just where to go, slipping and sliding on the pasture above the lane. When Ellie lost traction, she just backed up and drove forward again. In true Ellie fashion, she got through. Ellie always got through."

Whether legislation, hay bales, or snowdrifts, Ellie was still managing to overcome obstacles in her everyday life. Despite the loss of her husband, the hard work of running a ranch in a land of severe weather, and her constant concern for keeping the land healthy for her neighbors and friends, she was doing all right. Ellie said she couldn't do it without her many wonderful friends, including an incredible couple, who could fix just about everything. RJ and Paula Bragg hailed from western New York. They had friendship to offer, but they also offered Ellie an astounding array of skills, garnered from their service as volunteer firefighters in New York. These skills included RJ's training in mechanics, and Paula's in all things electrical. "We're handy, and we have the time," RJ said humbly.

When Ellie's old Ford died, RJ helped her find a reliable replacement and was always available for repairs, even on the four- and six-wheelers. When Ellie's old dryer went out, Paula repaired it. The couple assisted with the replacement of the 30-year-old furnace, replaced the old propane-fed hot water heater with an electric one, and installed a carbon monoxide detector, "although," said RJ, "we probably didn't need to because the wind blew right through that old house."

When the light bulbs went out in the west barn, Paula replaced them with even more LED lights and put everything on one circuit so that Ellie could flick one switch by the door, rather than pull many strings from one end of the barn to the other. When it became imperative that Flag get an improved watering system, one that wouldn't freeze and would eliminate Ellie's need to haul buckets, Paula put in a switch for Flag's hot water bucket. She also dug a hole for the eight-foot hydrant, which she wrapped in multiple layers of insulation, dug a ditch to the water line, put a new handle on the hydrant, and re-designed the hose system so that the barn area near the pump system would stay dry.

"We were there for her," RJ said. "Our goal was to make sure that the house was a bit more reliable and safer and less burdensome. While we worked, she paid us with her interesting stories and history of the neighbors and of Sodergreen."

The Braggs were as astounded with Ellie as she was with their skills and abilities. "Ellie never complained," RJ said. "In spite of the hardships of her life, she appreciated and was happy to be where she was. I think she could have lived anywhere, even in a cardboard box, and been happy. We weren't surprised anymore with her ability to adapt or to make something work with what she had. If it was too cold, she'd put on layers. If it was too hot, she'd sit under her cottonwood trees. If she had to haul hay or grain in the winter, she'd hook a plastic sled to her six-wheeler." The Braggs were astounded to see all that Ellie had saved to the basement, just in case it proved valuable. RJ described the basement as "an accumulation of everything ranch."

Just north, at another ranch, lived a horse named Smokey. Karin Schubert had purchased Smokey but was afraid to ride him. Karin attempted to learn to ride from the Cherry Hill horsemanship books and, later, a book by Eleanor F. Prince. It wasn't until Smokey, decked out in heavy Western gear, galloped like the master of Harriman Road to the lane leading to Sodergreen Ranch that Karin put neighbor and book together. The two women became better acquainted through their volunteer work at the Fire Department, and Ellie suggested some lessons for Smokey and Karin. At the first lesson, Ellie advised Karin to remove the cumbersome tack and "just try my saddle," which was one of the English pads Ellie used in her classes. Karin soon discovered the connection between horse and rider and was sold on riding English. She became a regular at Saturday School. A feature of their friendship was the trips the women took together. Their first trips were the nature walks that Karin, a former park ranger, led during the last summer session of Sodergreen Horsemanship School. The group hiked the property, while Karin lectured on history, geology, and the characteristics and benefits of the plants and animals in the area. At the tipi rings, Karin told of the local indigenous cultures.

Longer trips, including just Karin and Ellie, sprang from Karin's constant comment to Ellie: "Let's go to Nebraska." Karin always drove her noisy, old stick-shift ranch truck with the passenger door that wouldn't unlock. "I'd gas up, sweep the manure from the passenger seat, and Ellie would slide across the semi-clean seat. She didn't mind." Ellie supplied the picnic lunch, which always included chocolate cake. Sometimes the trips were planned, and sometimes the women got laughing so hard that they'd miss a turn and set out on an entirely new adventure. The best route changes for Ellie were the ones that yielded the purchase of chocolate chip cookies.

Adventures, especially those involving high speeds, were treats as well for Ellie. At Sand Creek Bridge south of Laramie, spring rainstorms had caused the creek water to rise. Karin questioned crossing the bridge. "Oh, just do it! Go!" Ellie yelled, her blue eyes sparkling. They shot over the bridge, and spotting funnel clouds in the distance, outraced them. Speed anywhere was a delight for Ellie. At the Denver Zoo, when Karin drove the cart, Ellie pestered her to drive faster.

"There was no end to our travel conversations," Karin said, "and every time we stopped at a museum or information center, Ellie was talking within ten minutes to everybody there, including the rangers. It was as if she got everyone warmed up, and, oh, how she loved learning." There was nothing fancy about the trips. With Ellie's packed lunches, featuring crab or tuna salad, and a log or picnic table to sit at, they avoided restaurants. "We also," said Karin, "peed by the side of the road."

According to Karin, Ellie appreciated that people took care of her but loved it when she could take care of them. It tickled Ellie when she and her friend Ann had to rescue Karin and her husband when their car had a flat tire. "It was a favorite time for Ellie," Karin observed. "She loved being able to turn around the care for someone else. She and Ann couldn't stop laughing about saving their friends. Because of her grit, I actually never felt that I had to protect her."

Like Ellie, the historian Karin was committed to preserving the past presence of indigenous people on the Sodergreen Ranch and surrounding lands and often vocalized her concern that utility poles and lines were making their way through the tipi rings. According to Karin, Saddle Back Mountain was a spiritual place for tribes, and old cowboys talked of the sweat lodge by the spring and evidence of vision quests along the ridges. A wanderer could find hints of hand holds near Chimney Rock, and the nearby Twin Mountains offered indications of buffalo jumps. Preservation of the tipi rings was of special interest to both Ellie and Karin. They worked with the Wyoming State Historic Preservation Office to make the area eligible for historic preservation, their efforts including a search for an original map of the area that was drawn by the deceased Dr. George Frisson.

A lover of the land that Ellie and her neighbors called home, Karin narrated perhaps the most accurate depiction of the "community connection" that Ellie worked to maintain. The story began on a dry summer day at the Walkers' ranch where Karin and her husband were caretakers. Karin was carefully monitoring trash burning in a large barrel, but the wind was tricky, and in moments, the fire jumped the barrel and caught the nearby grass on fire. Karin panicked and called 911. From the high hill where the grass burned, Karin could soon see the fire truck from the old fire station near the Colorado border racing north toward the ranch. Then she saw more trucks, and cars, lots of them. She recalled that "it was like a scene out of the movie *Field of Dreams*. 'Set your place on fire and they will come.'"

The first truck arrived "and Mary Rose, a short piece of dynamite and older than I was, jumped out, grabbed a shovel, attacked the fire, and declared it out."

Vehicles kept coming. Tailgates were dropped, food appeared, and everyone settled in and started visiting. "They looked like they were going to stay a long time. They seemed to have a lot of catching up to do. I didn't know any of them, but everyone was friendly." Someone even handed the bewildered Karin a package of food. The visiting went on for a couple of hours, and then everyone left. The event of a spreading fire had been a social gathering—a chance to catch up with neighborhood news. "That spirit caused me," Karin said, "to get involved in the neighborhood Ellie called home."

At one of the Fire Department Auxiliary-planned Christmas dinners, Ellie met "the other Bonnie," the one who lived to the north. It was Bonnie Lindenfeld, who had been hired by Lisa Pontoriero to cut Ellie's hay the summer that Lisa's swather broke down. Bonnie's very first conversation with Eleanor Prince started out on a precarious note, when, at a get-together, Bonnie L asked Ellie if, because Lisa supplied the horses, Lisa also taught the lessons.

"No," said the 90-plus-year-old Ellie, "I give the lessons."

"You get on a horse?" Bonnie asked, incredulously.

Ellie answered, "How else am I going to give lessons if I don't get on a horse?"

Despite the awkward moment, Bonnie L soon knew Ellie as "a dear, dear friend, who always invited me over for cookies and hot chocolate."

Bonnie L was soon in league with Ellie in opposing the presence of the Granite Canyon Quarry. She attended the many meetings and took a stand for the land, water, and lives that were being negatively affected by the lack of rules and restrictions regarding the truck traffic, the blasting, and the blowing dust. According to Bonnie L, even though Ellie insisted she hadn't much to say, she spoke at nearly every community and council meeting. Ellie was instrumental in researching, compiling, and documenting pertinent records and other material. Bonnie L saw her as a strong communicator, effectively opening her presentations by stating that she was often giving lessons when a blast occurred, a situation that could result in horses and riders being put in danger or injured, incurring liabilities.

It was clear to Bonnie L that "Ellie maneuvered the quarry owners and operators into a corner when she said that her business was in jeopardy because of quarry business. She asked why she should have to stop doing what she did to make money because another business was doing what they wanted to do to make money. Ellie scolded those owners, saying that, even though they had the wealth, they should try to be 'good neighbors.'"

Ellie reminded the audiences that the heavy, fast truck traffic on the unpaved road presented hazards to the residents, and the silica and selenium dust affected the health of livestock. She explained that fracture from blasting could cause damage to the thermal spring that flowed on her and others' properties. The springs were critical to at least Ellie's livestock because her school horses depended on the creek water that ran in the winter. She also presented the accusation that in doing whatever they wanted without restrictions, the quarry operators, deliberately oblivious to the constant winds that sometimes clocked at sixty to seventy mph, did not bother to supply water trucks to keep the dust down on the roads. Likewise, Ellie reminded the company that they had neglected completing the required geological study, and that the company was selling the gravel in Colorado, not Wyoming.

Despite the power of the company and the arduous and deflating confrontations, Bonnie said admiringly of her co-activist, "Her speeches gave us merit, and she vowed that they wouldn't run over us." Bonnie L saw Ellie the activist as "a brave woman who stood for what she believed. She wasn't doing this for herself. She was doing it for everyone, for both sides. Her intent was strong, and she stepped up to the microphone and spoke with the confidence of one who believed in a cause with her heart and soul."

Travels and Horse Treats

Chapter 22

Beth Buskirk and her husband Steve felt in their hearts a strong commitment not only to the preservation of the ancient history on and surrounding Sodergreen Ranch but to the ranch's present contribution to Wyoming's story. Steve served on the Wyoming State Board of The Nature Conservancy, and he and Beth believed it imperative to help Ellie place the Sodergreen property under the protection of the organization. The Buskirks contacted a Cheyenne representative, who met with them at the property and explained that the biggest cost to the Conservancy would be the establishment of easements. Easements, which are legal provisions attached to a deed after surveys and legal descriptions are completed, would allow for the right for specific changes or conditions, such as power lines or road access, to occur within specific components of the property.

The assurance that the property would stay "as is" was compulsory for Ellie and the Buskirks. The easement to maintain this assurance—which would allow for building new structures, a well, or even a house on only the twenty acres surrounding the existing buildings—would cost the Conservancy money, and Beth realized that donations would be necessary. She promptly set up a program to solicit donations to make the easement possible. Donations flowed in. The easement permission went through, to Ellie's joy, and thus, no development would ever occur that would disturb the property's landscape and any archaeological sites, such as Native American arrowheads on the property and the tipi rings. The Princes had always been adamant that the evidence of indigenous travelers on the land as well as the land itself—with its rock formations and flowing streams—be respected, admired, and maintained. In other words, according to Nola Shafer, "Ellie and Bill wanted the ranch to stay a part of Wyoming's landscape." Interestingly, the Conservancy indicated early on that the size of the property might be a problem since large parcels were preferred.

However, the Conservancy was quickly convinced that the property, regardless of size, should indeed remain part of Wyoming's landscape. It was relatively undisturbed, had scenic value, and indicated good stewardship regarding soil conservation, wildlife, and overall upkeep.

The process was time-consuming, but in 2018, the 792-acre conservation easement was finalized. In the Spring/Summer 2018 issue of *The Nature Conservancy Wyoming: Wyoming Update* (nature.org/wyoming), Ellie was quoted on page 6 as saying that she chose The Nature Conservancy because "I trust them to preserve, in perpetuity, the natural beauty of the area, the opportunity for my students to learn about and enjoy horses and riding, and the land's agricultural use." The ranch was described in the article as "rich with wildlife, native grass and shrublands, and streamside habitat. Mule deer, elk, and pronghorn are year-long residents of the land, which also serves as a migration route for elk and raptors."

Assured that the ranch would remain pristine, Vickie Engbretson decided, about three years later, that Ellie Prince was long overdue for a trip away from the ranch to an entirely different landscape. Vickie was President of the Women's Auxiliary of the Volunteer Fire Department when Ellie was highly involved in it, and was the one who had expertly cut Ellie's long hair into white ringlets when Ellie announced that she "just didn't think a woman my age should still wear a ponytail." Vickie, who with her husband had given Ellie the gift of a trusty six-wheeler to use in winter, proposed one day to take Ellie on a six-day trip to Portland, Oregon, where Bill's son Carl lived with his family. Ellie had never been to Portland to visit the family. She accepted Vickie's gift, but of course she was concerned for her stallion and dog, Stubby the cat now gone. Ellie's dear friend Ann assured Ellie that she would take excellent care of Flag and Awssie in Ellie's absence.

On January 11, 2021, Vickie and Ellie headed south to Denver International Airport. Ellie had worried that because of her knee, she would slow Vickie down, and Vickie was a bit nervous that Ellie would not want to ride in a wheelchair. To Ellie, though, it was merely a new experience, and according to Vickie, "Ellie rode around like the Queen of Sheba and was always getting ahead of me." In the large and bustling terminal, the ever-curious Ellie was fascinated with the abundance of suitcases on wheels and the many mechanisms in play. Vickie was concerned that the attendants in the boarding area would not allow Ellie to carry on her walking cane, but Vickie said "Please," and Ellie flashed her smile, and they moved to the head of the line. Once on board, Vicki was delighted that the flight attendants "treated Ellie like gold and even allowed her to do some of her daily exercises in the aisle. In fact, they told her to do whatever she wanted. She was a hit." When the plane started its taxi, Ellie squealed, "We're going! We're moving!" Vickie watched while Ellie, "looking like a little kid, watched out the window."

Once in Portland, Ellie couldn't get enough of Carl and Kim and their daughters, with spouses and grandchildren. On outings, Ellie bought mementos for her friends and was fascinated by the vegetation that grew on top of other vegetation, rocks, and even an abandoned car covered with moss. In awe, she studied the tallest of trees and the mountain peaks. She noted the "immaculate" state of the ranches, farms, and stables and was astounded that in Oregon, hay was baled year-round. According to Vickie, "We were always having to stop so that Ellie could take pictures and ask a lot of questions."

Vickie noticed that throughout the visit, Carl called Ellie "my mom" rather than "my stepmom." He explained to Vickie that Ellie became his mom, as far as he was concerned, many years ago. Vickie saw that Carl was "24/7 attentive to Ellie's comfort. He made meals that she liked, they watched the same films, and they talked of old times. He had on display the artwork Ellie had given him over the years as well as items they had built together. He's an amazing son to Ellie. In the past summers, he traveled to Wyoming to take on more of the ranch work and to just take care of Ellie. He was willing to do anything for Ellie."

Pampered during the visit, about the only experience that upset Ellie was that of a one-hundred-foot tree falling close to the house one night, the severance at its base reminding Ellie of a shotgun blast. Ellie feared for her Portland family's safety, but Carl quelled her fears by gently saying, "It happens. We're okay."

Back home, Vickie recalled, Ellie was content with the memories of her visit to see her Portland family as well as her return to the little things in her life: Flag and Awssie, a good book, a flashlight, chocolate brownies, and knowing that spring was on the way and Carl would again come to visit her at Sodergreen.

"I don't need much," Ellie maintained, "because I repurpose everything." There was one remaining material desire, though, that Ellie revealed to Vickie as she hung the yellow-bordered curtains she had sewn for Ellie. Yellow was Ellie's favorite color. "Overalls," Ellie said. "I like all their pockets. I love pockets."

More than pockets, though, Ellie loved her family. She treasured her long-distance phone conversations with her stepdaughter Lynn, and fondly remembered the times Lynn had brought her family from New England to Sodergreen. She treasured that Carl, tall and lean like his father, and with a ready smile underneath his moustache, made it a point to visit Ellie at least once a year, usually in the weather-permitting summer. A truck driver by trade, he made the 1,100-mile trip in one haul, sleeping and eating in his truck. Once, when younger, he had made the trip by motorcycle. Ellie remembered that even as a teenager, Carl was likeable. Noting that raising a teenager was supposed to be a difficult job, Ellie simply said, "Carleton and I got along very well." She always preferred to use Carl's given name.

As Carl grew to manhood, he and Ellie had found they had similar interests, including mechanics, solving problems, reading, and of course horses. He was grateful that he had learned from Ellie how to ride and care for horses and from

Bill how to maintain a ranch so that he could hire out to other ranches. During his summer visits to Sodergreen, Ellie and Carl enjoyed spending the mornings together. In the afternoons, Carl disappeared up the hill beyond the west barn to the tipi he erected and lived in during his months at the ranch.

Like Ellie, Carl was inquisitive and a good listener and learner. Like Ellie, he was a wood carver, creating duck-hunting decoys and presents for his grandchildren, such as trucks and stools. Ellie marveled at the intricacy of a suspended rocking chair, which Carl crafted for his daughters to use as new mothers for simultaneous rocking and feeding. Carl gathered flat-faced granite rocks and sawed and sanded cottonwood logs into discs. On the rocks and the wooden discs, Ellie painted vibrantly colored intricate designs of flowers, pets, and horses—thank-you gifts for friends.

Theirs was a happy relationship, according to Ellie. "Carleton has always been loving to me, always giving me a hug. Of course we disagreed, but I don't ever remember an argument." Carl and his family "were always sending me presents, like 'happy boxes' with all kinds of little presents in them." Love always went both ways, where Ellie was involved.

In the summer of 2015, Carl was no longer the only summertime resident on Ellie's land. While his tipi was to the west of Ellie's house, a large RV was parked south of the house and north of the hill on which stood the holding corral for the school horses. The RV bore a Georgia license plate and belonged to three members of the Huff family from the Atlanta area. The family would call Sodergreen Ranch their home for several summer months for nearly the next ten years.

Charles Huff had been on active duty in the early 1970s as a U.S. Army Captain assigned to the University of Wyoming as an ROTC instructor. When his path crossed with the Princes', Bill invited him to go deer hunting, and the Princes and Chuck soon became fast friends. In 1995, Chuck brought his wife, Lisa MacGuire Huff, and their six-year-old daughter, Michelle Nicole, to the ranch. Michelle's older and beloved brother, Sean, remained behind in Atlanta that summer—as he would in subsequent summers—studying for his bachelor's degree and gaining meaningful employment.

According to Lisa, "Michelle, diagnosed with autism, hid as usual behind either my or Chuck's legs during this entire first visit. It was just too painful for her to connect with anyone outside the immediate family." Years passed, with only Chuck returning to the ranch since Lisa saw the Wyoming environment as "too challenging to live in."

During a phone call with Ellie in 2014, Lisa asked Ellie "if she would be willing to think about writing a riding therapy program for Michelle." Lisa and Chuck were experiencing the serious challenges of raising a child with autism, and Lisa told Ellie of the exhaustion that came with their fierce desire to help their daughter. They saw helping Michelle to achieve the highest quality of life possible as their lifelong purpose. Lisa asked Ellie if she could write a hippotherapy plan tailored for Michelle. Ellie readily accepted the task. She began months of research to determine how this type of therapy could help people on the autism spectrum and how it had been effective in helping those with traumatic brain injury and PTSD. Lisa took on a more forgiving attitude toward Wyoming, and Michelle and her parents agreed that when Ellie put together a curriculum, they would spend anywhere from three to eight weeks every summer in Wyoming so that Michelle could benefit from this hands-on therapy with Ellie at the helm.

Up front, Ellie knew what would be required of Lisa and Chuck if Michelle was to have a positive and confidence-building experience involving a partnership with a horse. One parent would have to ride with Michelle during every lesson, and the other would have to walk with Michelle's horse and be ready for the unexpected. From Lisa Pontoriero's herd, two horses were selected because of their calm and sensible dispositions since Ellie figured that even a horse's cough or a toss of his head could startle the rider. They were then trained by Ellie to stand patiently at a mounting block. The companion horse was to provide company for Michelle's horse, a big, beautiful Quarter horse named Janey, since Ellie maintained that horses, as herd animals, respond better when one of their kind is nearby. Lisa agreed to ride the companion horse, even though she hadn't been on a horse since childhood. She would model for Michelle the movements Ellie described during therapy. Chuck knew how to ride but elected to walk beside the horse, citing the need for surgery on both hips and deep pain in his back.

Because safety was of the utmost for Ellie, Lisa and Chuck would have to watch constantly for anything that could startle the horse or the rider, at work or during grooming. Lisa spoke of such an incident that later occurred during a lesson in the arena. "A fellow unexpectedly threw the arena door wide open, allowing sun rays to spray across the arena during an early therapy session; his body presented a featureless black shadow blocking part of the sunlight. The sight startled Michelle's horse Janey, who gathered herself to rear at this surprising and frightening shape."

Ellie knew that daily and weekly repetition would be necessary, and the same skills would have to be re-introduced and reinforced each summer. It was agreed by instructor and parents that ample time and patience would be allowed for Michelle to learn and relearn groundwork: how to communicate with the horse through touching, grooming, talking, haltering and leading, picking hooves, saddling, bridling, and longeing in the arena, all before getting on the horse. Physical exercise sessions on the ground would also be required, to warm up Michelle's muscles and prepare them for the many movements required to properly guide and ride a horse. "In Michelle's case," said Lisa, "these physical exercises were especially critical as she struggles with weight gain and prediabetes, as do many on the autism spectrum." Michelle loved the exercises Ellie prepared for her, especially the windmill and the shoulder, upper back, and neck massage. Afterwards, she said, "I felt like a fluffy cloud."

Aware of safety herself, Michelle was glad that Ellie planned to start with lessons off the horse. Practicing on the reining board and "mounting" Ellie's four-wheeler would give Michelle skills for confidence-building and also help her to connect with her horse's feelings. She quickly learned that "if I plop down on the horse's back, the horse will say, 'Oh, boy, what next?' If I do it quietly and gently, the horse will say, 'This person knows what she's doing.'"

Once Michelle was on her horse, there would be additional confidence-building and stretching exercises. Lisa explained that "there were exercises that required reaching across the mid-line of the body, which is difficult for many on the autism spectrum." The accumulation of ground work and exercises, Ellie knew, would benefit someone on the autism spectrum, especially in regard to fine and gross motor skills and sensory perception. This was, Lisa and Chuck realized, "the start of year after year of high focus on touch learning. Ellie had correctly planned. Every summer, it would be about a week before Michelle would mount up to ride an actual horse."

Lectures and quizzes were a part of the curriculum, necessitating positive study time between Michelle and her parents. Some of this work was designed to relate directly to horsemanship, but Lisa remembered that lessons also touched on animals, insects, flora, and fauna—usually those indigenous to Wyoming. Ellie believed it her responsibility to introduce her students to a wide range of topics and instill in them a love of learning, maintaining that "not everything is about horses."

All winter long, Ellie collected word-find puzzles, quizzes, human interest stories, and articles on flora and fauna. These lectures satisfied Michelle, who loved to hike on the ranch and be out in nature, especially walking to collect rocks. She and Ellie discovered a shared love of art, especially that of painting rocks, one of which Michelle adorned with an animated dragon. Ellie treasured a gift from Michelle, a striking paint-by-number portrait of a horse, which hangs in an important spot in the Prince home. The two also loved photography, and Ellie saw talent in Michelle's skillful photos, including the one of April—a beautiful chestnut horse that Michelle's mom usually rode—munching some long grass. The photograph displayed awareness of angle, lighting, and composition. When asked what other views in Wyoming she liked to take pictures of, Michelle mischievously answered, "Horses." Perhaps everything *was* all about horses.

Ellie believed, as she always had, that her instruction was not just a one-way experience with Michelle. To the contrary, she was learning much from her student, including a heightened form of patience and the need to think ahead as to what might or might not happen. Humor and jokes always crept into the lessons, and Lisa encouraged these moments, explaining that "humor often unlocks barriers to learning." There were chuckles when Chuck stood in for a horse so that Michelle could practice putting on a halter. Quoting a favorite joke, Michelle asked, "Why the long face, Dad?"

The curriculum was nearly identical to that of Ellie's school and the UW program, but her delivery was different. In videos taken by Lisa and Chuck, in which Michelle exercised and practiced mounting Ellie's four-wheeler—nicknamed the "steel horse"—and then longed Janey, Ellie's attitude resembled that of a loving adult soothing a child. Her voice was soft and low, and her movements were slow and gentle. She kept just far enough from Michelle to give her the time she needed to think and make her own correct decisions. Ellie encouraged, directed, and affirmed in repeated murmurs. She wisely broke simple steps into series of smaller, more achievable tasks. If change or something new was imminent, Ellie always cued with, for example, "Now, this time—." Any modifications to the skills introduced were made for the sole purpose of instilling confidence and self-trust in both horse and rider.

The benefits of Ellie's style of instruction soon became apparent. As Lisa divulged, "Folks on the autism spectrum often have other associated issues like sensory processing disorder, high anxiety disorder, and language and learning delays. Rhythmical stroking and touching a horse challenged Michelle, but with repetition, she began to lose her tactile sensitivity challenges and came out of her shell." At first Michelle was afraid to put tactile pressure on her horse, but with Ellie's coaching, she soon discovered that her horse loved that firm attention. She also learned that she could talk to her horse as if she were a friend, a welcome breakthrough since she had problems talking with anyone outside her immediate family. She was elated when she remembered something she and her new equine friend had learned a day, week, or even a summer before.

The necessary constant repetition of skills, even within sessions, did nothing to deter Michelle. Clearly, she couldn't wait to be with the horses that she reacquainted herself with every summer. "I love horses," she shared, one summer day in 2022. "They have a free spirit." One of her favorites, April, she described as a good listener. "Grooming and talking to a horse is important. Ellie tells me to talk to them."

Michelle's favorite early morning scene was seeing "all the horses coming down the hill. We watched from our RV window, as they came through the gate from the pasture at a gallop and into the corral." Michelle agreed with her mom that "it was a great start to every day." Ellie admitted that there were days when the lessons were difficult and frustrating for both instructor and rider, "but through the difficulties, Michelle's determination and her love of horses spread sunshine."

Michelle said she was never frightened on a horse until she remembered the time the fellow abruptly opened the big arena door and her horse threatened to rear up. Michelle said she "scrunched down and around that horse and held the reins." A remarkable feat for more experienced riders, Michelle kept her seat. Grinning broadly, she said, "Ellie was happy, and I was proud."

With the same exuberance that Ellie used to praise Michelle for her accomplishments, Michelle looked forward to treat time. With no exception, after each session's end, the horses groomed and the tack and saddles put away, the waiting horses turned their heads in one direction. "The horses were happy," Michelle stated, her lips mimicking how they reached and nibbled the air. "They knew," she said, correctly holding her hand flat, palm upward, "that they were all going to get a reward they loved, a horse treat!"

Michelle might have asked to cut a day's lesson short, but in no way did she ever want to quit a lesson. She loved them too much. In fact, her parents said that "since the first therapy trip to Ellie's for the first summer, Michelle began reciting in January or February, 'It's getting closer to time for Wyoming horses again!'" Each subsequent year, Chuck and Lisa wondered if Michelle would announce that caring for and working with horses was just too much work, and that she didn't want to spend her whole summer in therapy. Instead, Michelle continued every year to eagerly and joyfully count on her time with Ellie and the horses, even though her parents knew that the trip meant "unplugging Michelle from everything that is routine and comfortable and bringing her to an alien place with dust and dirt."

On their return to Georgia at the end of each summer, Michelle grew more comfortable working part-time as a popular bagger at a grocery store, as well as going to events and meeting people. Ellie noticed each summer as well that Michelle "was less and less concerned if people made comments about her. She wasn't the least bit bashful and displayed the attitude that her disability didn't bother her in the least. Even though she had her down days and needed her meds, as a young woman she showed strength and confidence." Although the lessons had to be repeated each day, each week, and every summer, Michelle carried the essence and spirit of her work with Ellie home to Georgia.

After her third summer of therapy with Ellie, Michelle volunteered to shop alone at a busy grocery store if her parents would hand over the shopping list. She also voiced her desire to help her parents with various daily chores. In fact, each year saw positive changes like these in Michelle's behavior. Several years later, Michelle accepted the invitation from a different instructor to ride with four adults she had never met. She joined a trail ride and attempted some advanced riding maneuvers, and, with Ellie's help, learned to sit and post the trot. "We saw," shared her parents, "that Michelle was developing coping skills in seemingly totally unrelated ways to deal with our world, which seems a strange and confusing place to those on the spectrum."

Ellie's loving intervention in Michelle's life yielded some other benefits as well. With her increased understanding of human interactions and of the needs of horses and dogs, Michelle, in Georgia, was granted an internship in training rescue dogs to become certified service dogs for people with disabilities. Equally important, according to Lisa and Chuck, was that Michelle was becoming a more verbal advocate, not only for others, but also for herself.

According to Lisa, "The beauty of therapy with Ellie had been that Michelle retained well over 90 percent of each summer's gains and growth, including increased comfort level for being around large groups of people and strangers, willingness to tackle new tasks and skills, greater self-confidence, and increased ability to advocate for herself. Most rewarding was that the gains lasted all year and beyond and, with years of repetition, built on each other. Ellie gave Michelle the gift of expanding her world and facing new possibilities with more excitement and less fear. Her comfort level and survival skills in our mainstream world grew year after year with Ellie's calming, consistent hippo-therapy."

Working with Michelle was, for Ellie, "a gradual thing. I learned by doing. I wasn't fearful, but luckily, I didn't make many mistakes." However, she attributed a good part of the program's success to the support and plethora of information that Lisa and Chuck gave her. "They gave so much of themselves to Michelle, all in the form of love. They were good and generous friends to me as well. They were a big part of my life."

The love, according to the Huffs, went both ways. Lisa shared that "Ellie was a huge part of our life as a family and as individuals. We treasured her as a loved member of our immediate family, even as we lived most of the year thousands of miles apart. We were blessed and thankful to have her work with our struggling Michelle for over ten years."

In 2021, Michelle's beloved and loyal horse Janey died. Ellie began training Johnnie, another of Lisa Pontoriero's horses, but Johnnie was not ready by the time the Huffs arrived for the summer. When it was time for Michelle to work with an actual horse before riding, Ellie was perplexed until she realized, "Well, there is Flag." Despite not having been ridden in years, the well-trained stallion was an excellent helper. He accepted the cinch even though he surely felt, as a shorter-backed Arabian horse, overshadowed by the western saddle. He even graciously lifted his hoof for Michelle to check. The amazing old horse and the amazing young rider became immediate and forever friends.

The Last Horse

Chapter 23

ASK ANYONE ALONG UPPER HARRIMAN ROAD TO DESCRIBE WINTER IN MARCH, April, and May, and they will tell you it's a stubborn critter. Spring is often in danger of being relegated to a once-upon-a-time memory, but Mother Nature, teasingly tardy, doles it out in bits and pieces. Wyomingites pay dearly for Spring.

On a rare day of seasonal benevolence, a proud bald eagle assumed a perch atop a telephone pole just south of the cluster of buildings called Sodergreen Ranch. Had he been interested in more than the young gophers racing erratically on the hill above the ranch, he would have noticed that the two-story house with moss stonework had withstood what Eleanor Prince called the harshest winter in her Sodergreen years. The redwing blackbirds screeched, a fat meadowlark trilled its message of meadow happiness, and to the west of the house, in the paddock that opened off the south side of the west barn, an aging Flag trotted briskly to Carl, who had come to spend time with Ellie and help her care for Awssie, who was recovering from surgery to remove a lump on her leg.

As is the pattern every year, Winter 2021 blew even more violently into 2022 and nastily eroded the two-track road from the main gate to the house. Determined friends' pickups had dislodged rocks as the motors were gunned, tires spinning, to plow through ice-packed drifts. Fearing that the cars her friends drove would be too low to navigate the ever-deepening ruts, Ellie insisted that intrepid, determined visitors turn off Harriman Road at the Bjores' gate, just south of hers, follow Bjores' gravel road up the steep hill, and turn north just past a gate onto a newly scratched two-track path that would descend to Ellie's house. It is true; Wyomingites drive across prairies when the roads aren't good enough.

On this new trail, the visitor traveled past the holding pen on the left, where Ellie's many school horses had once milled about, anticipating the approach of their student riders. Not much further, on the visitor's right, the outdoor riding ring sat adjacent to the large indoor riding arena, where UW classes continued each season. On this late spring day, though, the visitor, giddy in the hint of warmth, ready to make that right hand turn downward, braked for a moment to savor the scene at the bottom of the hill, a scene packed full of years and memories of both hardship and accomplishment for those who had dwelled at Sodergreen Ranch. The house was, by modern standards, small. Dotted about were corrals and barns, old equipment and shelters, all set in a remote width of Wyoming prairie, cottonwoods, huge rock outcroppings, and a vast blue sky. A soft wash of green touched the trees' high branches, and short stubs of grass were visible. Nothing fancy, but it was home to Eleanor Prince, and it gave off a freedom feeling.

Over the years, the ranch had been home to five Princes, 35 horses, twenty-some live-in students, a handful of counselors and assistant instructors, another twenty-some UW and individual student riders per semester, a herd of Polled Herefords, some chickens, grown dogs and pup litters, and a goodly number of cats. In the late spring of 2022, it was just Ellie and Awssie and, at the west barn, Flag. Stubby, the last cat, had died years earlier.

Flag was the last horse of Sodergreen. His importance was no less diminished by this standing. In Ellie's eyes, he, like Awssie, was one of her reasons for being, for waking up each day. Early every morning and early every evening, in below-zero wind chills, heavy snows, and the brief season of summer, Ellie donned the requisite layers of wind-resistant, sensible, and sturdy clothes. She served Awssie breakfast and then made her way outside to one of her two ranch vehicles. Her four-wheeler was best for summer weather. The six-wheeler, which she rode side-saddle and which had to remain running while outside and until the end of Ellie's chores, included a bed for transporting items and the means to drag a plastic sled. The vehicle was also heavy and therefore more reliable in snow and ice. Ellie used the stout rope she had tied to it to pull herself over snowdrifts and to clutch to keep from falling, being blown about, or becoming disoriented, or a cypher, in a snowstorm. It was truly Ellie's lifeline. The fierce Wyoming winters are merciless.

At feeding time, Ellie climbed aboard her vehicle, revved its motor, and turned it with the agility and skill of a Harley driver. She drove fast on the rutted, rocky road up to the west barn. Just as she seemed about to crash into the big wooden barn door, she slammed to a halt and climbed off, without capitulating to the fact that a 6-wheeler is large and she was a small woman. Watching her steer and bounce to her destination, one might have easily forgotten that she was born in 1926 and, yes, this was 2022. She always drove too fast and wildly for her friend, Esther McGann. "Ellie was intrepid on that four-wheeler and that 6-wheeler. She invited me to ride up to the west barn with her, but, 'No thanks,' I always said, 'I need the exercise.'"

As if a metaphor for Ellie's life, the west barn door sported a home-made door pull that simply and efficiently served its purpose. A rope dangled outward from a drilled hole. On the inside of the door, the rope was tied to a wooden latch that raised and lowered into a trough, which, when the door was pulled sharply with the rope, welcomed the latch securely and tightly. Lisa's nosy horses, traveling about in search of mischief, and critters of the day or night would be hard-pressed to manipulate the strong rope and its rancher-rigged mechanism.

Critters were no nemesis compared to the Wyoming wind, which adjusts its direction on a whim, often crashing without warning from the southeast when it chooses to haul in a blizzard or two. The main door of the west barn faced east. As Wyoming's unique law of physics would have it, the barn acted every winter like a snow fence, the blizzard-heavy wind cresting up and over the length of the barn and dumping mounds of snow in front of the east barn door. It never took long for a drift to gain the height and density of a nearly impenetrable wall. The sun's weak rays, post-blizzard, added to the harrowing situation by causing just enough melting to make any attempts at drift-climbing treacherous. In the cities, a plow might make several attempts to clear such a drift. In the dawn of the winter morning and in the dusk of the evening, a small figure, tied to the rope that was tied to her 6-wheeler, armed with a shovel, climbed the steps she formed in the drift and began to chip away at what was barring the door and preventing her from getting to Flag. Often, her good neighbor Zach Bjore drove his plow to her aid, but when he could not come, Ellie managed. This was the woman who did not believe in missing a feeding for any animal who depended on her. There was no excuse for a breach, even minor, in excellent and thorough care. Breaking through, Ellie bundled herself into the refuge of the old barn.

What is it about an old barn that comforts its visitor's heart? The west barn in winter staved off the harshest blasts of the frigid wind. In the longer days of summer, the structure was partially illuminated by shafts of lowering sunlight, its wide planks and posts and beams aged to a soothing darkness, smelling of old wood. The shadows and the luscious green smell of the stacks of hay bales wrapped around whoever walked from the entrance down the quiet aisle toward a large, well-kept stall. One wanted, in respect to the barn's interior, only to whisper and to welcome the memories linked to such massive, benevolent structures. The scent of horses was still strong.

At the old Sodergreen, Ellie and Gay Collier spent much of their time discussing topics for their books on horsemanship, caring for the horses, and once, in what Gay referred to as an intimate time, waiting in the beautiful old barn, in the dead-of-night chill, for a mare to bring forth her foal. It is likely that, in the still of Flag's barn, Ellie would be reminded of that intimacy of two friends who were so very much alike, as revealed in the tributes to Gay at the memorial service celebrating her life, from June 28, 1935 to January 18, 2013. Gay, the writer, bookstore owner, and recipient of the 2004 Wyoming Governor's Arts Award for Literature, was, in Ellie's words, a woman "who touched so many lives with love, courage, and humor," and who was as well "a great friend and a special lady who I miss sorely." Other close friends and colleagues brought forth Gay's own words, which could have easily been crafted by Ellie. In her online March 21, 2012 "Story Circle Book Reviews" interview with Gay, soon after *Just Beyond Harmony* was published, author Susan J. Tweit quoted Gay as intending to write "a story of a not-so-easy life that could still appreciate humor and beauty at least most of the time. … Lose hope? No. Become discouraged? Oh, yes. … But there was humor, as you mention, and beauty—the beauty of the land, the skies, the river, the animals. … Who can lose hope when surrounded by these things? … I tend to see the glass as half full rather than half empty, tend to emphasize the good, no matter what the circumstance, even while in the midst of it."[77] Gay's life story was indeed Ellie's.

Linda M. Hasselstrom—co-editor, with Gay Collier and Nancy Curtis of High Plains Press, of *Leaning into the Wind: Women Write from the Heart of the West*—quoted the words Gay wrote in her contribution to the anthology, words which mirrored Ellie's life philosophy: "The important thing is to touch the earth and stand in the wind, to know you are part of a whole—not superimposed like asphalt. On the plains, in the mountains, you learn that you are as important as the beaver, the hawk, the dragonfly—but not more so. You are part of the circle."[78]

For Ellie, the memories she savored as she stood just inside the west barn were surely tucked away safely to allow space for more practical matters. There was the matter of nourishment for Sodergreen's last horse. To the right, in critter-resistant containers, were Flag's performance minerals, several minerals for weight acceleration, a mixture of minerals for overall health, oats, equine senior feed, timothy pellets, and—of course!—from Ellie's coat pocket, three baby carrots. Using the ranch-ubiquitous empty metal coffee cans, Ellie blended all but the carrots together. Hearing the rattling of his feed, Flag trotted in from his large paddock and nickered an eager and grateful greeting to his human pal and protector of almost twenty-four years. It was difficult to see Flag through the wooden slats as he munched heartily, blowing air from his nostrils as if to move the food around to his liking. He was not a large horse. Ellie was concerned that he had lost weight, but she was hopeful that the summer months would be restorative and was grateful that some time ago, her veterinarian had floated Flag's teeth, a procedure that involved humanely rasping an old horse's teeth to allow for more balanced chewing of hay.

Ellie kept hay in two areas of the barn. Closer to Flag's stall was her own hay, cut shorter because, she explained, horses preferred shorter lengths of grass. Every morning, Ellie cleaned out the old hay and tossed in new. She sometimes repeated the routine in the evenings. Flag deserved a solid meal and a clean stall. He had been a loyal friend to Ellie.

"Flag," according to Bonnie Lindenfeld, "was Ellie's baby. The stallion was so used to her and so trusting of her that he never minded her bustling about in his stall or paddock. She could even walk right behind that horse. They were best friends." Karin Schubert described the relationship in simple but touching words: "She loved that last horse so much."

Before Paula Bragg intervened to set up the new water system, this part of Flag's care was incredibly hard for Ellie. Deb Matthew explained that, to her amazement, when the water system was acting up, Ellie "carried large jugs of water out of her kitchen, down the house steps to the six-wheeler, and loaded the jugs up, just to get water to Flag. Nobody was there to help her. She couldn't afford to be weak, but the heavy lifting was hard on her. She even took the time every day to scrape the surface scum from Flag's water."

Beth Buskirk was concerned that "Ellie had to deal for a long time with freezing water heaters, and just getting the water flowing for Flag. There were lots of people who loved her dearly and were willing to bend over backwards to help her get Flag's water, but she knew she could do it, so she did it."

That Ellie, in her nineties, could still do so much on her own, was no mystery to her. "I exercised every day," she stated, with the subtext of, "Doesn't everyone?" The daily plan was a substantive one. At the west barn, after caring for Flag—moving the huge hay bales an exercise in itself—Ellie walked nearly the length of the eighty-foot barn, two laps. "I was limited somewhat by my knee that was injured, but," she began to explain, delighted for yet another chance in her life to impart knowledge, "our knees are greased by synovial fluid, just like horses. As we get old, our knees dry up and our joints get painful, what with bone on bone. Walking enough but not too much helps to grease the joints."

When the weather was nice, and after Flag's breakfast and her own, Ellie walked from the house to the arena, and on to the east hay meadow, the return from which involved an uphill climb. Using the old farm equipment, such as the swather, she completed standing pushaways. She then ducked her head down, between her arms, then way back, bending her back, a stretch that she said was "great for my back, which I really don't have any trouble with now." Then, she executed three sets of leg and torso stretches and got in a walk of the whole of the arena before heading back to the house, where she had a bit more breakfast that on occasion included her favorite indulgence second only to chocolate: a donut. Weather did not rule the exercise regimen. On nasty days, Ellie walked the length of the house, stopping at each designated point to complete a stretching, limbering exercise.

The blizzard that blew into 2022 was nearly too much for the strength and spirit that Ellie still exhibited on a daily basis. "The storm gathered strength with a vengeance in March, blowing in from the northeast," Bonnie Walno recalled. "It hit Ellie's place hard. She had it tougher than the rest of us, her nearby neighbors. No one could get to her, and she couldn't get to Flag. It was all just a nightmare. Lisa Pontoriero couldn't get Ellie on the phone. Ellie's flip phone was dead, as was her home phone." But Ellie knew how to read the weather and had made adequate preparations for Flag for what she thought was the first and only nasty day of the storm.

When storms were harsh, Lisa Pontoriero had made it a practice in the past few years to ride her stallion over to Ellie's to feed Flag. As the March blizzard developed, Lisa knew that Flag would have water and feed, but she was concerned that Ellie had no electricity, phone service, or water service for the house. Ellie, though, always had a stockpile of food, so Lisa decided that all was relatively well on the storm's first day. Soon, reports came in that Interstate 80 and Harriman Road were closed, and no one could get to the Fire Station. By the second day of the raging blizzard, Lisa knew that Flag would need food and water. She set out to make the trip over the wind- and snow-drifted prairie to care for Flag and check on Ellie. Ellie recalled that Lisa's daughter, Evelyn, riding Myrtle, may have made the exhausting trip with her mother. To get over the tremendous drifts, the two women rode across the bare spots of prairie and dismounted at each drift. Holding the reins securely, they crawled up a drift, slid down the other side, and then pulled their horses over with the reins. Unable to walk through the deep drifts, the horses took short leaps. The exhausted riders and their horses soon made it to the Sodergreen house.

Meanwhile, and there is always a "meanwhile" in the drama of Wyoming winter storms, Ellie had, on that second day, sensibly dressed in her many layers of clothing and accoutrements known to defy Wyoming's weather and set out to care for Flag. Heading home from the west barn, Ellie made it to just below the house, to the long picnic table where so many summer meals had been enjoyed under the warm Wyoming sun. She knew that her safest move was to stay put, and that is where Lisa and Evelyn found her and helped her back to the warmth of the moss-rocked house. Ellie was all right, but in that storm, she realized her limits. As Cheryl Mair said, "Ellie always dipped her toe into feeling vulnerable, but Ellie never thought, as she grew older, that she was in the wrong place. She only thought of how to stay safe. Her fear was that she might not be able to take care of herself, to live alone, to go on with life, to care for her animals."

With the help of her friends, Ellie made it through that one more blizzard. Her friends witnessed that the recent long winters had worn on Ellie. Robbie Wenske Wilson noted that "Ellie seemed beaten down by the weather." As springtime came, and the fields were touched by the hue of green, Ellie alone was convinced that "I was just at a low point."

There had been earlier low points, one occurring in 2007, when a similarly ferocious blizzard raged. Val Scott, who was used to the milder winters in Great Britain, was immediately on the alert when she received a phone call from Ellie, "who was quite distressed that her stallion, Flag, was snowed into a corner of his run. Ellie could not dig him out alone and asked if we could help." Glad that Ellie called, Val treasured this rare occasion which would allow her "to give back to Ellie when she had given me so much." Val and her husband contacted a neighbor named Dale, who owned a small Bobcat digger, and the trio, with the Bobcat, headed to Sodergreen Ranch. "Dale and Bob made short work of the snowdrifts," said Val, "but the poignant memory that will stick in my mind was of Ellie finally being able to get to Flag and the two of them standing head to head in the door of his stall, reunited at last."

Flag's nearby acquaintance, in an adjacent paddock, was a horse belonging to Carolyn Rowe. Flag's real buddy, however, was the elderly woman who cared for him. She was the friend who was not stopped by the relentless winds of sometimes 60 miles per hour and was not deterred by the uphill drive to the barn and the climb over snowdrifts. She was the friend who never missed a feeding, even if the meal was blizzard-early or blizzard-late. She was the one who loved him.

Sensing Ellie's love and commitment was probably one reason Flag was a calm and trusting horse. That trust could be seen in his big eyes, placid but not dull. Flag's sire was Kamars Sharif; his dam was Dhar Aziza. Kamars Sharif passed on to Flag the famous Al Khamsa "willing ability and gentle disposition." Flag carried himself with pride and sensibility. It was as if he remembered, even in his autumn years, that his sire was the Kamars Sharif of Sodergreen Ranch who had posed for an advertisement for the movie, *The Black Stallion*. Flag seemed to sense that he was important, not for any potential breeding legacy, but for his purpose in providing Ellie with a purpose: a reason for rising from her bed every dawn and making her way into life and into the west barn.

This last horse, SG Sharifs Flag, was born on June 14, 1997, Flag Day. He was listed as a bay, although Ellie explained that according to his markings, he was a black bay. Deb Matthew insisted that "he looked just like the Black Stallion." He may have looked like the flashy Black Stallion, but he was a docile, sensible fellow. With pride in her voice, Ellie insisted that "it was his breeding, his lineage." And yet there was something more. "I did a really thorough and good job of ground training him," Ellie said, "and that makes so much difference in a horse. He never offered to buck or kick, and I often didn't put a halter on him." Ellie was alone when training Flag, "so I had to be especially careful. I had to be alert for anything. Safety was everything," she said, "but so was trust, and we trusted each other."

Lisa Pontoriero was Flag's first rider. Ellie soon rode him in the paddock, far from the mares, and delighted in his performance: "He handled beautifully, as if he'd been ridden before." He also had a second and equally enjoyable job: "to tease the mares when they were brought down." When Carl came to visit, he enjoyed riding the well-mannered and well-pampered Flag.

The ground training paid off in other ways. In caring for Flag, Ellie and the stallion were in close proximity. She often bumped him inadvertently with the plastic hay fork as she raked the old hay and manure onto the sled to be taken out to dump. She maneuvered all around him, including under his neck, chatting all the time and noisily moving things about. He never shied. He knew Ellie's routine, stepping aside or back with nary a command from her. She took solace in the huge animal, who in his recent prime had weighed 950 pounds. "He's laid back, he's gentle, he's just my pet now."

In 2021, Flag suffered a bad bout of colic. Luckily, he had not progressed to rolling. In fact, the colic might have cured itself, but Ellie didn't want to take a chance and have to transport him in the night. Ellie and Lisa had to get him to their veterinarian, about an hour's drive. The trailer ride would be Flag's first in twenty years. Ellie couldn't recall the last time he had worn a horse blanket, if ever. Nevertheless, while Lisa led him from the west barn down to where the trailer could be backed, the strange blanket whipping in the frigid wind didn't faze the horse. It was as if he knew that the blanket was necessary to ward off a chill. At the trailer, Flag sidestepped and hesitated a bit but then loaded right in for the trip to the clinic.

Before leaving Cheyenne, Ellie and Lisa, relieved at Flag's recovery, stopped at a fast-food restaurant to eat. Flag stood contentedly in the trailer, still wearing his blanket because Ellie didn't want a draft or chill coming in from the open sides of the four-horse trailer. All was quiet, all was good. "He was a good horse," said Ellie.

Bonnie Walno, who often took Ellie into town for groceries, said that Ellie never tired of taking care of her last horse. "She'd use her wagon or sled to get her groceries and Flag's feed from her car to the back porch and to whatever four-wheeler she was driving in whatever weather. I'd offer to help, even to feed, and she'd say nope, she was just fine, in spite of the steep steps to the house or her bad knee. A woman of her age, in all that snow? But she was inventive. Once, she used the shovel to make stairsteps in a snowdrift. She'd figured out all she had to do at her age, with her limitations. She never stopped, and that was the trick. She never quit, never stopped doing what she was doing." A visitor could not leave the west barn without looking back and thanking Flag for taking care of Ellie. For never quitting. For giving her purpose.

Her spirits raised by her time with her horse, Ellie made a wild return ride to the house, the six-wheeler bouncing over the rocks, ruts, or snow, Ellie gunning the motor and shooting straight downhill or sideways on a ridge. All that was missing was a "Yeehaw!" from the driver. Perhaps the exclamation was gobbled by the wind. If it was morning, Ellie, back at the house, enjoyed her second cup of coffee and the rest of her breakfast. Then it was back on the four- or six-wheeler for a trip in the opposite direction for daily exercises. If it was evening, a healthy meal and a good book beckoned.

Ellie's stepson, Carl, slipped in the adjective "amazing" when speaking of Ellie. "She was not on prescription medicine, she didn't wear glasses—although she probably should have—and she had her own teeth. She had a positive attitude, she laughed a lot, had a good memory, and rattled off many phone numbers. She was always busy, always helping out, and when I was there, always insisting on doing half the cooking and buying the groceries." When Ellie visited Carl and his family in Oregon, his friends were all impressed that, as Carl shared, "she still drove, went shopping, paid her own bills, and did her own taxes." Carl might have been joking just a bit, or not, when he attributed her longevity to not only "not smoking or drinking" but to the Wyoming wind. "Many of their animals," he said, "lived long lives on the ranch, as Ellie is doing now. It's all the fresh air going through that house with all its cracks and joints. It's how the animals got to be ancient. And the people too. Yes, I would say she was one amazing independent pioneer woman." Add to that Julie Wilkinson's words: "You can't not be happy with Ellie."

During one of the last interviews with Ellie, she was asked, "Why horses?"

Not surprisingly, she said it was in her DNA, "like my grandfather and my father, both of whom had a love for horses. On a horse, a person can be seen and heard. I liked the smell of horses, even the manure, and the challenge of working with such a large animal who is also a companion. There's always something new to learn with horses. A horse changes a person's life. Why horses?" Her voice grew a bit feisty. "Isn't that what we've been talking about all through these interviews? It's that freedom feeling of being on an amazing animal."

Ellie lived that freedom feeling her whole life, doing what she wanted to do with the horses and people she loved.

Awssie, close to thirteen years old, died on February 4th, 2023. She ate a good breakfast, went outside, and suffered a seizure. On February 17th, his body in distress, Flag had to be put down. When the ground fully thawed, Lisa Pontoriero promised, she would bury Awssie and Flag on Sodergreen land.

There would be no more feedings for Ellie to attend to. She would miss them. They had been her reason for living.

On March 19, 2024, Ellie passed away peacefully, under Lisa Pontoriero's care, at Lisa's ranch, just up the hill from Sodergreen Ranch.

Endnotes

Chapter 1

1 Galbreath, Robert M. Walter S. Fracker Jr.'s Ancestors/Personal Unpublished Genealogy. 2022. Collection of Robert M. Galbreath, Wyoming.

2 Edwin Carl Kemp, *Melrose, Massachusetts, 1900–1950, commemorating the One hundredth anniversary of the Founding of the town of Melrose and the Fiftieth Anniversary of the Incorporation of the City of Melrose*, online pictorial images, access date March 31, 2023, https://archive.org/details/melrosemassachus00kemp

3 Ibid., online archived text. This book is the supplement to *The History of Melrose*, by E. H. Goss, published in 1902 (https://archive.org/details/historyofmelrose02goss).

4 Gray, Lori. "True Grit," *SunDAY Magazine, A Local Weekly Supplement to the Sunday Wyoming Tribune-Eagle*, June 8, 1980.

Chapter 2

5 Galbreath, Robert M. Walter S. Fracker Jr.'s Ancestors/Personal Unpublished Genealogy. 2022. Collection of Robert M. Galbreath, Wyoming.

6 Ibid.

7 Ibid.

8 "Black, Frank Swett," *History, Art, & Archives: United States House of Representatives,* accessed 5/8/2023, history.house.gov/people/detail/9418.

9 Galbreath, Robert M. *Walter S. Fracker Jr.'s Ancestors*/Personal Unpublished Genealogy. 2022. Collection of Robert M. Galbreath, Wyoming.

10 www.images-of-new-hampshire-history.com, access date June 5, 2023.

11 Ibid.

Chapter 3

12 Galbreath, Robert M. *Walter S. Fracker Jr.'s Ancestors*/Personal Unpublished Genealogy. 2022. Collection of Robert M. Galbreath, Wyoming.

13 Angie Fracker's Mocha Icing: ⅓ cup strong coffee; piece of butter, size of an egg; 1 tablespoon cocoa; 2 teaspoons vanilla; 2 cups confectioners sugar. Soften butter. Add coffee, sugar, cocoa, and vanilla. Beat all together.

14 Galbreath, Robert M. *Walter S. Fracker Jr.'s Ancestors*/Personal Unpublished Genealogy. 2022. Collection of Robert M. Galbreath, Wyoming.
15 Ibid.
16 Ibid.
17 Ibid.
18 Ibid.
19 Ibid.
20 Ibid.
21 Ibid.
22 Ibid.
23 Ibid.
24 Ibid.
25 Ibid.
26 Ibid.
27 Ibid.
28 Ibid.
29 Ibid.
30 Ibid.
31 Ibid.
32 Ibid.
33 Ibid.
34 Ibid.

Chapter 4

35 liveboston617.org (no longer available), access date January 11, 2023.
36 Galbreath, Robert M. *Maxine Griffith's Ancestors*/Personal Unpublished Genealogy. 2023. Collection of Robert M. Galbreath, Wyoming.
37 Galbreath, Robert M. *Walter S. Fracker Jr.'s Ancestors*/Personal Unpublished Genealogy. 2022. Collection of Robert M. Galbreath, Wyoming.

Chapter 6

38 Gaydell Collier, *Just Beyond Harmony* (Glendo, WY: High Plains Press, 2011), 13–14.

Chapter 8

39 Dena Hansen, "Popp-Harmony," in *Cow-Belles Ring School Bells: A History of Rural Schools in Albany County, Wyoming*, ed. Albany County Cow-Bells (Laramie, WY: Albany County Cow-Belles Club, 1976) 60-62.
40 Mortensen, Billie, "Harmony School" in Chapter 4, "Sodergreen Harmony," in *Cow-Belles Ring School Bells: A History of Rural Schools in Albany*

County, Wyoming, ed. Albany County Cow-Bells (Laramie, WY: Albany County Cow-Belles Club, 1976), 65, 5 61.
41 Gaydell Collier, *Just Beyond Harmony* (Glendo, WY: High Plains Press, 2011), 56–57.

Chapter 9

42 Longe, pronounced "lunge." The long longe line is held by the trainer and attached to the horse's halter. The trainer stands in the center of the circle and uses a whip and voice commands to direct the horse to walk, trot, canter, reverse, or halt. The trainer rarely touches the horse with the whip. Longeing can be used as preliminary work for saddle training and as exercise for any horse at any time.
43 Ellie's recipe for Sodergreen Horsemanship School Hot Chocolate included: 8 quarts of powdered milk; 1 pound of Nestlé's Quick (now Nesquik); 3/4 cup powdered sugar; 6 ounces Coffee Mate; dash of salt.

Chapter 12

44 Galbreath, Robert M. *Maxine Griffith's Ancestors*/Personal Unpublished Genealogy. 2023. Collection of Robert M. Galbreath, Wyoming.
45 Ibid.

Chapter 13

46 "Mary O'Hara: My Heart Is in Wyoming," American Heritage Center Wyoming, accessed January 9, 2018, ahcwyo.org.
47 "Remount Ranch," wyoshpo.wyo.gov, accessed October 25, 2022.
48 Mary O'Hara, *My Friend Flicka* (New York: Harper Collins Publishers, 2003), 17.

Chapter 14

49 Quoted in Raymond W. Settle and Mary Lund Settle, *Saddles and Spurs: The Pony Express Saga* (New York: Bonanza Books, 1955), 8.
50 Settle, *Saddles and Spurs*, 8.
51 Ibid., 44.
52 Ibid., 45–46.
53 Ibid., 42.
54 Ibid., 43.

Chapter 16

55 Gaydell Collier, *Just Beyond Harmony* (Glendo, WY: High Plains Press, 2011), 116.
56 Quoted in Collier, *Just Beyond Harmony*, 116.
57 Gaydell Collier, "Monarch of the Mountains," in *Western Horse Tales*, ed. Don Worcester (Plano, TX: Republic of Texas Press, 1994), 126-135.
58 Gaydell Collier, *Just Beyond Harmony* (Glendo, WY: High Plains Press, 2011), 118.
59 Ibid., 120.
60 Ibid., 172-173.
61 Eleanor F. Prince and Gaydell M. Collier, *Basic Horsemanship English and Western: A Complete Guide for Riders and Instructors*, (New York: Doubleday & Company, 1974), Introduction xxii.
62 Ibid., xxiv.
63 Ibid., 11, 18.

Chapter 17

64 Photo caption, "FT. D. A. Russell, Establishment of the Fort," accessed March 18, 2022, www.wyomingtalesandtrails.com.
65 Rebecca Hein, "Horses for War: A Market For Wyoming Stockmen," accessed March 18, 2022, www.wyohistory.org.

Chapter 18

66 "Arabian Horse History," accessed April 6, 2022, www.arabhorse.com/arabian-horse-history
67 Ibid.
68 Arlene Magid, "How to Read a Pedigree," accessed April 6, 2022, arlenemagid.com/readpedigree.
69 Joe Ferriss, "Strains in Arabian Horses," *Al Khaima: A Publication of the Institute for the Desert Arabian Horse*, Vol. 1, #1. 8, 9, 14.
70 Donna Ott, "An Introduction to Al Khamsa's Desert Arabians," *Khamsat*, Vol. 16, #2, Summer 1999. 9.
71 *Al Khaima: A Publication of the Institute for the Desert Arabian Horse*, Vol. 1, #1. 52.
72 Nancy Palmer, "Making a Difference: An Enduring Partnership: Dorothy Feldman and Eleanor Prince and Their Al Khamsa Horses," *Khamsat*, volume 16, no. 2, Summer 1999. 2.
73 Gaydell Collier, *Just Beyond Harmony* (Glendo, WY: High Plains Press, 2011), 227.

Chapter 19

74 "Attractive Nuisance," accessed February 28, 2022, www.law.cornell.edu/wex/attractive-nuisance.

Chapter 20

75 "Horse Play," February 1990, Vol. 18, #2. 54–55. The authors of the review are not credited by name.
76 "Book Review: *Basic Horse Care,*" *Arabian Horse Country.* January 1987. 58. Again, the authors of the review are not credited by name.

Chapter 23

77 Susan J. Tweit, "Story Circle Book Reviews," March 21, 2012, www.storycirclebookreviews.org/interviews/collier.html.
78 Gaydell Collier, "Wyoming Bound," in *Leaning Into the Wind: Women Write from the Heart of the West*, eds. Linda M. Hasselstrom, Gaydell Collier, and Nancy Curtis (New York: Houghton Mifflin, 1997), 3–5.

Acknowledgments

I HUMBLY ADMIT THAT I COULD NOT HAVE WRITTEN THIS BOOK ALONE. ELLIE'S passion and personality were too large for one person to capture in words. I owe huge and heartfelt thanks to so many.

First, to Ellie. I may be the only person grateful that she never threw anything away, including her memories. I will cherish our interview sessions and her loving friendship. She taught me so much, whether I was riding a horse or negotiating life.

To all who agreed to be interviewed. It was my interviewees who fleshed out this book, providing me with lively, poignant, and humorous accounts of Ellie's life. Too many to mention, they are in my heart as well as forever in my spiral notebooks.

To Deb Matthew Brown, for her amazing business savvy and ideas as well as her constant support, encouragement, hope-filled laughter, and Ellie Project emails. And to Ken Brown, for being my Pony Express.

To Joyce and Bill Tyrrell, for introducing me to the big barn and Ellie's early Wyoming years, for their Western hospitality in hosting the reading of the book's first chapter, and their friendship. They are the epitome of what is good in Wyoming.

To my forever friends and family who are scattered near and far. They never doubted the book would be published.

To my dear friends at Prairie Sage Writers, for their constant encouragement.

To Andrea Graham, Senior Research Scientist, University of Wyoming American Studies Program, for providing early and invaluable information regarding the interview process.

To Jay Bress, Manager of the University of Wyoming's Copy and Print Center, for his patience and enthusiasm and his skill in turning grainy old photographs into works of art.

To my diligent readers, for their time and skills—John Galbreath, Diana McGahan, Dr. Donna Marburger, Mary Prather, and Vanni Prichard.

To Mary Beth Baptiste, Linda Dunlavy Johnson, and Vanni, for writing book blurbs.

To Maggie York, Managing Editor, and the staff at *WREN* Magazine, for publishing the article, "Time for Wyoming Horses" and thus supporting the publication of my book.

To Oliver, now in horse heaven, who reinforced everything Ellie taught me.

To my son Robert, for his amazing research acumen and his expertise in researching and compiling Ellie's genealogy. To my son Andrew, who reminded me how to confront and conquer challenges. To my son Daniel, for reminding me to seek the force and eloquence of words. To daughter-in-law Ali and son-in-law Collin, new to the family and ever so supportive.

To my beloved husband, my rock, for his unwavering belief in my ability to write Ellie's story, his constant encouragement, his ever-present help and advice, his patience, and his love. He saved me from computer nightmares and the dark and doubt-filled moments. It was he who, many years ago, bought Oliver for me and introduced me to Ellie Prince.

To my former Managing Editor, Rebecca Didier, and my Managing Director, Martha Cook, at Trafalgar Square Books, for believing in the value of Ellie's story and guiding my manuscript through the initial stages of publication. To Rebecca Didier a second time, and to Abbey Gregory, for their work as cover designers. To Managing Editor Neleigh Olson, Chief Operating Officer Brooke Warner, and Assistant Editor Lizzie Gray, and the additional staff of Trafalgar Square Books and the Stable Book Group, for their literary artistry in creating the book that holds Ellie's story.

About the Author

Pamela Galbreath holds an MFA in Creative Writing from the University of Wyoming. She was awarded the 2011 Wyoming Arts Council Creative Writing Fellowship in Creative Nonfiction (judged by Lee Gutkind) and received WAC honorable mentions in 2024 and previous years. Her nonfiction earned her a nomination for the 2015 Pushcart Prize and, in 2024, first place in the Wyoming Writers Inc. state contest. Her work has been published in the anthology Unruly Catholic Women Writers: Creative Responses to Catholicism and in magazines and literary journals. A retired teacher of writing and literature at the high school and university levels, Pam resides in Laramie, Wyoming, with her husband, dogs, and horses (pamelagmusings.com).